Cecile's Secret

A Novel

Ruth E. Hill

Part One

Cecile

Prologue

Cecile Antoinette Isabella Andre Legrand was born on the 1st of May 1922. She was a full month premature, and the birth proved so difficult for the young wife of Andre and so dangerous to her health, that it was reluctantly decided that she would be their only child. This was a great disappointment to Andre, who was 20 years senior to Isabella, his aristocratic, half-Spanish wife. He had hoped for a brood of siblings and naturally a son and heir.

Cecile clung onto life in those first few perilous weeks with a feisty fortitude that was to remain with her throughout her life. She was small, indeed puny at birth, and only the experienced care of Isabella's own childhood nurse ensured the tiny bundle began to thrive. Her mother was petite with flowing black hair, huge dark eyes, expressive long fingered hands, and a tiny waist. Cecile was made very much in her image; however, she inherited her father's quick thinking and curiosity about the world.

She may not have been a son, but it soon became clear that Cecile did not fit the usual mould of a girl in the early 20th Century. There became a strong bond between Cecile and her Papa, as her mother remained fragile in health and temperament for many years after the birth. Papa spent as much time as he could with his daughter and engaged tutors at an early age for her with explicit instructions to allow Cecile to learn about all aspects of the curriculum, not just those normally taught to girls.

Andre Legrand was a wealthy industrialist with Jewish heritage, who profited considerably from the war of 1914-18. He ran a successful business and enjoyed spending time in his workshop where he worked on his imaginative inventions which he shared exclusively with Cecile. Often clockwork, he would produce moving toys that initially amused her and later inspired her to dismantle them to find out how they worked.

Living in a grand house with servants in a wealthy enclave in Paris and spending the summers at a villa in the hills above Nice, Cecile had an enviable upbringing. Sharing the summer months with her mother's extended family of aunts and cousins, at the villa with its huge, forested grounds where the children could build tree houses and play endless games of make believe, saw Cecile at her happiest.

However, her sheltered life ended abruptly with the storm clouds of war gathering over Europe again. Her paternal grandfather was Jewish, and although her father had little contact with his family following his marriage to Isabella, who had been considered totally unsuitable, the events in Germany unsettled him greatly. Reluctantly he decided to make arrangements for his wife and child to travel to England to keep them safe. They would stay, temporarily he hoped, with a good friend while Andre would remain in Paris to look after his business with the expectation that they could return very soon.

At first Cecile and her mother stayed in London and enjoyed life in a social circle not unlike Paris, but with the outbreak of war and the danger of bombing raids in the capital they moved to a small house on the estate of another friend in Dorset. The communication from her father abruptly ceased, the house was cold and damp, and they socialised with no one. The health of her mother declined rapidly, and she died from pneumonia within the year. Cecile was left alone before her 20th birthday and, returning to London, she was determined to do her part to help her country.

No one had foreseen this disastrous war and how it would tear the continent of Europe apart and change the course of many lives for ever.

The Special Operations Executive. S.O.E.

The S.O.E. was formed in June 1940, following the retreat of British soldiers from the mainland of Europe via Dunkirk in May, and the surrender of France a month later. The outlook for the future of the war effort in Britain looked bleak.

This new volunteer force, called the Special Operations Executive was set up to wage a secret war on the German Reich, tasked with sabotage, subversion and espionage behind enemy lines. The Prime Minister, Winston Churchill, was famously reported as saying to the S.O.E. recruits, 'And now go and set Europe ablaze.'

Following training, the agents were parachuted into enemy occupied Europe, sometimes in small groups but often alone, to work with the local Resistance. At that time only men were allowed to serve as soldiers on the front line, but women were allowed to join the S.O.E., with many enlisting in the First Aid Nursing Yeomanry to disguise their real position.

It was discovered that actually women made excellent secret agents as they were not seen as a threat by the enemy, they could easily blend in with the local population, and so move around without causing suspicion. When assessing potential recruits one of the most important qualities was the ability to pass as a native of the country and especially by use of its language.

Initially women were trained as wireless operators and couriers but were still instructed in the use of weapons and unarmed combat. Later, with the development of a wide range of explosive devices including the use of so-called plastic explosives, women brought knowledge of these areas of combat to the Resistance movements in the German occupied territories. These brave women came from all walks of life, from the working classes to aristocracy, but they all had one thing in common, a desire to help liberate Europe from the stranglehold of the German occupation.

S.O.E agents understood their missions were dangerous, the average life expectancy of an S.O.E. wireless operator in occupied France was just six weeks, with many agents captured, killed in action, executed or sent to concentration camps. More than one third of the female agents did not survive the war.

There are conflicting views about the efficacy of the S.O.E but it is widely accepted that the moral contribution of this secret war made possible the resurrection of self-respect in the occupied territories, allowing the general population to unite in their resistance of the enemy.

Chapter 1

Spring 1944 South-East France

I couldn't breathe. I was gasping for air. It was all around me but speeding past.

"Come on. Deep breaths. Concentrate." Talking to myself might just make a difference as, almost unexpectantly, the ground was coming toward me very fast. Thankfully training kicked in, I could hear the instructor shouting in my head, ′Feet together, grab the guide ropes, hit the ground, and roll away′. Then, with no time to waste, ′Get out of the harness, bundle up the chute and get into cover as fast as possible′.

I scrambled over the rough, grassy field, all the time heading for the tree cover lit by the clear full moon, with the sound of the plane's engines gradually disappearing. Then nothing, just nothing, no sound at all. Once under the cover of the trees I sat completely still and listened to the silence. If all remained quiet for five minutes, I could then move to the next part of the plan.

A full, silent, five, very slow, minutes passed. Now I could go, moving further into the prickly dense tree cover, systematically hiding the parachute bundle, getting out my compass and moving purposefully south through the trees. It felt good to have my feet back on the soil of my homeland, even if the enormity of my task was becoming even more daunting. The dawn of harsh reality was beginning to break, but it was no time to get distracted by cold feet, I needed to remember the instructions.

'Continue south until a forest track running west to east is found. Take this track west for about one mile until a further track crosses. Wait there.'

Clear and precise but it wasn't quite so easy on the ground. The patchy undergrowth was dry, my shoes made far more noise than I wanted, the trees seemed to stretch a long way ahead in an untidy sequence, and the moonlight that had enhanced my arrival was disappearing behind clouds.

In the distance I could make out a change in ground cover, there it was, a wide forest track cutting through the trees, and a compass check agreed that it ran west to east. A deep sigh of relief escaped my lips, at least it seemed I was in the right place. Double checking the direction, I set off west, keeping to the shadow on the side of the track, all the time listening and scanning the dimness.

About 20 minutes later, just as my thoughts began to be preyed on by possible misdirection, a path appeared in the distance cutting across my progress.

"This must be it," I murmured reassurance to myself. "But where should I wait?"

I left the rough road and climbed into the thicker forest choosing an elevated position seated with my back to a mature pine tree, so that I was well hidden, but I could clearly see all four forest tracks. For the first time since plunging out of the plane my breathing slowed and my hands stopped shaking. This was ridiculous, I thought, I had to control my anxiety or the whole reason for the mission would be put into doubt.

I waited, sitting perfectly still, and continuing to breathe deeply and evenly to control my emotions. Time seemed to stand still in the darkness, I shivered in the cool of the night, my thin dress and coat seemingly an incongruous set of clothing, but the neat, worn, lace up shoes on my feet were more practical, though not the best for walking through a forest.

I thought I heard a rustle in the bushes across the track, perhaps a fox or other predator, searching for prey but I couldn't see anything in the now patchy, moonlight. Another rustle, I strained forward, listening intently. Without warning there was a hand across my mouth, my arm was twisted up my back and a whispered question hissed directly in my ear. They were better at this than I was, at least at the moment.

"Tricolour." I hissed back.

My arm was released, and the hand removed. I half turned to see a young man dressed in dark clothing, a peaked cap pulled down over his face. He gave a low whistle, another similarly dressed youth emerged from the opposite bank. I realised a clever distraction trick had been played on me making me feel foolish, but I resolved to know better next time.

"Come on, we must go quickly now, it will be light soon." He moved away, I followed.

We set off down a narrow uneven path, and I followed as quickly and noiselessly as I could, but he had meant it when he said to go quickly. My pride would not allow me to call out to slow the pace and I repeatedly stumbled and scratched my legs in the undergrowth. The moonlight was now gone replaced with a rosy glow in the east, as dawn was beginning to arrive. I had little idea where I was going, and knew not to ask, all three of us were silent concentrating on moving as swiftly as possible. At one point the one who had distracted me moved off the path and disappeared into the bushes.

Eventually we reached a field with rows of lavender, the long spikes that would hold the purple flowers forming, then this gave way to stunted olive bushes, and further on mature, well-tended cherry trees, their blossom getting ready to bloom. In the scant dawn light, I made out an unkempt stone farmhouse and some rundown outbuildings. Approaching from the north, the windows were small and shuttered ready for the Mistral winds.

My guide gestured for me to wait in the barn to the side, so I tucked myself behind the door hanging limply from its hinges. The whole barn had seen better days, and there was a distinct air of neglect mixing with a strong odour of goats who, it seemed from the evidence had not long exited this place. I hoped I was not staying in here for very long. The house had a dim light showing from one of the small unshuttered rear windows latticed with strong iron bars.

Within two minutes my guide came out of the door and beckoned me inside. I dashed quickly from barn to house finding myself in a large kitchen with a dark wood and plaster ceiling, a cold stone floor, a white sink with a single tap, and a large scrubbed wooden table. Around that table sat an old man dressed in farm workers' clothes, and a younger woman with a welcoming but exhausted expression.

"This is Monsieur Redoubt and his daughter-in-law," it was explained. "They are going to look after you for a few days until we have everything in place elsewhere."

I shook hands with the Monsieur and Madame of the house and smiled. They looked as anxious as I felt, then the old man turned to my guide and in guttural, but understandable French patois, made an unflattering remark about my use to them being so young, small, and female. I manged to keep a straight face even though I completely understood his words, and perhaps, in my in the depths of my own heart, echoed his sentiments. But I was here to do a job and though small of stature, I had an iron will and that would show if needed.

"It's who they have sent us." Replied my guide. "We must work with her skills to a common end." The old man tutted and looked away, but my guide looked me straight in the eye for the first time. He had taken his cap off and I could see his deep brown, slightly hooded eyes and curly mop of hair.

"I am going now, daylight will soon arrive, and I need to get back to the village. Do everything they ask, as they are risking more than you realise to help. I'll come back soon." Then he was gone, and silence fell in the large kitchen. Madame turned and smiled.

"You must be hungry. Come, sit and eat, we kept you some supper." She placed a bowl on the table and reached for the pot on the stove pouring out a thick dark stew which she passed with a chunk of bread and gestured to eat. The old man slowly got up and took his place in the armchair by the range, not even giving me a second glance.

"Take no notice of my father-in-law," she confided quietly. "He is from a different world where men did all the dirty work. He lost his son, my husband, in the last war. He hates them and the fact he can do so little about it. Eat up and I will take you to your room, you must be tired."

"But listen," she continued. "This is important for us all. If you hear the dogs bark, then someone is coming up the track. We get very few visitors; they have been here once and damaged their vehicle on the rough track so I doubt they will be back in a

8

hurry. But, if the dogs bark, get out of the back of the house, I will show you how, and hide in the barn. If I don't come out for you in two minutes, go as fast as you can up into the hills and wait. One of ours will find you, do you understand?"

I put my spoon down, the hot food having given me more strength than I realised I had, and I tightly grasped the Madame's hand looking straight into her eyes.

"Yes, whatever you want me to do," I said. " Just tell me, I am here to help as much as I can. My name is Cecile."

Chapter 2

Madame took me upstairs to the room apologising for it being so small. I looked around the room, it was scrupulously clean, had bare wooden floorboards, a well-worn chest of drawers with a pretty wash bowl and jug on top, a narrow wooden single bed with faded counterpane, and one shuttered window.

I had only the clothes I was wearing and smiled briefly to myself, 'travelling light' had never been one of my strong points until now. Taking off just my shoes, I lay fully dressed on the bed, alert and listening for barking dogs, but exhaustion must have overwhelmed me and lurched me into a deep, dreamless, sleep.

I was woken, startled by a banging door, saw the light filtering through the shutters, then realised the next day had begun. A quick splash of cold water in the washbowl made me feel more wake, I dragged my fingers through my hair, and listening again for barking dogs, I cautiously went downstairs to the kitchen. Madame Redoubt was alone and busy cooking on the old range, she turned, smiled, and greeted me warmly with milky coffee, more rough baked bread, and honey from her own hives. I looked around grateful that her father- in-law was not in the room.

"He's gone off doing bits and pieces on the farm," she explained when she saw me looking. "Happiest, if you can ever call him that, when he is out on the land. Not that it brings us any money now, and God knows we could do with some."

"Was your husband his only son?" The Madame nodded, sadness suddenly in her eyes.

"The cussed old thing won't sell any produce to them, if he can get away with it. So, we sell next to nothing as no one has any money. If they have, they don't buy cherries! Used to have wonderful crops of cherries, huge ones before all this. Had a stall at the market, but nothing now."

"How can I help today?" I interrupted, trying to change the subject. "There must be something that needs doing to keep me

10

occupied." Madame sighed and thought, it was a long time since she had anyone to help in any way, and eventually suggested I could weed the plants in the small vegetable garden behind the house.

"Only fresh stuff we can have," she explained. "And he thinks I have time to look after it on top of all this."

Madame loaned me a set of rather large overalls, but then I thought, most clothes were large on my small frame and set me to work on the patch of dry stony earth that was supposed to yield up precious green vegetables. Onions were recognisable in one row, then some straggly green plants were fighting each other and the weeds for space, so I began methodically pulling up the obvious weeds and hoeing the ground. I had never done any gardening before, as my life had encompassed walking in well-tended gardens not digging in them, and I sincerely hoped I wasn't pulling up anything worth eating. It all seemed so unreal, but yes, I was here in occupied France, willing and waiting to engage in the tasks I had been so meticulously trained for.

The sun continued to rise in the sky, a small portion of the vegetable patch was now in order, and I was leaning on the hoe just thinking about how to tackle the next part when I heard the dogs barking. I stood motionless, felt a deep, sudden, chill in my blood, caught my breath and dashed into the barn. My heart was hammering against my chest as I tried to listen for any tell-tale noises of people arriving, then I heard a low whistle from the direction of the house and my guide from the previous evening entered the barn.

"We need you now," he announced. "Come on, no time to waste. I'll explain on the way."

"My clothes." I spluttered, "I'm in overalls, and they are far too big."

"A great disguise," he retorted. "Just what you need today." But I noticed he had a brief smile on his face, it seemed there was a first time for everything.

"I must tell Madame."

"No need, just come, you'll be back before dark. We don't have time to waste."

Realising I was here to do exactly what was wanted, I followed him to the track at the front of the stone farmhouse, where a horse and four wheeled cart stood with straw bales on the rear.

"Get up behind and ride down in the bales, keep well down if you hear an engine, only they can run cars around here now." His instructions clear, minimal, and precise. He jumped up into the driving position and I clambered into the back of the cart lying between two bales of rather prickly straw.

The horse moved off at a slow walk over the bumpy track. So many questions filled my head, but I knew, we had all been taught, it was all about 'need to know'. If you only knew just enough, then you couldn't give others away if something went wrong. *Something going wrong,* I had to get that idea out of my head and concentrate on what was needed here and now, not what might happen.

"Don't ask questions, you won't get answers," we were all told. "You're there to do the job required, just get on with it." The horse began to trot over a better surface, and I could see the sky and tops of spiky pine trees going past. At one point, something noisy like a motorbike passed, but we didn't stop until after another rough road, where the horse halted in the shade next to a tumbledown barn.

A hand appeared over the bales, surprised and thankful I was going to be helped, I grasped it and jumped down from the wagon. We seemed to be in the middle of nowhere, a derelict barn with the roof falling in standing at the end of a stony track deep into a rocky gully. Without a word, my guide went immediately into the barn and motioned me to follow. All was quiet, and once my eyes were accustomed to the change in light, I could see another young man, hands on hips looking me over. It appeared he was decidedly unimpressed. There was another quick exchange in guttural Provencal French, but I got the gist, he too had expected someone different, at least someone who didn't look like me, but no time on pleasantries was wasted.

"We need you to make something for us, today. Can you do it?"

I guessed what they had in mind, this is what, after all, I had been trained for. Nervous anticipation and a fear I wouldn't manage their task bubbled to the surface, but I nodded and glanced past the young men for any tools and equipment.

"Tell me exactly what you want, and I will try but I don't know till I see exactly what you have here." A wooden box was dragged out from under the ancient bales of straw, revealing a motley collection of what looked like wires, tools, clips and other rusty items. I knew that some supplies of ammunition and explosives were coming in on air drops, but these were few and far between, what was here was very old. They explained their problem and what they wanted me to construct, it wasn't impossible, but it was not going to be easy with minimal equipment and a short timescale. Quickly I looked in the box and decided I needed two extra items if I was to make what they wanted and explained what I needed. My guide disappeared and left me at work using the dim light through the barn door. The second youth sat on a bale and silently studied me, with not a word passing between us.

Time passed, and eventually my guide returned with the necessary items, and before long I had what they wanted, a delayed detonator switch for an explosion. It was small and pretty sure to work, but it would be unstable when attached to the explosive.

"I really should put the last items in just before you put it in place," I carefully explained. "It's not safe otherwise." This was met with an audible scoff and grunt, with the two young men eyeing each other.

"We'll take the risk. We're not taking you that's for certain."

"Alright, but don't fasten that wire tight until you are ready and move away quickly." There was no point in arguing, I had done what they asked, it was their decision not mine.

Riding back, low down in the straw bales I wondered what the trigger was to be used for and when, and if I had passed the test. It was probably better I didn't know the details, but I sincerely hoped it would work.

The horse stopped well before the rutted track to the farm, with the last daylight fading quickly, I realised I had been away all afternoon. My guide appeared over the side of the cart and spoke softly.

"Go down the edge of these trees and follow the track to the back of the farm, don't knock just walk in, they will have some food waiting."

Again, he helped me down from the cart and held onto my hand for just an extra split second allowing me to look directly into his dark brown eyes.

"Tell me your name." I said quietly.

"Etienne, they call me Etienne," he replied, before jumping back on the cart and setting off along the track.

Darkness was closing in as I reached the farm. Approaching from the back I could see Madame through the barred window busy in the kitchen and, as I placed my hand on the door handle, I felt a wave of sheer exhaustion sweep over me realising it was not quite twenty-four hours since I had arrived. Such a lot had happened, was it all going to be like this?

Inside Madame greeted me warmly but asked no questions, and the old man sat with his back to me, reading. Again, food and drink appeared on the table, and we fell into easy conversation about the 'potager' and the plans for planting it with vegetables, with not one mention made of the afternoon's excursion. I excused myself after helping to clear up and made my way up the narrow wooden stairs to my bedroom.

This time I did undress, but kept my clothes close by for any unexpected arrivals. Falling asleep quickly I slept soundly but was woken suddenly in the dark by a vivid dream where I saw a solider with his legs blown off by an explosion, but when I looked again, he had the face of Etienne.

Chapter 3

The strong sunlight filtered through the shutters to wake me for a second day. It had been a better night's sleep until the abrupt shocking dream, after which I had lain awake for some time, trying to get the picture of the body, with the legs blown off and the face of Etienne, out of my head.

Lying still for a moment, I tried hard to make sense of this sudden change in my life. I knew I had volunteered for this dangerous work; I had been told I was exactly what they needed, but I was most probably naive, and it wasn't until I arrived that I began to comprehend the enormity of my choice. I seemed to be constantly in a state of heightened anxiety, wondering if I would ever be able to relax again. Yes, I had been taught all the skills to help 'harry' the occupying force, if the Resistance in the area were prepared to use my full potential. My appearance of petite, feminine and youthful, didn't tell my full story, but at this moment seemed to be counting against me, though I had been assured it would help me blend into the local population. Etienne and his associates were going to have to trust my knowledge and nimble fingers to allow me to play the vital part I had been sent to do.

Hearing Madame in the kitchen already hard at work, I knew I ought to get down to help. Again, the old man was missing, and we had an amicable chat about mundane things that partially helped to settle my nerves. After breakfast, I suggested getting on in the garden, but Madame however, had a message for me.

What now? I thought, as I caught my breath.

"You are leaving us today. You need to go to the place you were left yesterday for 3pm. That's all I know." No point in asking for more information, it wasn't there, anyway I didn't need to know, yet anyway. I must have gone pale or looked even more anxious than I had done before, as Madame suggested, as if to distract me, I went with her to collect some herbs, milk the goats, and check the rabbit snares.

"I don't often have anyone to talk to," she explained. "It'll be good to have some company." We set off through the cherry trees where the blossom was beginning to set, and came upon a small, stone walled field where three goats grazed the rough ground in seeming contentment. While Madame milked two of them, I gathered soft deep fragranced thyme from the woodland nearby with some spiky new green growth of rosemary. Two snared rabbits were collected and placed in the basket, and on the way back we chatted like old friends.

Madame told me about her husband, taken so soon after their marriage by the horrors of the First World War. She explained she had just married and moved to the farm when he was called up to fight. He did not return, and her life since then, was one of caring for his father and working on the farm. As her husband had no brothers, it was just her and her father-in-law. At first things had not been so bad, but now they existed very much on what they could produce, and just waited with hope, that it would all be over eventually. I could only imagine what Madame's life must be like, and it spurred me on with even greater resolve to do what I could to help.

The sun was well up in the dazzling blue sky by the time we arrived back. A quick bite of bread and goats cheese set me up to tackle more work in the vegetable garden, as I was determined to make some headway into making it into a neat, tidy and possibly productive area. It was the least I could do.

In good time, I gathered my few things and made myself as presentable as possible, finding a comb in my coat pocket to tease my unruly hair into some sort of tidiness. I felt a distinct sense of loss as I kissed Madame goodbye on the cheeks, for in just two days I had gained a remarkable sense of friendship. I had felt safe at this remote farm, and I had no idea what I would face next, so I thanked Madame profusely and, grasping her hand, promised I would do all I could to end this dreadful situation.

"Bonne chance." she said quietly, smiling and waving as I set off uphill to find the place where I had been told to wait. It was quite some way over rocky ground, and I was out of breath by the time I reached the poorly surfaced road, so I stood carefully out of sight in shade of the trees until I heard the approaching sound of horses' hooves.

Would it be Etienne? At the very least a known face, even if not too forthcoming, would give me some extra reassurance. I stayed hidden in the trees until indeed Etienne arrived and pulled the cart to a halt, giving a low whistle. Smiling and happy to take his hand I climbed up into the back of the cart to find, very much to my surprise, a man was already ensconced in the bales. He was older than either of the other two I had seen, had more of an air of authority, and was more smartly dressed. The cart moved off slowly. I said nothing, sat down opposite him, but could sense I was being judged again, though eventually he spoke, directly and without any introduction.

"We have a plan for you, we've everything in place, but you must follow these instructions exactly."

I nodded and listened with curiosity, then disbelief and finally horror at their plan. It had been decided the easiest way to hide me was out in the open, 'in plain sight' and to that end I was being sent to take up a job as the school mistress in the nearby village. It was presumed my education and background, I had grown up in Paris in a wealthy family, would give me the knowledge I needed, and the thousands of displaced French people gave me good reason to be here with no completely traceable history. My papers, false of course, were partially correct, no one would suspect anything, if any checks were made they would lead back to pre-war reality, the easiest way to hide a falsehood. The School Master would have no idea of my real identity, it was much safer that way, and I would live at the schoolhouse above his flat. He was, apparently, a widower with a lady friend with whom he spent most evenings and nights, so I could come and go undetected.

It seemed they had it all worked out, and I knew to ask no questions, but the enormity of the situation was daunting. I had to admit it was a daring and simple plan, but it was up to me, working alone, to carry it off. I didn't have a choice, but my hand was trembling as I grasped the worn leather handbag and felt hat that he had given me.

"This contains everything you will need." He gestured toward a small suitcase by his feet. "The Schoolmaster, Monsieur Foix,

17

is meeting the train from Cavaillon at the Station in Apt this afternoon. You will have 'travelled' today from Paris. Do you understand? Follow my instructions exactly and there'll be no problem."

I had just about taken in all the information when Etienne drew into a dilapidated courtyard in the town, and I got out with the other man, both of us brushing straw from our clothes. Doing exactly as I was told, I followed him out of the old wooden double gates and up the street at a safe distance, arriving at the imposing station building, where regular trains stopped on the way to the Alps from the Rhone Valley.

We entered the station building from the rear, and I tried very hard not to at look the two soldiers, guns at their sides, who lounged against the café doorway opposite, thankfully showing little interest in the people passing.

The man had carried the small suitcase, and as planned, he placed it on the tiled floor by the doorway while he studied the train timetable. I waited, as arranged, by the entrance to the platform as if meeting someone from the next train. The station was quiet, but anyway, no one seemed to pay any attention to either of us, I just hoped they could not hear my heart thumping against my chest.

Just then the noise of the train arriving filled the small space. The man left the suitcase and engaged the ticket seller in conversation, while I joined the disembarking stream of people leaving the platform, collecting the suitcase as I passed. Now, with felt hat on my head and carrying the small suitcase I looked for all the world as if I had just arrived on the train.

As I emerged to the square behind the station, a short, balding, man in a worn, but well-kept suit, emerged from a battered Citroen car and limped toward me.

"Mademoiselle Andre?" he said, hand outstretched. "Welcome to Apt, I do hope your journey wasn't too tiring." I smiled, greeted him formally, and followed him to the car.

Thankfully, Monsieur Foix talked for most of the short drive to St Saturnin, he obviously liked the sound of his own voice, but it did allow me to relax a little and try to settle into my new role. Quite simply I must be myself but be very careful how much I revealed to anyone, I was part of an audacious plan but it ought to work, at least I had to keep telling myself that.

"The two ladies from the village who have been looking after the younger class of children mean well and have tried hard, but we needed a properly qualified person," Monsieur Foix went on. "I am so pleased you have arrived."

He explained what I already knew that I would have the rooms at the top of the schoolhouse, and he lived below with the school rooms on the ground floor.

" I have the key to the front door, but there is a back door through the kitchen, you can have that key to that as I go out a lot in the evenings," he said by way of explanation as we arrived at the front of the building.

There was a low wall with iron railings much in need of a coat of paint alongside the road, with the school set back behind a dusty gravel playground with high creeper clad walls either side. Two doors marked 'boys' and 'girls' were at each end with two rows of identical windows with painted shutters and two attic windows above. The ground floor had two school rooms and a small kitchen, with the stairs to Monsieur Foix's rooms, and then steeper stairs up to the two rooms above.

"A woman from the village cooks a meal each lunchtime for the children, we eat with them, but you can use the kitchen whenever you want." He said, as he showed me up the narrow stairs to the small attic rooms. "Tomorrow is Sunday, Mass is at 10am, the church is just in the village. Perhaps we can meet after to prepare for Monday?" I nodded my agreement and was glad when he eventually left me alone, allowing me to sit down wearily in the worn leather armchair. I felt drained but curiously settled, I now had a purpose and a means to do it.

At a quarter to ten the next morning I set off up the village street toward the stone church with its magnificent octagonal bell tower. I had found, amazingly, that the suitcase I had picked up at the station, contained a good collection of suitable clothing, most of it in my size. I walked steadily toward the church realising that religion in times of war brings people together, and as expected, the church was well filled. It was obvious the news of my arrival had spread, with most of the congregation taking a furtive glance at me as I walked up the aisle to take a place in one of the side pews. At the end of the service, I left the church having smiled and acknowledged so many people. They were all very welcoming.

I sincerely hoped I could be of use to them.

Chapter 4

I was down early in the schoolroom on Monday morning. Anticipation and fluttering nerves had not made for a restful night, although long holidays in the summers spent with my younger cousins, before my life was turned upside down, had given me some insight into my new role. Luckily my father had insisted I was taught all subjects, not just those normally reserved for girls by my private tutors. I was very willing and, it seemed, able to learn, but I was, by no stretch of the imagination a trained teacher. A set curriculum was going to help, but it was not going to be easy. I had been well educated, but mostly at home, so the classroom was something altogether new.

At 8.30am Monsieur Foix opened the school doors and my class of children came flooding in. They were obviously expecting someone new and quietly sat in their desks, their eager eyes staring at their new teacher. Boys and girls, their ages ranged from about five years old to eleven, they all looked thin and wore clothes that had seen better days, but the war had gone on for years now, so it was impossible to expect anything else. They looked anxious, not knowing what was going to happen next, though some of the older boys had a more defiant expression.

"I'm Mademoiselle Andre." I said by way of introduction, and I tried to engage them by greeting each child with a handshake, expecting them to reply and hoping they didn't notice how nervous I was.

"Now I need to learn your names," I announced. So, trying to ease the stilted atmosphere I initiated a game using the children's names, making deliberate mistakes to encourage some laughter, until most of their names were well rehearsed in my head, and we all began to relax a little.

I coped with the formal work that followed, and the morning passed quickly. After lunch, where I assured Monsieur Foix that the morning had gone well, the class seemed happy to continue with lessons until I read them a story later in the afternoon, then suddenly the first day was over. The children were smiling and so was I. Breathing a sigh of relief, I stood at the school door and shook hands with each child using their name, smiling and waving a goodbye. They skipped and straggled across the playground, some to waiting elder brothers or sisters or family members when out of the corner of my eye, I glimpsed a tall figure in familiar work clothes. Was it Etienne? I could see his dark curly hair under his cap. One of the younger boys ran up to him and they set off down the street chattering together. A younger brother, a cousin or perhaps a nephew, I hoped I had not stared for too long or made any sign of recognition, I needed to be very careful.

Those days of that first week began to merge into a routine, with the boys and girls I taught willing and most of them eager to learn. They had the carefree innocence of youth, despite the atmosphere of oppression and fear that surrounded them, and they brought enthusiasm and hope with them each day. However, the occupying army had a noticeable presence in the village with soldiers in uniform often seen and conveys of troops frequently rumbling along the main road travelling north. The children went quiet when the troop-carrying lorries went past, glancing at each other, waiting until the noise had faded before resuming their activity.

On Friday, whilst we were all eating lunch, a picture drawn by one of the young children appeared on my desk. Smiling at the 'gift' I turned it over to see message *tonight 9pm at the church*. An involuntary shiver ran down my spine. Fear but also excitement, at last I was going to do something to help, perhaps they would begin to trust me more, allow me to do what I had been trained for, but I knew I had to wait for them to make decisions.

That evening, I slipped out of the school by the back door and made my way up the darkened street toward the church. There was as yet, no official curfew, but most villagers chose not to walk the streets at night in case they met a patrol and were accused of being involved in some clandestine activity. I had to be careful not to draw any unwanted attention. I could hear the noise from the cafe on the corner of the Main Street, mostly off duty soldiers, otherwise the street was deserted. I kept to the shadows thrown by the tightly packed, tall houses, grimacing at my shoes making unwanted noise on the cobbles. On reaching the church I furtively glanced around in the dim street lighting, and seeing no-one, approached the huge, deeply carved, wooden doors. A hand touched my shoulder, I swung round to see Etienne.

"Come with me."

He was, it seemed, a man of few words. I walked with him side by side along the narrow street that curved round the back of the church. Not one word passed between us, though I was longing to ask questions and engage him in conversation. Either his nature was as taciturn as it seemed, or I was not of interest. All the houses were shuttered against the dark with the smell of wood smoke from the chimneys hanging in the air. Etienne led and turned down a narrow alley and then abruptly through a lower ground floor door. It was dark and musty smelling in this cellar with piles of wood and other unrecognisable objects littered on the damp floor, with the only light coming from the rudimentary torch Etienne was carrying. He dug under some old blankets.

"Can you get this working?" He revealed what appeared to be a radio transmitter in a suitcase which was damaged on one side, no further explanation was forthcoming. Had it been dropped as its operator was fleeing, or worse still apprehended, the words formed in my mind, but stopped there, I knew not to ask questions. I simply didn't need to know; however, my curious mind couldn't stop thinking. I knew how important the radios were and how dangerous it was to be found with any of this sort of equipment. Although trained as a basic radio operator, all agents were, I didn't know anything about repairing transmitters, but in childhood I had loved, and been encouraged by my Papa, to take apart, and reassemble anything I could get my hands on. This memory surfaced in my mind.

" I'll try but I may need some new parts, is that possible?"

A long silence. I wondered if he had heard me. Did I perhaps intimidate him? My mother had once told me that overtly intelligent girls didn't encourage the opposite sex, as men liked to think themselves superior, such was my mother's message. Although catching a good gentleman to marry may have been my mother's preoccupation, it had never been mine. Etienne was intriguing though.

"Do what you can here. I don't know about new pieces."

Setting to work in the dim light, I patiently dismantled the contents, made all the connections sound again and bypassed some of the damaged items hoping, but not knowing whether they were vital to the receiver's function. I put the box back together as securely as possible.

" Can we test it?" I asked cautiously. I knew radio equipment was being regularly tracked, and the signal would give our position away.

" Not here."

"Then I've done as much as I can without new pieces."

I showed him the parts that were needed if it didn't work, with no idea how they were to be obtained. No doubt if they needed me again, I would be summoned. I waited in silence as Etienne slipped the radio away under the shelf and covered it with the same pile of old blankets.

We left the damp, musty cellar and emerged onto the moonlit street just as the church clock struck ten. Etienne took my arm, tucking his under mine, and we set off down the street.

"No-one will suspect a couple walking together in the street in the evening." He said with a smile, by way of explanation. I returned his smile, remained silent but leaned in closer to him.

Let's act the part then, I thought.

Chapter 5

Sleep wasn't coming easily. I was lying thinking, which was never a good way to drift off, yet it was quiet, no troop lorries passing through. My attic bedroom was airless, and I tossed and turned feeling frustrated, being unable to use the skills I had been taught, as it seemed those in control locally were unwilling to trust me beyond basic tasks. I was well aware that being small, young, and female didn't seem to improve their confidence in me, yet I was not here to do tasks that relied on strength but rather on nimble fingers and a trained mind. How could I prove to them my worth if they didn't include me in the planning? I decided to try to talk to Etienne, he was my only contact, but I guessed he would not have much influence. Perhaps I just had to be patient, though that wasn't one of my known virtues. The church clock struck twice, turning over in the lumpy bed I pushed Etienne's face from my mind, concentrating on tomorrow's lesson plans which brought a fitful sleep.

The following afternoon was warm, it seemed summer was coming, so the windows in the schoolroom were open wide, along with the door to the corridor. I was helping two of the youngest children with a rather old wooden jigsaw on the classroom floor, when the rest of the class went unusually quiet. Looking up, I could see a tall, slim officer clad in the uniform of the occupying forces standing in the doorway. I rose to my feet.

"Good afternoon, Herr Captain." I recognised the insignia. "Children, remember your manners and stand to greet our visitor."

"Good afternoon," they chanted, without enthusiasm, as they stood up.

"Monsieur Foix, the teacher in charge, is just next door, I'll send one of the children to fetch him for you if you will wait?" The Officer smiled.

"No, don't disturb him. It was you I came to see." I felt myself go pale, and my breath quicken, and I fought to control myself as I walked across the classroom as steadily as I could, keeping my back to the children. Playing for time, I tucked a loose strand of hair behind my ear with one hand.

"How can I help?" My voice as normal and as helpful as I could make it.

"I was passing through St Saturnin today and wanted to check some information I had received." I looked straight into his pale blue eyes and noted the blonde hair curling under the peaked cap, the insignia on his lapel, and the service medal ribbons on his chest. Noting details helped keep panic from rising, a technique we had been taught. But I kept quiet, for it was up to him to explain.

"My informants told me a pretty young teacher had arrived at the village school." A knowing smile played around his lips, and I realised he was enjoying the anxiety he was causing. I just wanted to spit in his eye but managed to stop myself, as I knew that really wouldn't have done anyone any good. Thinking fast, I decided I could perhaps turn this to my advantage if I tried. I opened my eyes wide, turned my head slightly quizzically to one side and replied with a teasing voice with a faint smile dancing on my lips.

"And so, were they right?" Silence. The officer at first looked momentarily surprised, it wasn't the answer he was expecting, then he threw his head back and laughed loudly.

"They didn't tell me she was amusing as well." I kept the half smile dancing on my lips looking directly into his steel blue eyes.

"But you're busy now. I will come back sometime soon." With his black gloved hand, he took mine very formally, gave a sharp nod of his head, and left as noiselessly as he had arrived. I stared at the empty doorway and taking two deep breaths, could feel the colour slowly returning to my cheeks. I needed to remain calm as I turned to face the class, speaking to them all.

"We must always remember to be polite when we have a visitor. You should stand and greet them to show respect." I glimpsed two of the elder boys grimacing at my remark, and whilst I fully understood their sentiments, I dare not show my approval. I was walking a difficult tightrope here, and they had to understand my position as a teacher, not as an assistant to the Resistance, so I used volume and tone to emphasis the point.

"It isn't for us to decide whether we will be polite when a visitor arrives. You must follow the school rules for the good of everyone." Silence filled the classroom. I had rarely raised my voice before, I didn't need to as the children were usually polite and compliant, but this time I felt I must make myself clear to all the children. I just could not be seen to be taking sides.

I had no doubt the news of the visit of the officer would travel very quickly around the village, as would my reaction. I had to be careful. I tried to restore normality by smiling and saying in my usual way,

"Come on now, put your books away and let's have some more of our story we began yesterday. Its nearly time to go home." Noisy chatter again filled the school room, but I kept an anxious watch on the door.

I didn't have long to wait, as he returned after the children had gone home the very next day. I would have very much liked to consult with the local Resistance on how the situation ought to be played, as nothing like this had been included in any of my training. Surely word of the officer's visit would have reached someone, and I needed some means of contacting them. I would need to discuss that, if I saw Etienne again, as there had to be some way for me to communicate safely in an emergency. However, any time for that had gone, for now anyway.

He stood in the doorway as before, immaculate in his dark uniform, this time a smile already playing on his lips.

"Good afternoon, Mademoiselle." Again, in perfect French.

"Good afternoon, Herr Captain, back so soon?" I was trying to keep the conversation light-hearted, though my heart was pounding in my chest, deciding that without instructions to the contrary the safest option was to play along with him, for now anyway.

"Better timing today, your pupils have all gone, now we can perhaps have a proper conversation." I swallowed, breathed deeply, and kept the smile on my face. I didn't want to rebuff this officer and cause annoyance and possible unwanted attention; however, it was so difficult to fraternise this way with the enemy.

27

I realised that I could perhaps, use his attention to my advantage, but it was going to be a risky strategy.

"I am sorry I can't offer you any refreshment, but conversation, well that I can probably manage." I forced myself to look directly at him.

"Actually, I thought a ride in my car may appeal, such a lovely evening. It won't be dark for some time." Refusal, it seemed, was not an option. I realised I might as well get the encounter over as soon as possible, so glancing at my unflattering floral dress that more or less fitted my petite frame where it touched, I snatched my worn red cardigan and followed him to his immaculate open top staff car. This was blatantly parked directly outside the school entrance. I felt as if the whole village was watching, as he held open the door and holding my hand to help me in, closing it securely, while rarely taking his eyes off me. He climbed into the driver's seat, started the engine, setting off out of the village along a quiet road into the mountains. All the time I kept my eyes fixed ahead.

"They tell me you come from Paris," he remarked over the roar of the engine and the wind whistling past. "You must notice a big difference; a sleepy Provençal village won't offer much excitement."

"I have my job which I enjoy, it takes up most of my time. It's good to be doing something rewarding and useful".

"But why here?" He persisted. "It's a long way from Paris." A seemingly innocent remark yet it rang alarm bells, and I wondered how much he really knew about my background, invented and real. Was he playing with me to get me to make a mistake?

"When I was young, I used to visit around here, staying with a relative in Pertuis. I heard of the schoolteacher's position, so I applied. It was good to get out of Paris, the atmosphere isn't good there at the moment." I was feeling braver.

Make what you want of that remark, I thought. He fell silent as he pulled the car into a viewpoint over a deep limestone valley, stopping the engine. The sun was starting to disappear behind the Mourre Negre, the highest point in the Luberon, with a rosy sky contrasting with the deep shadows in the wooded valleys.

Taking the initiative, I decided to turn the conversation away from myself, it would be safer that way I thought.

"Herr Captain, you have the advantage of me. You seem to know all about me, and I know nothing about you, except that you speak perfect French." He turned to look me straight in the eye again then returned to look at the fading sunset.

"How remiss of me, I speak perfect French because my mother was French. I find it very useful now." He paused. I didn't rush to fill the silence.

"Living in the Rhine valley where France meets Germany it was natural that we spoke both languages, but I was educated in Berlin. Captain Otto Kaufman at your service." He finished very formally, taking my hand in his and holding on to it. "Is that enough information for you?"

"Well, for the moment yes," I teased, feeling rather reckless. "Please understand, I don't usually accept car rides from strange men." He smiled, directly looking at me.

"Can a gentleman not have a conversation with a pretty and intelligent young lady without causing anxiety? I am not going to bite!" When he smiled, I suddenly felt something akin to attraction. This shocked me. I had little experience with men, my upbringing keeping me confined to my parent's elite social circle. More recently the training camp had thrown many different kinds of people from all backgrounds together, but I had kept myself apart, not through snobbish reserve, rather total inexperience in mixed social situations. I decided I just had to follow my instincts, for now anyway.

But what is the true nature of this man's attention? I thought, and more importantly. *How am I going to deal with it?*

Taking a deep breath, I decided the best way was honesty.

"Herr Kaufman."

"Otto please."

"Herr Kaufman, we are not in normal times, you are a German officer, and I am a French civilian with an important job in the community. I have a certain standing that I need to maintain. I fear that does not include trips out with a member of the occupying army." There I had said it and felt relief that I had been honest and straightforward, but I had yet to hear his reply, as I doubted most French civilians would be so direct.

Silence again, this seemed to be one of his favourite conversation tools.

"So," he replied slowly. "If we had met casually away from here and all your concerns, would your hesitation be the same? Do you really suspect my intentions to be dishonourable? We are not all the same you know!"

This time the silence was mine.

"I see you cannot answer that, perhaps I am pressing you too hard and too soon." He took my hand and waited until I looked at him.

"You don't seem to want to believe this, but I mean no harm. There is much in my life at present which I do not enjoy, over which I have no control. It is so refreshing to have different company and get away from all my problems."

Again, I chose to remain silent, to be quite honest I didn't know how to reply and didn't want to say the wrong thing.

"An hour or two of your time, some simple pleasure in company and conversation. We can be discreet if that is your worry. Is that too much to ask?" Incongruously I felt sympathy for him. In different circumstances, I started to allow myself to think, but no this was here, and this was now. I needed to decide, and quickly, what was for the best. Perhaps I could play for time.

"Herr Kaufman, Otto, I don't want to offend, but I have explained I need to keep my standing in the community. Please let me think about how this could, perhaps, work." He seemed at least a little satisfied, as I suspected he was used to getting his own way immediately.

Dusk was now well upon us. He turned the car toward the village, the last rosy glow of the sunset showing over the mountains. We rode along in silence, and he stopped by the turning to the old windmill just outside the village. Grateful that he was showing some awareness of my situation, I quickly climbed down from the car and turned to walk back to the village. But it wasn't going to be that easy, as he called after me.

"May I contact you in a few days' time to perhaps arrange an afternoon together?"

He seemed solicitous and genuine, what should I do? I hesitated, then almost without realising it, nodded my head.

Somehow, I had made a decision, set a path for the future from which there seemed to be no turning back.

Chapter 6

What had I done? What on earth was I thinking about? Why did I agree to meet him again? What should I have said? Urgent, anxious questions flooded into my head as I watched the rear lights of the car disappearing into the gathering dusk. Had I really just agreed to meet a member of the hated occupying forces willingly? I could try to tell myself that it might produce some useful information to pass on, or had I just taken the easiest way out for the moment? However, the difficult question remained. *What was I going to do when he contacted me again?*

Deep in thought I realised I couldn't stand at the side of the road for ever, as I was now shivering in my thin cardigan in the cool evening air, so I walked on toward the village as the darkness intensified. Having in fact agreed to nothing, in omission I had actually agreed to everything. I tried telling myself that rejection would have led to far more scrutiny and that was dangerous, however acceptance of his advances, however minimal at present, started down a frightening slippery slope without little chance of escaping.

The troubling thought that kept resurfacing in my mind was that the conversation with him had not brought about the disgust for my actions that I had assumed it would. Damm it. He was handsome, very considerate and gentlemanly toward me, and although I tried to stop this thought, I did have some empathy for his situation. Had I actually enjoyed his company and moreover his attention? I shuddered, but that thought which had been impossible yesterday, niggled away in my brain.

It was almost dark, the lights from the café on the corner ahead lit the way. I suppose I wasn't really concentrating, being deep in thought, so that when I felt myself being lifted off my feet, my arms held tightly against my sides, with a hand over my mouth, I had no time to react. My body was swung deep into a side alley between two houses where it was completely dark. I came to my senses and kicked out catching the heel of my shoe on my assailant's shin. I heard him gasp, but he only seemed to grip tighter, and with his hand clamped over my mouth he whispered fiercely directly into my ear.

"What do you think you are doing?" Etienne's voice. I stopped struggling and he dropped his arms releasing me. In shock but also shaking with anger, I stepped back against the wall of the narrow alley. There was hardly any distance between us, though I could make out very little in the dark, but before I had a chance to say anything he spoke.

"Do you know who that was?" I clearly recognised the anger in his voice.

"Of course I do," I spat back, equally angry. "A German officer."

"Not just any Officer, he is the personal assistant to the director of all the troop movements in south-eastern France." It seemed Etienne was well informed.

"And his father is a General with close links to the inner circle in Berlin." Even more information. My eyes, having now adjusted to the dark allowed me to see Etienne's exasperated expression. Before he could utter any further accusations, I unleashed my fury at his unjustified attitude. I whispered angrily knowing the last thing we both needed was unwanted attention from any passers-by, however unlikely that may be.

"What was it you expected me to do? Reject and antagonise him? Bring down scrutiny upon myself and through me on others?" I heard a sharp intake of breath, I seemed to have got the message home, though no reply followed.

"Where were your instructions as to what to do when, as I am sure you did, you knew of his arrival at the school yesterday?" The question hung in the air between them. Could I sense not just anger but perhaps jealousy at my actions? Or was I just reading too much into the situation, as frayed tempers on both sides didn't make for rational thinking.

"I had no choice but go with him this evening, he made that perfectly plain. I told him nothing about me that he could not have already found out, and most probably had." There was no reply, but I could just make out him staring at me, but the darkness was making his expression difficult to read. Perhaps Etienne had nothing further to say to me, but I wasn't finished

33

with him yet. My dissatisfaction with the whole situation spilled out.

"Exactly when am I going to be included in your planning? Does all my training count for nothing? Arrange a meeting with someone who can make some decisions if you can't and let me know."

I abruptly turned back down the alley before he had a chance to reply and emerged in the now total darkness on the village street. I was still shaking with anger, exasperation and, I had to admit, fear. I had to get back to the schoolhouse, try to feel safe again and attempt to put all the days happenings into some sort rational understanding. At that precise moment I didn't know what to think about anyone or anything, I just needed to get away.

Stumbling, almost running, toward the lights of the café I felt a hand on my shoulder. Swinging round, it was Etienne, cap pulled down over his eyes. I tried to shake myself free.

"You need to get home safely. Here take my arm." A command not a request, and for the second time that day I didn't feel in any position to refuse. Exhaustion and an overwhelming desire to be alone with my thoughts swept over me, so I slipped my hand through his arm and walked silently toward the dim lights of the café ahead. Silence hung in the air between us. I don't know what I had expected, perhaps an apology of some kind, or maybe even some attempt at conversation, but Etienne remained stony faced holding tightly onto my arm.

Two can play at this game I thought and stared steadfastly ahead.

Opening the school gate Etienne detached his arm and, with a cursory "Goodnight," disappeared into the darkness. Suddenly overcome by the enormity of the past few hours I wearily let myself into the back door of the schoolrooms and made my way slowly up to the top floor. I then just sat for a long time in the worn leather armchair trying to put my thoughts into some kind of sensible order.

Gradually my heart returned to a normal beat, my breathing slowed, and I slowly sipped a glass of water, as I had to think this through carefully. Seemingly, I had two problems, but they could not be dealt with separately. Uppermost in my mind was of course what on earth was I going to do about Otto? Stringing him along, getting his confidence, finding out some information might be useful, but it was a risky strategy. It could prove worthwhile, and probably was the simplest option right now, as I had no idea how to get out of a further meeting. However, how far would I have to go and more importantly, was I prepared for possible further involvement? I had felt empathy for him, so how could I be sure to keep my emotions in check? Otto filled my thoughts but with no obvious answers I turned to my second problem. How then could I possibly get the local Maquis Resistance to use any of the potential information profitably when I had no means of communication. My anger was revived, the local Maquis seemed unsure of my capabilities and unwilling to use any of my knowledge of explosives to their advantage. There was so much I was trained to do that could help, but would they listen and take me seriously?

I hoped I had sent a clear message with Etienne but had no idea what might come of it. One thing was sure though, I didn't think I was Etienne's favourite person right now.

Chapter 7

Two days passed. I had not heard from Otto and began to think this probably would be the best solution. If he never contacted me again then a huge problem would just disappear. More importantly, I had achieved the meeting I wanted with the Maquis, but it hadn't gone too well.

The rendezvous in a dark, lower ground floor room in a house on the edge of the village had been difficult to say the least. I smiled ruefully at the recollection. Etienne had silently taken me there, then withdrawn, leaving me in a small dimly lit room with three older men who clearly were not impressed by my demands.

I had ideas about planning and executing attacks on the occupying force and expected to be taken seriously. After all, if they didn't know what I could do they couldn't use me to their full advantage. My task was to help them 'harry' the opposing army, to debilitate their ability to concentrate on the main occupation and, in the future, to distract their forces when the invasion began. I explained all this, they listened in silence and my suggestions seemed to fall on deaf ears. Only one spoke but he told me, quite forcibly, to await their command and their instructions, I was to be included but only when they were ready. As for the 'Otto' conundrum they instructed me to 'play the Nazi Boy along' as I may get some useful information, but I would be on my own working entirely on my own initiative. The meeting was short, my reception frosty, and it was obvious they felt I didn't know my place. I very soon realised I would get no further antagonising them and left the meeting with a frustrated feeling that I had wasted my time.

Etienne emerged out of the shadows to walk me home, again arm in arm, as we would create least suspicion like that. Walking in silence, I tried to make conversation, asking about the child he often collected from school. He relaxed a little and began talking about his nephew, but all too soon we were back at the schoolroom.

"Thank you for helping me," I said quietly, I was trying to make up for the fiasco between us last time. A nod came as a reply, but as he turned to go, he looked directly at me for the first time that evening.

"You must take care, don't trust that man, please." Before I could reply he had slipped into the shadows. A shiver went down my spine. What did he know about Otto?

Otto's courteous, handwritten note was waiting for me the next day at school. It assumed I would meet him again it seemed, so there was no means of getting out of the rendezvous. Not knowing what to think or feel I tried to come to terms with what I was going to do.

The Provençal Spring was delightful, warm sunny days with the countryside bursting into life. The vines were just waking up with their first tentative leaves exploring their way out of the twisted gnarled branches. The pink and white cherry blossom now coated the valleys, just a hint of the crop to come.

Otto had suggested meeting at the turning to the old windmill outside the village on Saturday afternoon. The sun was shining and, grateful that there were so few villagers about, I casually strolled along the road hoping not to attract any attention. I heard the approach of his vehicle and felt my heart beat faster, my breathing becoming shallow. I needed to get myself under control and not to show my anxiety, but my thoughts drummed loudly in my head.

You don't have to do this. I knew it would certainly make everything much less complicated if I didn't but, having come this far there seemed no opportunity to turn back.

The car stopped level with me and there was Otto, now out of uniform, with a broad, youthful, inviting smile. He leaned over, opened the door and I climbed up into the car without any apparent hesitation. My body was doing the exact opposite to the screaming thoughts in my head.

"I am so pleased you came." He looked me straight in the eye. It felt as if he could read my mind. I had to just get on with this and act it out. "Such lovely weather for an afternoon away from work for both of us, don't you think?" I stayed silent and nodded in reply.

Just let him do the talking, make all the suggestions. Just play along with whatever he wants.

"I've planned a surprise for later, but now let's get some fresh air in our lungs." He put his foot on the accelerator and roared out of the village. Thankfully the engine noise and the wind rushing past in the open topped car made any further conversation difficult. However, he turned from time to time and smiled encouragingly at me. He took the road out toward the mountains again, turning up a track just before the plateau, and switched off the engine. Turning to me and fixing me in his direct piercing blue-eyed gaze he said.

"I thought a walk, then I have a picnic I hoped we could share." Again, I just smiled my agreement, I really didn't know what to safely say. I was going to just let my instincts take over. We set off together along a track heading to a viewpoint over the Calavon valley. I stumbled over some stony ground, and he caught my hand, keeping hold and looking directly at me again. He spoke jovially,

"You're very quiet. Where's the independent feisty young lady who put me in my place last week?" I looked away not knowing how to reply. His tone changed abruptly "Has someone said something to you? You must tell me, and I will protect you." He kept hold of my hand, now tightening his grip.

It was so near the truth it shocked me. The local Maquis group certainly didn't approve of 'independent feisty', but the agreement to continue this dangerous liaison was one item on which we had managed to agree, however I knew I was on my own. I had to think quickly, or the afternoon would turn into a dangerous disaster. I found my voice and tried to sound calm, but the trouble was I had never been very good at telling lies.

"No…. no… It's just well……. nice to have an adult talking to me! My days are spent conversing with children. It's just so pleasant to be out, my life this week has been pretty mundane actually." It was, even I could see, a pretty feeble excuse but on the spur of the moment it was the best I could manage. He looked at me enquiringly. Had I convinced him? I had to try to be more genuine or this was just not going to work. I forced what I hoped was a casual smile, and he gently lifted my hand and touched it with his lips, watching my expression the whole time. I kept the smile on my face, I had to get out of this situation as I began to fear he could sense my unease. So, trusting to luck and with a somewhat cheeky expression in my voice, I said,

"Come on, race you to the top!"

Taking him by surprise, and being quite fleet of foot, I got ahead of him, reaching the boulder strewn summit a few seconds before he did. He was laughing now and, looking straight into my eyes, whispered suggestively,

"You won't get away next time so easily." He slipped his hand round my waist, and as I looked up into his smiling eyes, he smiled back and I let him kiss me, slowly, full on the lips.

What was I doing? This should have disgusted me, but I had never been in anything akin to this situation before. Having had a very sheltered upbringing I had absolutely no experience of men, so I was following my instincts now, and had really no idea where they were leading me. Otto held me close and began to gently stroke my hair as I relaxed leaning into his body. Excitement and fear gripped me, and perhaps sensing my trembling as he gently took my hand and gestured to sit down.

"Come on let's sit and look at the splendid view." Sitting close beside him, his arm protectively around me, I felt safe and stopped trembling. My thoughts were screaming at me to get away and stop all this before things got even more complicated, but I took no notice. Otto began to talk again about everyday things, his home in Germany his two elder sisters, and his love of the outdoors. Out of uniform it was easy to forget he was the enemy. He was just a handsome, considerate young man who enjoyed my company, but I was finding it difficult to concentrate with feelings aroused within me that I not experienced before.

Was I actually enjoying this? I really did not know what to do or think. Acting on pure instinct I tried to lighten the conversation and teased him about his sisters and made him laugh.

"Cecile." The use of my name brought me rapidly back to reality and my senses. "I do so enjoy being with you. I hope we can do this again, soon?" Another kiss stopped any reply, but there was no hesitation on my part.

I should stop this while I can. I realised this, but also that it just wasn't going to happen. We retraced our steps to the car with Otto holding my hand.

"I'm not letting you get away again," he explained with a broad smile on his face. A basket of food was waiting on the back seat of the car. Food the like of which I had not seen for a very long time. Properly baked bread with real flour, soft creamy cheese and cold roasted meat nestling in the basket along with a bottle of white wine. As we shared the picnic as I listened contentedly to more stories about his childhood. Otto then asked to meet again soon, all too readily I agreed.

Later that day I sat deep in thought in the old armchair in my attic room, the small window partially open, with the cool evening breeze drifting through. Conflicting opinions were racing round my head. A large part of me was disgusted that I had not only spent the afternoon with the enemy but had enjoyed it. Yet Otto was so engaging, and it was just wonderful to be treated with such consideration and be in the company of someone who so obviously enjoyed being with me. Every logical angle on the situation told me I needed to stop now before I became involved deeper in a situation out of which I could not extract myself. Yet the rest of me tried rationally to ask what harm I was actually doing? If I enjoyed his company was that wrong? If I continued to see him purely to extract useful information, then it was a means to an end, and I would, of course, resist getting emotionally involved. How realistic was this? By the time I went to bed I was certainly no clearer in my thinking.

Chapter 8

I stood watching in the darkness from the higher ground. I had been told, ordered in fact, to be far away before the action started, but I needed to know all was going to plan. If the execution was as good as the planning, then any transfer of armaments to the north would be hindered for a considerable time. Some of it would always be down to luck, but my skill, for the first time, had been central to this operation. I had wanted to be right there, in the thick of it, but had to agree that the risk was just too great.

Simply stopping a convoy of lorries was simple, but to make maximum impact and disruption I knew we needed to do more than blow up the first truck. With careful use of explosives, a precious commodity for the Maquis, it could mean the road was blocked for some time and the total confusion would hinder the arrival of any reinforcements. I had engineered a pretty audacious, but basically simple plan using the resources to hand.

A deep rumbling could be heard in the far distance as heavily laden lorries came through the village heading up towards the plateau in the north. They would have a fully armed escort, but surprise would be to our advantage, however the convoy needed to reach the tree line before any action could begin.

A light from the torch in the distance was to be the initial signal. Hidden in the trees by the roadside, a shadowy figure waited for this sign, ready to pass the prompt to the next man just in sight by the following bend in the road. The noise of the approaching trucks echoed in the darkness of the limestone valley heightening the anticipation.

Quickly he flashed his torch uphill toward the next bend where they would do the same. Then nerves jangling, he waited, as instructed, until the initial truck followed closely by a second, had rumbled past before lighting the first long line fuse. It fizzled away slowly, almost innocuously, in the darkness toward the base of a large pine tree, as more lorries passed. He moved a short distance downhill, alongside the road, keeping in the trees the whole time, counted 100 and lit the second fuse. This one headed for an explosive device hidden at the side of the narrow road. His task was now complete, and he moved quickly away, disappearing into the forest. Further down and up the road similar fuse lines had been set and activated.

The first explosion ripped through the air further up the valley, a large pine tree splintered and fell across the road. With the road blocked the driver stopped, and almost immediately, a second explosion threw his lorry across the road setting it on fire. Another explosion followed, further down the road, another tree down followed by more explosions, more lorries on fire. Yet more explosions, and the road was very effectively blocked by fallen trees and flaming lorries. The armed escorts let fly with machine gun fire into the forest, but the perpetrators were long gone, safe in the trees and on the deserted rocky paths as they hurried home.

Nervously I had waited until the first explosion ripped through the night air. Then another, a burst of noise and flames and then another, lighting the night sky with flames, and the silence ripped apart by gunfire. It was time to go, so I turned around and hurried down the narrow track back to the village, filled with delight that the operation seemed to have been a success.

I knew my information had been crucial to the planning and success of the action. Yet I felt a stab of betrayal, as I came to terms with the fact that the information I had passed on I had gleaned from Otto. I completely understood that my role, in theory at least, was to use our private time and conversations to gather any knowledge that may be of use to the Resistance. However, I was finding it extremely difficult to reconcile that role with Otto. Just thinking of fraternising with the enemy should have repulsed me, but deep down I knew I enjoyed the time spent with him.

Somehow, I just couldn't see him as the enemy but rather a kind, considerate handsome young man who clearly reciprocated the enjoyment of our time together. His boyish blue eyes lit up when I stepped up into his car. He treated me with respect and kindness, taking nothing that I was not ready and willing to give. I had tried so hard to distance myself, to act a part, but I knew my feelings for him were becoming much too strong for me to easily disengage from this exercise.

Previously, any time together had revealed little of use, that I could tell anyway, and I could just relax and enjoy his company. Then, at our last weekend foray into the hills some important information just seemed to fall from his lips.

"I think of you so much when we are not together." He revealed tenderly. We were sitting on a flat rock at what had become our special viewpoint over the valley, with Otto's arm protectively around me, so close I could feel the warmth of his body mingling with mine. I felt relaxed and yet feelings were heightened with excitement spreading within me. I returned this tender thought with an upturned face searching for a lingering kiss, but Otto was staring into the distance with an uncharacteristically concerned look.

"Is there a problem Otto? You are quiet today. Have I done something to upset you?"

"Of course not, meine Liebling," he grasped me closer. "It's just I have to go away and won't be able to see you for a while." My heart sank, I wasn't acting the part now, I actually did feel a sharp pain of loss.

"I must go to the coast to help organise a special convoy, but I will be back." He added rapidly. "It's odd really," he smiled contentedly, "We could actually watch it pass from our special place here." I leaned in closer to him, I was deep in thought and distracted about what he had just let slip. At last, some useful information. My thoughts began to race.

Shall I ask innocently for more information? However, my instincts were to not ask, let him forget what he had said to me, distract him as I knew I could. I looked up, turned his head gently with my hand and kissed him slowly.

"Let's not waste this precious time then." I whispered into his ear.

The light was beginning to fade that afternoon as we drove back toward St Saturnin. Otto stopped the car some distance outside the village as we both realised, we had to be very careful about being seen together. I had discovered an old bicycle in a shed behind the school giving me a project to work on. Before long, and with a good deal of ingenuity, I had a working bicycle

43

which gave me so much more freedom. I had become a familiar figure most evenings cycling to explore the country lanes around the village. If I was meeting Otto I would cycle some way out of the village, hide the bike in the undergrowth, and wait hidden for his car to arrive.

Tonight, the goodbye kiss was more lingering than usual.

"When will I see you again?" I said quietly. "Please say it won't be too long."

"Soon after the 18th, when the convoy passes, I promise I will be back". He stroked my face tenderly and pushed the loose strands of hair behind my ear, he was so gentle, I just longed to be in his company. Smiling my sweetest smile, I jumped down from the car, blew a kiss and disappeared into the trees to find my bike.

I listened for the noise of the engine to disappear, emerged from the woods, and cycled slowly back to the schoolhouse frantically working out what I should do with the information. However, I was certain of two things, the significance of what Otto had let slip, and the determination that I would pay a central role in any action taken.

Chapter 9

The ambush on the convoy certainly disturbed a hornet's nest. The Resistance went to ground with the occupying soldiers seeking to make the lives of the local people even more difficult. Retribution and revenge fell upon the surrounding area. As there was no hint of the identity of perpetrators of the deed, the planning of the operation had seen to that, the resulting repression was widespread and impossible to predict.

Seemingly random, brutal, searches of isolated farmhouses, obviously trying to find hidden explosives, revealed nothing, with a number of local young men arbitrarily taken as forced labour to work in the armament factories in Germany. The towns and villages were subjected to soldiers on the streets, relentlessly checking identities and arrests were made for trivial indiscretions.

Throughout it all, I tried hard to keep the schoolroom a place of safety, security and routine, however some children arrived in the mornings traumatised by late night raids on their houses. Others saw fathers, uncles and brothers taken away, not knowing if they would ever see them again. The familiarity of the school day was something on which the children needed to be able to depend, and I tried to act normally but feared for the people I had come to know, especially Madame Redoubt who had been so kind to me. Their isolated farm was exactly the kind of place that was ruthlessly targeted. Whilst I felt sure nothing incriminating would be found, she was much too clever for that, I still worried for the safety of her and her father-in-law.

Etienne appeared most days collecting his nephew from school, and I wondered if this was as a reassurance to me. I allowed myself to think as little as I could about my own safety, after all nothing could link me with the ambush, except of course Otto, and there I must hope my innocent guile and his infatuation for me would blind him to any association. I was gambling that his inherent Teutonic arrogance would not let him even consider that it could be he that had given the intelligence away. After all

I had been very careful not to ask any questions of Otto, the information had occurred in the passage of normal conversation. At least that is what I kept telling myself, but in the depths of the night I was woken by agitated dreams of soldiers marching into the schoolroom, and I felt real fear deep in the pit of my stomach.

Some of my group of S.O.E. recruits had been destined for specific tasks, targeting certain pieces of infrastructure, working in twos and threes with routes into and out of enemy occupied territory, but my task was open ended. There existed an escape route, but I knew my work was, as yet, far from finished. The ambush was just the beginning if I had any influence. I had been sent to this area exactly because of the strength of the A.S., the "Armee Secrete", who managed the Resistance in the Ventoux and Luberon. With this latest action I had shown them what could be done and hoped now they would use me to continue to disrupt the occupying forces.

Minor incidents of a nuisance nature were one way of keeping the soldiers on their guard. Any vehicle left unattended for just a few seconds would find itself damaged or had engine problems a few miles away often due to an obstruction in the exhaust. One good sized potato less at dinner was sometimes the price a hungry family gladly paid. Power and water supplies to the barracks in Apt were frequently interrupted, but they were soon repaired. Larger, and more lasting disruption was what was needed, and I was ready and waiting to do the planning if the local Maquis would let me.

One afternoon, around a week after the ambush, I heard a disturbance at the entrance to the school yard as my class were going home. Stepping out into the playground, I saw two soldiers demanding identity papers from the people collecting their children. More of these occurrences had happened lately, but the school had not been targeted before. One of the mothers had been singled out and pushed aside roughly, in sight of her young, fair-haired daughter, who stood, her worn school clothes hanging on her slight frame, sobbing silently a few paces away, still in the school yard. Anger flared inside me. I wasn't having this in the school grounds, and almost without thinking I strode forward to confront the soldiers.

"What is the problem?" I addressed the soldiers carefully and directly in clear precise French, knowing that their comprehension of our language was poor, with the heavily accented local dialect another excuse for confusion and brutal behaviour. The soldiers just ignored me and jostled the woman, who fell against the railings.

"I asked what the problem was." My voiced raised this time, as I stepped closer.

The taller of the two soldiers turned to me and immediately lifted his rifle to strike and push me away. Out of the corner of my eye I saw Etienne watching, holding his nephew's hand, standing in a group of people. He made as if to move toward me.

"DON'T you DARE touch me!" I used my school mistress voice. I was angry and had no time to be frightened, luckily the tone of my words carried sufficient authority for the soldier to hesitate. "Can't you see you are upsetting the children." I gathered the sobbing child in my arms.

"What do you want of this woman? Please let me help." I decided being conciliatory was perhaps a better plan, I certainly didn't need to further provoke a soldier with a rifle and increase the danger to us all by getting Etienne involved.

"Identity papers, out of date, she comes with us." A minor, petty, offence, but in the current atmosphere I knew it was enough for someone to be held for days.

"Please let us go to the Mairie now and I will help sort this out. I am sure this is a simple mistake." I wasn't going to back down, but I knew that I needed to persuade the soldiers that taking the woman was more trouble than they needed. One of the soldiers stood right in front of me glowering down. Looking straight back at him, I refused to accept his intimidation. The seconds ticked away, and the impasse was suddenly broken by the child screaming out for her mother and rushing between the soldiers to her side. They turned away, pushing the woman roughly for one last time.

"Next time the right papers understand?" He threw the identity papers in question to the ground and looked directly at me. I nodded, being sure my voice would betray my anxiety and determined not to show any weakness.

Satisfied, the soldiers marched off down the street searching for their next victim. I sensed the whole watching crowd breathe a sigh of relief and felt the surge of adrenaline that had given me the courage to stand up to the soldiers ebb from my limbs. I sensed myself start to shake. The young girl held onto her mother and silently wept, as the woman grabbed the papers from the ground and looked up at me with relief etched on her face.

"What can I say," she whispered. "Thank you is not enough. They were going to take me away." She was close to tears but held back not wanting to further upset her daughter.

I just smiled and reassured her all would be well, making light of the incident, but encouraging her to get her papers in order as they were certain to come back soon to check.

The crowd of onlookers gradually broke up, moving away from the schoolyard as I waved to the little girl, who had just about stopped crying as she walked away holding tight to her mother's hand. I caught Etienne's eye, and he touched the peak of his cap in recognition, giving a quick smile as he turned to go up the street with his nephew.

Another day was over.

Chapter 10

It was clear the rumour machine had been at work since my confrontation with the soldiers. Emerging into the bright sunshine from Mass the following Sunday, I was greeted by smiles and handshakes from members of the congregation who previously had merely acknowledged me with a nod or even completely ignored me. There were times when I worried that my liaison with Otto was not the secret I firmly wanted it to be, however the incident with the soldiers had certainly increased my standing in the village community.

Lingering in the square in front of the large, white stone church with its imposing octagonal bell tower, groups of villagers chatted. Under the single plane tree stood Etienne in his formal clothes, with a group of women and his nephew who was in my class at the village school. Jean gave a shy wave to me and smiling I returned his wave. Etienne bent forward and whispered something to the boy who set off in the clear bright morning sunshine across the square toward me.

"Bonjour Jean," I said as I greeted the boy formally shaking hands. Jean like so many in the school was thin and small for his age. I noticed his clean but worn, Sunday Best clothes, it was clear the deprivation of war was taking its toll in so many ways.

"Bonjour Mademoiselle Andre," he replied politely. "Uncle Etienne sent me," he paused and then finished the sentence in an embarrassed rush. " Would you like to come to tea this afternoon, it's my birthday and we are going to have a cake." His eyes lit up at the word cake.

"Thank you so much Jean, of course I would like to come, especially if there is going to be cake," I added playfully. Walking over to the family group, I smiled and held Jean by the hand, letting him chat away now his shyness had almost disappeared.

"Thank you so much for the invitation." I addressed the group as a whole on arrival and was formally, as a well brought up young Frenchman should, introduced by Jean to his mother, his Grandmother, his Aunt and his two younger cousins. Etienne laughed and shook my hand warmly last, remarking that his nephew felt no need to introduce him as he saw Mademoiselle Andre at the school gate most afternoons.

"It's Jean's birthday," continued his mother. "He would very much like you to come to share his birthday tea. He talks all the time about you at home. Mademoiselle Andre says this, Mademoiselle Andre says that, we are all learning so much from him." I laughed, a little embarrassed at the thought of my name coming up so often in Etienne's household.

"He's a pleasure to teach," I replied. "Yes really, he has such an amazing capability to remember things and asks sensible questions all the time."

"He's so happy at school now, since you have arrived, there is no need to shoo him out in the morning anymore." The family group laughed again, and Jean put his head down intent on studying the ground to save further embarrassment. So it was arranged, I would attend the birthday tea that afternoon. The Fournier family lived out of the village at Les Andeols, a tiny hamlet in the middle of the plain leading to the large town of Apt. I agreed to cycle to there, with Etienne volunteering quickly to meet me in the hamlet and show me the way to the small family farm.

That afternoon, cycling into the small group of houses that were the hamlet of Les Andeols, I spotted Etienne sitting on a small stone wall looking thoughtfully into the distance. There was much that I wanted to find out about him and his family, as so many of our previous meetings had been fraught with misunderstandings on both sides, but I realised I needed to tread carefully. For one thing, Etienne didn't approve of my liaison with Otto, perhaps guessing that I was having great difficulty keeping my feelings in check, and there was something vulnerable about Etienne. Had his feelings been hurt before? Seeing him relaxed, deep in thought in the shade of an oak tree, I had a moment to study him. Broad shouldered, his thick brown hair hiding part of his face, his long, almost gangly, legs swinging slowly, I felt a rush of well what? Empathy, attraction, gratitude for his help, I was so mixed up I just couldn't tell.

The scrunching tyres on the gravel let him know of my arrival, and he turned, smiled, jumped up, and walked toward me. The standard Provencal greeting of three kisses on alternate cheeks was dispensed with enthusiasm on both sides. Having insisted he push the cycle, I gave in far too easily, we set off toward the farm and the birthday tea. Gentle questioning prompted Etienne to tell me the family circumstances, and thankfully, he seemed equally relieved to spend time with me that was not tainted with anxiety and danger, and he talked freely. For once I could relax too, I didn't need to act a part with him – he knew the truth.

The family story was much like those of the population as a whole. Life under the occupation was difficult and dangerous. His elder brother, Jean's father, Pierre had been taken almost a year ago on the STO, ´Service Travail Obligataire´, with the forced labour being used in the armaments factories in Germany. The family had heard once from him since his arrival, but knew not when or, knowing about allied bombing of the German cities, if they would even see him again. Etienne was the youngest in the family, the only other son. He had been training to be a mechanic in Cavaillon but returned to help his sister-in-law run the family farm as there was much work to do to on the upkeep on the acres of vines, olives and cherry trees. They were also successfully growing vegetables which helped supplement their meagre diet and feed others in need in the community. With his widowed mother still living on the farm, Etienne felt a great sense of responsibility for his family which made his actions in the local Resistance perhaps hard to understand. He was actually putting not only himself at risk but the future of the entire family, however, the hatred for the occupying forces, outweighed the personal risk, and Etienne felt strongly he had to do his part.

We approached the neglected farm buildings from the track, entering the courtyard through a huge wooden double door in the surrounding high wall. There was set a long table under a single plane tree, with Jean and his cousins playing a noisy game of football close by. Verdant green creeper clad the walls, and shutters, in much need of paint, were mostly closed against the spring sunshine. Jean's mother hurried out of a wide-open doorway to greet them.

"Thank you so much for coming, Jean has been so excited." Traditional greetings followed and I surprised Jean with a small birthday gift I had quickly made that morning, a book of handwritten puzzles with spare pages to draw and write. Politely rejecting my offer to help in the kitchen, Etienne, the children and I were sent away for a walk while the final preparations for tea were completed. We set off in the sunshine to visit the pond where at the moment frogs could be found, Jean's choice of course. I'm afraid I shuddered at the thought as frogs were not my favourite attraction.

"Don't worry he won't catch one," laughed Etienne. "But it will keep the three of them occupied." Arriving at the pond the children were quickly engrossed in the frog catching exercise allowing Etienne and I to sit on a fallen tree in the shade. There was silence between us, something hung in the air that needed to be said. In the end Etienne spoke first.

"You must be careful, don't trust him, please. He is not what he makes out to be." I knew it was Otto he was referring to.

"If you know something you must tell me." I simply replied. Silence again.

"He has done this before, that's all I can say."

"Done what before?"

"Taken advantage of young women for his own satisfaction."

"So?"

The question hung in the air. Etienne got to his feet and kept his back to me so I couldn't see his face.

"She was expecting his baby and told him, then she just disappeared, no-one saw her again." This information was, of course an unpleasant shock, but I said nothing steadying my thoughts and feelings.

"All I am doing is trying to get information," I began.

"But that's not all is it?" He faced me again, his voice low but sharp. "I have seen you together, yes you think no-one knows, he is using you, playing with you, and you are lovingly believing every word he whispers in your ear. Can't you see that? I just want to protect you. It's too risky what you are doing. You must stop."

So, Etienne had been spying on me. I felt instantly betrayed by him and suddenly very angry, and yet incongruously grateful that he cared about me to this extent.

With impeccable timing, a squeal of delight indicated the children had in fact caught a frog and were running toward us with it in a makeshift wooden box. Despite Etienne's protestations Jean was determined to return to the farmhouse with his prize capture, though needless to say his mother was not too enamoured, but there was praise all round for his determination and skill. With all the attention on Jean, no-one noticed the brooding silence between Etienne and me.

The birthday tea was a delight with thin toasted pieces of bread topped with warm creamy goat's cheese drizzled in honey. The cake itself was a little flat and lopsided, but it tasted sweet and was warm from the oven. There followed hilarious party games with even Jean's grandmother joining in, but as the shadows lengthened in the courtyard, I made my excuses, kissed everyone on the cheek and turned to leave.

"Etienne will accompany you," his sister-in-law suggested.

"No need, honestly, I won't get lost. Please stay and continue the party." I really wanted to be alone. However, Etienne already had hold of my cycle and began pushing it along the track away from the house. I had no choice in the matter it seemed, though spending time alone with him was not what I wanted at this precise moment. We walked in silence, my initial seething anger at being spied upon had subsided, but I felt I would have difficulty having a civilised conversation. Yet I knew we had to work together, so arriving in the hamlet with Etienne propping the cycle against the wall, I took the initiative.

"Etienne please don't concern yourself about me, I will be fine, honestly."

"That's what she used to say".

"She, the woman who Otto......"

"No," he cut across me. "One of ours. Like you, she was stubborn, fearless, brave and yes, pretty. She always said, 'I'll be fine' and she was. She was there in the thick of it with us, and then," he snapped his fingers together. "One bullet from the crossfire and she died in my arms." Without hesitating I took his hands in mine, looked straight into his deep brown eyes, so this was what was haunting Etienne.

"I am so sorry, I didn't know. She was obviously special to you." He nodded, and without warning, took me in his arms and hugged so tight I felt as though I couldn't breathe. I looked up at him, saw the sorrow in his eyes and not really being sure why, moved to kiss him gently. He responded equally as gently, then more fiercely and passionately arousing similar feelings in me. He stopped abruptly, let go of me, then looked away not meeting my gaze, and simply whispered,

"I'm sorry I shouldn't have done that, please forgive me."

"Oh Etienne," I sighed gently. "There is nothing to forgive." I leant forward, stroked his face, smiled, gave him a simple kiss on his cheek, and retrieved my cycle riding off with my heart thumping.

Chapter 11

It's never a very good idea to start thinking seriously at two o'clock in the morning but as I lay awake in the airless attic bedroom sleep, again, had been difficult arriving. Eventually, deciding that I was just too wide awake, I got out of bed, poured a glass of water, and curled up in the worn leather armchair, and tried to order my thoughts. I hadn't heard from Otto for over two weeks, and while at first my heart, and body, ached for him, his attention, conversation, and caress, gradually I had learnt to live without him, but he was far from forgotten. As each day passed after the ambush without the feared attention of the occupying forces, I breathed a little easier. Mentally I rehearsed scenarios of conversations with him as I needed to be prepared, so I could persuade him I had nothing at all to do with the ambush, should he indeed suspect anything. Deny, deny, and deny, had to be my mantra. I just had to be quick thinking and convincing, but that was easy to say.

Pretending to be someone who was not really me, was increasingly difficult with Otto. Did I actually love him? What was love anyway? I certainly enjoyed being with him, I missed him when he was not there, and he aroused feelings within me I had never experienced before. The unpleasant information about Otto's previous girlfriend revealed by Etienne had come as a shock, but it just didn't seem to fit 'my' Otto. He wasn't cold and calculating, or perhaps he was, and I was too naive to recognise this. Maybe his youthful front was just a game to reel me in, and yet, he was very considerate towards me and certainly asked for nothing that I was not all too ready to give. Despite the sultry night, I shivered at the thought of Etienne watching us together, ashamed of my intimacy with someone who was supposed to be the enemy.

Etienne, now there was another set of thoughts to stop restful sleep. It all began to add up now I knew about his loss, he lacked the arrogance and self confidence that somehow attracted me to Otto, but he drew my sympathy, compassion and a depth of feeling that I realised I may have revealed in our kiss after the birthday party.

But I reminded myself, all this was of minor importance compared to my reason for being here. The local Ventoux Maquis was at last using some of my expertise, and after the success of the ambush my creative, innovative ability with explosives was beginning to be incorporated in their planning. I had accepted they did not want me on the 'front line' in operations, where in effect there was no need for me to be, but my explosive devices needed to be.

The occupying forces must surely now be alert to the fact that someone from outside was helping the Resistance, making it all the more important for me to remain hidden and known only to the least possible number of contacts. I knew my work was of vital importance, as by April 1944, plans for the invasion into northern France were in their final stages, and their success depended on the allies being able to create a strong base on the coast of Normandy. The fewer German troops that were available to defend those beaches the better, with as many soldiers who could be, occupied with anti-insurgence manoeuvres in the south of the country. All this would mean a greater chance of the invasion succeeding.

My job was simple, keep on causing problems for the occupying forces and tie up as many soldiers as possible. The Maquis had the manpower, many young men had escaped to the wild, remote, Ventoux Mountains to avoid the enforced labour conscription to the German armaments factories, and these men were ready and willing, but unskilled. The Maquis had created an army of volunteers; however, they needed direction and expertise. Living in remote farmhouses and derelict mountain huts, the occupying army searched extensively for this ramshackle force, making many surprise raids. However in recent times the soldiers had to watch their step as explosive booby trap bombs had become a successful method of defence.

The next morning, seeing the recognisable handwriting on the note left on my desk caused a sharp intake of breath. I had readily convinced myself I never see Otto again, yet here was his usual flourish of an invitation as if nothing had happened. Was it some kind of trap? If I refused, I gave myself away, yet acceptance could lead to a very difficult, dangerous meeting though, in reality, I had little choice.

Just two days later I found myself waiting in the trees at our usual place in a state of heightened anxiety. I had considered telling Etienne as a precaution but felt I would get little sympathy for my actions, as I was on my own with 'the Nazi boy' as the local Maquis had put it. The sound of his car broke the silence, and I remained out of sight until he stopped, as was the usual plan. The car pulled off the road into the trees, but before I could move forward Otto leapt out, ran round the car, and grasped me tightly in his arms nuzzling my hair, whispering softly over and over again,

"Meine Liebling, meine Liebling."

A flood of relief flowed through me, I turned my face up to meet his and our lips met in a passionate kiss.

"I have missed you so much," he lifted me easily off my feet and twirled me round in the air, laughing and kissing all in one movement.

"It has been so long, I thought you might have forgotten me," he was teasing me, obviously waiting for my reply. A test perhaps? I stroked his face, ran my fingers through his curly blonde hair and replied with a kiss that made sure he knew my feelings. He relaxed and grasped my hand, at least I had stopped shaking, but I was really running on instinct and shocked at my delight in seeing him again.

"Come, let's go for a walk and you can entertain me with everything you have been doing since we last met." He led me back to the car and drove out into the mountains stopping by a wide track which we walked along hand in hand. I entertained him with stories about the children at school which I knew he would like and would keep me safe from any difficult references.

Stopping in the shade of a rocky overhang we sat close enjoying our time together. I was, by now totally relaxed, leaning my head against his shoulder, holding onto his hand while playing gently with his slim, perfectly manicured, fingers. Then I felt him tense slightly.

"Cecile, you must be careful, I may not always be able to protect you."

He knows.

Feeling as if icy fluid had been injected into my veins, I released myself from his grip, stood up and took two paces away. I had practised this very scenario, I just hoped I could act it out. I turned and looked quizzically at him, asking for more information with my facial expression, thinking all the time.

How much did he know?

He looked straight back at me, not giving much away, but showing a determined resolve in his expression. Involuntarily I glanced around for an escape route, but there was nothing obvious, the only way was to bluff this out, so I needed to hold my nerve.

"I was able, this time, to stop them bringing you in for questioning, which I am afraid would not have been pleasant. But you must not do anything like it again." He spoke calmly, but firmly.

Let's continue to act the scenario, I know nothing of what he is talking, deny, deny and deny.

"Otto, my love, what on earth are you talking about?" I moved back toward him, but he also stood up, confronting me. This wasn't going to be easy, but I had prepared for this.

"You can't be seen to oppose the legitimate government and get away with it. It would encourage others." He spoke strongly, but not raising his voice.

What is he referring to? I must hold my nerve; I have done nothing. Deny, deny, deny.

"Otto, please, what do you think I have done. I really don't know what you are talking about."

"Cecile, you interfered with the checking of permits outside the school. You must not set yourself against authority, it just cannot be allowed. They were going to make an example of you, so you were lucky I heard about it and could persuade the Commandant that it should ignored for this time."

The soldiers, school………… So, this isn't about the ambush. The relief of knowing that I had not been connected to the ambush on the convoy was only momentary as uncontrollable anger swept up inside me. I could not stop myself.

"Checking permits, you don't know the truth." I looked him directly in the eye, spitting out the words in disgust. "Two soldiers set about one of the mothers collecting her child, throwing her to the ground in front of her crying daughter. All because the permit was two days out of date. I will stand up to bullies whenever I see them, whatever side they are on. Tell that to your Commandant." I turned away from him shaking with anger unsure now I could take enough care with what I was saying or admitting to.

"Cecile, you must be careful, please. There are far too many illegal rebellious acts around here for anything to be ignored." He was almost pleading with me.

Illegal, rebellious acts… … How dare he?

I clenched my fists, inwardly screaming at Otto, but I knew I had to control my emotions if I was not to give myself away. I wasn't sure I could stop myself from showing my true feelings, realising Otto couldn't protect me if I said too much and inadvertently let slip more and possibly, incriminating details. But what was I to do now? I had to stop this questioning from him before things got even more difficult.

Let's try the last and best trick in the book to get out of this. If he has any feelings for me, it will work.

I breathed deeply, counted to ten, waited, and then turned toward him, with tears streaming down my cheeks,

"I'm sorry Otto, so sorry. Please…." And I broke off sobbing softly.

His face softened, he moved toward me, holding me tight and rocking me like an admonished child who needed reassurance. I clung on and cried silently onto his shoulder.

"Shh, Shh," he wiped my eyes with his handkerchief and looked directly at me. "I could not bear to lose you, please for me, be sensible."

Chapter 12

It was a subdued walk back to the car. Otto seemed ready to accept my apology and have some understanding of the situation that had caused the problem. After all he loved me for my independent feisty character, and that he cared so much to intervene on my behalf made me feel safe in his company. However, protecting me from a minor indiscretion was one thing, if he knew the full truth, I knew I would not get away so easily. Seeing him steely, but calmly, angry had frightened me, as obviously he was used to his own way and getting answers. He was not easy to deceive, and I shuddered at the thought of his reaction if my full deception was discovered, as I realised it would take more than a few tears to get out of that.

I barely spoke as we walked, with Otto keeping a tight grip of my hand, moving to kiss it tenderly many times, but I did not respond. He, no doubt, took my silence to be contrition and acceptance that I needed to take care with my future public behaviour, however I still could not trust myself to remain calm and say the right things. I knew he craved my love and affection, what I didn't know was all this something he had done before? I guessed there had been other girls, but perhaps they were merely playthings to satisfy desires and divert him from the mundane everyday tasks, but it seemed it was different with me, at least that is what I hoped. I imagined it hadn't been easy for him to deflect attention from me with the commandant without revealing our relationship which we both knew was better kept secret. The fact that he was actually aware of the problems that I would attract in the village, should it be known I was openly courting a German Officer, showed his understanding, and I hoped, his real feelings for me.

I had no idea he harboured secret ideas to take me away from the village and my country to keep me safe till the end of the war, but realised I would never agree and would dare not even suggest it for fear of causing a rift in our relationship.

On reaching the woods where my cycle was hidden, we sat in the car in silence. He turned and took my hands gently in his, looking directly at me with my eyes, red rimmed from crying.

"Cecile, please I only want you safe," he spoke gently, then he dropped my hands, turned away and slammed his fists hard on the steering wheel, his voice raised, "I hate all this conflict, this hatred and killing. You need to understand I have to follow orders; I have no choice. If I had my way, I would take you far away from here and forget all this." He stared ahead fighting to control his feelings. I had never seen him so distraught, as he was usually so controlled and calm. Slowly I stroked the nape of his neck where today's sun had turned his fair skin pink and caressed his blonde curly hair. Feeling him relax a little, I turned his head toward me and kissed him gently on his cheeks, his forehead and eventually his lips. The invitation was accepted, and he returned a gentle, then more violent kiss allowing some of his tension and anger to pass. Reluctantly he pulled away.

"I'm sorry Cecile, it's getting late, I must get back, just, please, promise to see me again soon. I hate to see you upset." He gently kissed my cheeks that had been covered in tears just a short while ago.

"Otto my love, of course, next time we will be happier, promise?" I smiled at him as best I could.

"Promise," he whispered in my ear as he gave me a farewell hug.

I watched as the car sped off down the road and walked quickly into the woods to retrieve the cycle, when a rustle in the undergrowth startled me, then Etienne appeared from behind a large oak tree. He had been waiting for me and perhaps even spying again. I sighed; I really did not need his intervention at this precise moment as my head ached from the tension of the afternoon. I just wanted to get back to the schoolhouse and rest, but Etienne had other ideas. He stared at me.

"You've been crying. Has he hurt you? The bastard, I'll break his neck with my own bare hands."

"Etienne, please, you don't know the truth, just let him go and then walk down the road with me and I will explain everything." Pausing, Etienne looked around, then nodded, and that was a relief as the last thing we all needed was a confrontation with Otto.

Otto resisted the temptation to look back for a last glimpse of Cecile before he drove off. The tension of the confrontation that afternoon lay heavily on his shoulders. What he did know for certain was that he wanted Cecile more than any other women he had met. He had scoffed, as everyone does at 'love at first sight' but from the moment he first saw her in the schoolroom just a few short weeks ago, she had dominated his thoughts. She was so unlike any of the other women he knew, her independence and intelligence and, yes, her stubbornness attracted him. Her fearless way she had put him in his place on their first drive in his car had made him stop in his tracks. Everyone previously had always agreed with him, he came from a privileged background and his Teutonic nature and outlook virtually ensured his views and actions were not questioned. He wanted her for his own, yes, he readily conceded, he wanted her for his wife. He had a flash of an image of them walking in the mountains, with two children running through a flower filled meadow in the sunshine, one with blonde hair, the other dark, it was miles away from here and now. He just had to protect her, he felt he had no choice, and he was sure, with his connections, he could get a valid travel permit and papers to get her away to his grandmother who lived on a remote farm in those Bavarian Mountains. But he realised he was also sure she just wouldn't go. She would laugh at his suggestion.

His father would understand, after all he too had married for love and against his father's wishes, which Otto had only discovered recently. His mother was French, not at all aristocratic and his paternal family felt her connections were not good enough for the only son of someone of their standing. However, the marriage had gone ahead, with Otto seeing much love and happiness between his parents. He did remember not seeing his paternal grandfather but thought nothing of it as his mother's parents were ever present in his and his sisters' lives. It was only after his grandfather's death that Otto formed a lasting, loving relationship with his other grandmother. As the last child and longed for son, his mother and two elder sisters had somewhat spoiled him, however his father was strict but fair. Otto respected him greatly, and as the son he was expected to follow his father's, and grandfather's footsteps into the army where the Kaufmann family had a long and distinguished history of service to the Reich.

It would not have been Otto's choice, while he was self-confident, some may say arrogant, he had a creative, sensitive side to his character, but he knew not to question his father's wishes. During a long 'father to son' talk just before Otto left for his officer training school in Berlin, his father had impressed on him the importance of 'doing the right thing', following orders and learning to command. He had also mentioned women and love, which is when Otto had discovered the true story of his father's love for his mother.

Now he had found his love, Cecile, but how could he keep her safe? She was never going to agree to go to Germany, short of kidnapping her against her will there was no way it would happen, he could just hear her laughing at him at his plan. It was not actually difficult for Otto to understand the attitude of the local people, as he would feel the same if an outside power was occupying his homeland. He felt the oppressive nature of the occupation was in fact, causing more problems than it solved, but he kept quiet as he knew his voice was in the minority, and it was not his place to suggest such an opinion.

He feared for Cecile because of her stubborn bravery, and despite their fraught conversation and her abject apology, he felt sure she would do exactly the same thing again and again. Somewhere in the back of his mind a thought that he was trying to supress bubbled to the surface. He couldn't pinpoint it, but a nagging idea troubled him. Was Cecile more involved in other activities than he realised? What made him think that? Whatever the truth, it was even more important to get her away before things got out of his control.

Driving across the flat, vine planted plain toward the barracks at Apt he still felt tense and anxious. He knew what he needed, and where he could find it. Forgetting the pressing need to get back to his barracks, he turned his car into the centre of the old town, deciding to call on his 'Belle-de-Nuit' She would know exactly how to ease all his tensions.

Chapter 13

When the sound of the car had disappeared, I walked with Etienne down the road towards the village. My head was still throbbing with the tension of the afternoon, and the last thing I needed at that moment was yet another fraught conversation. The wheels of the bicycle clicked in rhythm, breaking the silence as we walked. As briefly as possible I told Etienne all about the afternoon, emphasising that Otto had helped me, guessed nothing about my involvement with the ambush and just wanted to ensure my safety.

"But you have been crying, did he hit you, hurt you or make you......."

"No," I was emphatic, and I stopped him right away. "He wouldn't do that, he's too kind and considerate. He is a gentleman"

"He's a Nazi." Came back the retort.

A Nazi gentleman – is there such a thing? But quite honestly, I hadn't the strength to argue with Etienne.

"Then why were you crying?" He wasn't going to let this drop.

"Because it was the easiest way to stop him asking more questions," I snapped back, then immediately wished I hadn't let my temper get the better of me. I did realise Etienne was only trying to protect me, and I knew I really ought to be grateful for this.

So, we walked on in silence. In the distance beyond Apt, up in the Calavon valley, dark clouds were gathering and there was a rumble of thunder.

"I only came to find you to bring a message." He explained. "You are wanted at a meeting tomorrow evening. Something big is being planned. I don't know any more. I will collect you from behind the school at 9pm. OK?"

As I nodded, a flash of lightening, now closer, lit up the sky for an instant, with the thunder rumbling ominously again. We had reached a point where a path led off through the vines to the valley.

"I'll be alright from here. You get back before the storm breaks." I suggested, hoping that I could get away from any further questioning.

Etienne made eye contact for the first time that afternoon, and I saw the sadness in his deep brown eyes again. He nodded in agreement, kissed me on each cheek, as I made an effort to smile for him, then he left, running quickly down through the vines to get home before the rain.

I cycled on to the village, where large, angry raindrops were just starting to hit the ground as I opened the back door to the school.

"What is it you want me to do?" I knew by now simple direct questions got the most sensible answers from those who controlled the local Maquis. I guessed it had something to do with the imminent invasion from across the channel for which we had all been hoping and waiting. General de Gaulle in his Free French radio addresses, listened to in secret by so many of the population, had said as much. I huddled each day with Monsieur Foix, who had an old, battered, but just serviceable radio, to listen to the news broadcast by the BBC from London. It was about the only act of defiance that Monsieur Foix managed, but still it kept me informed.

The room where I met the Maquis was always dark, lit only by a small lamp, so I could not see their faces clearly, but the one who did most of the talking spoke with an educated accent. There was also always a strong smell of pipe tobacco which I recognised as my father had smoked a pipe. So, someone must have good connections I thought, as tobacco was hard to get unless you had German friends. Perhaps he too was playing both sides, I was not to know, but more importantly, at least now, they seemed to accept I was useful.

"We know to expect a drop of arms and ammunition soon, so we need you to create a diversion to ensure no patrols are in the area. It will take time to unload and hide all the supplies sent. These supplies are vital for the next few months." As ever

65

clipped, precise and to the point with no unnecessary information given

Night-time patrols along the local roads were infrequent but an ever-present danger to any clandestine operation. There were certain routes the occupying army would just not travel in the dark, as it was too easy for an impromptu ambush. A log across the road, sharp objects to pierce tyres, then an immobilised vehicle just waiting for an incendiary device, with shadowy figures ready to dispatch the soldiers within if they left their means of transport. The main routes were different and if, as I suspected, the drop was to be on the plain between Gordes and Goult, any activity could be seen from the main road. I needed to think quickly.

"With just a bit of explosive and a few helpers I can make it seem as if the Barracks in Apt is coming under attack. The patrols would be called back to help defend, but we need the timing to be right to work at its best. This ought to start well before the drop arrives, so you need to keep me informed."

A long silence and then nods of agreement. It became apparent I didn't have long to make final plans as the drop was either Wednesday or Thursday night that week, depending on the weather. A coded message would be sent via the radio broadcasts, so I had to know what to listen for, and I needed access to a cache of explosives. Eventually, all the knowledge required was relayed to me, and I was able to withdraw from the meeting, my head spinning with ideas. As usual Etienne appeared out of the shadows, took my arm protectively and we set off down the street.

"I can help prepare, but on the night, I am needed for the main activity, so I will make sure you get some good people to help." He understood what I had to do, and I knew he did care, for which I was very grateful .

The next evening, I cycled out of the village into the foothills of the Vaucluse mountains, pushing the cycle for the last stretch to find a broken-down circular stone building previously used a shepherd's hut. These Borries were a common sight in the landscape and regularly used by the Maquis for storage of weapons and explosives. Working quickly with the equipment, I made the small triggers and explosive devices I would need for my part in the operation. Normally I would prepare long lines to detonate the bombs, it was very much safer for all concerned and helped to ensure the person most at risk was well away before the explosion. However, they were not always reliable and this time the explosions had to work, or the supplies drop could be compromised, so I just had to accept more risks would have to be taken on the night. That meant I needed to be with the activity to ensure all went correctly.

Direct radio contact with England was always risky, any messages were easily intercepted and the radio transmitters all too readily detected. Instead coded instructions were sent as personal messages read out on the BBC radio broadcast at specific times, with most of these messages making little sense to anyone except members of the Resistance waiting for something specific.

"Uncle Albert still enjoys eating barley sugars." I heard the message as clear as a bell on the radio two days later, so the drop was on for the following night.

When Etienne introduced them I was dismayed at my helpers but tried not to let it show. Accepting that the main business of the evening was the drop and that the local groups would be expecting more than one drop at different pre-arranged sites, I did understand that the men were needed to transport the heavy arms, equipment and explosives as fast and as far as possible from the landing zone. However, the three young lads now standing before me looked no older than sixteen at the most. Willing yes, but able to follow my instructions under extreme duress, I doubted it, but they were all I had to work with, so I quickly briefed them on the task to come. We were wearing dark clothes with caps pulled well down over our darkened faces, but I did wonder if they might guess who I actually was. I rather hoped not, though my clear intention was for us all to get safely home that night.

The plan was to set the explosives, build as much foliage around each as possible to create a longer lasting fire and leave a small amount of ammunition in the flames to mimic the sounds of gunshots. Each explosion would then be set off seemingly randomly, and the guards at the barracks would think they were under fire from all sides. However all this would need precise timing.

Crawling around in the dark at some distance, but within sight of the watch towers of the barracks, I showed the boys how to lay the explosive, set the trigger, unwind the short detonator lines, and light them. They then moved off individually to set three lines each, while I took the three nearest the main gate, where the searchlights were brightest. I impressed on them we needed to rendezvous within twenty minutes down by the main road with the detonator lines ignited, if all was to go to plan. I left it until the very last minute to light the detonator lines for my devices, then silently retreated to the agreed meeting point.

But when I arrived only two of the boys were there. The first explosion began, with a fire starting at the furthest most point, bullets cracked, and with the second explosion ringing in the silence, a siren went off inside the barracks. Searchlights began to sweep the whole area, as I grabbed one of the boys.

"Where is he? We can't wait here." I tried to sound calm, but I certainly wasn't feeling so. The last thing I wanted to do was to leave anyone here, as it could jeopardise everyone's safety, yet if we remained close to the scene of the explosions we could easily be caught up in the subsequent search. The two boys frightened faces lit up momentarily in the light of the explosions as they shrugged their shoulders and shook their heads. The whereabouts of their accomplice was unknown, so I needed to take control before any more time was lost.

"Right, you two go on home now, keep to the fields, away from the roads and remember not a word to anyone." They were reluctant to go, but I shooed them away and, with just one backward glance over their shoulders they ran into the darkness. Turning back toward the barracks scanning for the third boy I heard the sound of the multiple explosions now echoing round the valley. Suddenly, stumbling out of the thick undergrowth the third boy almost fell onto me, and I could clearly see his leg bent at an awkward angle, so he could barely put weight on it. Putting my hand on his arm, I whispered urgently in his ear,

"Make as little noise as possible, follow me. I'll get you somewhere safe, but you have to move quickly." I saw terror in his eyes and felt his head nod, at least he understood, hopefully the fear in him would overcome the pain from the damaged leg which looked suspiciously like a break to me. The sky was lit up with multiple fires, and explosions were now ripping through the air, as I led him away toward the path which followed the old railway line toward the disused ochre quarries.

Chapter 14

At least the ground was flat, so walking as if in a three-legged race, with completely mismatched participants, we made slow but consistent progress. Thankfully, the boy was slightly built and, although much taller than me, carried little weight. We needed to hide in the bushes a number of times as vehicles sped along the road toward Apt. At the very least, the diversion seemed to be working, with the fires lit by the explosions still burning behind us lighting the night sky. Only when we reached the safety of the railway cutting, well out of sight of the road was I prepared to allow the boy to rest for a moment. His face was a grimace of pain, with fear predominant in his eyes.

"What's your name?" I asked gently, I needed to get his confidence and steady his nerves. He hesitated, then spoke.

"Rene"

"Well, Rene, we need to get going again. I know a safe place where you can wait until I can fetch someone who can help. I know it hurts a lot, but we don't want the soldiers to catch us, so please let's go as fast as possible."

"You're Mademoiselle Andre from the school aren't you? I know your voice," he said cautiously. I hesitated, dressed in dark men's clothes with my hair hidden beneath a large, peaked cap and my face blackened, I had hoped not to be recognised.

"It's not important who I am and best you don't know, come on, we've got to get going."

Reaching the end of the cutting, we turned across the fields of vines and approached the now disused Ochre mine workings, where there were endless caves and tunnels, with one in particular I knew, as equipment has been left there for me. If I knew where it was so would others in the Maquis, so it made sense to use it, but of course, I needed to find it again.

Luckily, I had a good memory for the detail of places and an uncanny sense of direction, so very soon afterwards I spotted the entrance covered in brushwood, which I moved aside and helped Rene crawl in. After a few metres the cave opened out to a sizeable chamber, but it was completely dark, with no light and it was very cold. I made Rene as comfortable as possible before I turned to go, but he clung onto desperately to my hand, and I could feel him trembling.

"Rene, I must go and get help. Someone will come soon, I promise." But I had to prise my hand away from his grip and scramble out of the cave, replacing the brushwood and scuffing up any footprints in the red ochre dust.

Without my encumbrance I was able to move much more swiftly. Whilst helping Rene along I had formed a plan in my head about what to do next, so cut hurriedly across the vines, their foliage now almost tall enough to hide me. I only had one contact so I must go to him, as I realised Etienne's home was not too far away, and he would know what to do next. I presumed he would be back from the arms drop as it has taken a long time to get Rene to the cave, but if not, I would leave a message. I was not going to abandon Rene; I had made a promise.

Approaching across the fields toward the rear of the farmhouse there were no lights showing, with only small, barred, darkened windows visible. The perimeter wall enclosing the property was high, the only way in via the huge wooden front doors. I crept as silently as possible around the walls but before I reached the doors, two hunting spaniels loose in the courtyard set off barking and howling. I stopped in front of the big solid wooden doors, guessing there must be a spy hole in the wood somewhere, as immediately Etienne, still fully dressed, opened one door with a look of astonishment and concern on his face.

"Cecile, what are you doing here, what's wrong?" Without waiting for an answer, he pulled me hurriedly inside, silenced the dogs with a hissed command then waved to someone in the upstairs window, it was clear the whole house was awake. Gratefully, I sat down on one of the old iron chairs under the plane tree, now rapidly growing its full summer foliage ready to shade the entire courtyard.

"It didn't all go to plan. One of the boys, Rene, got hurt, though I managed to get him away and he is hidden now in the ochre mines. We need to get help to him. I didn't know where else to go." One of Etienne 's silences followed. So I continued.

"I think he has broken his leg or ankle; he was probably too near one of the explosions. Etienne, he is so young, and very frightened, we need to rescue him quickly."

"Not too young to watch his father put against a wall and shot two years ago. He's been working for us since then, he knows the risks." I was shocked and completely taken aback by the callousness of his answer, he was talking about the young boy as if he were a throw away item. He went on.

"Cecile, you cannot risk yourself helping others. You are too important and know too much, he knows very little if he is caught." I stared at him not able to comprehend his remarks.

"He was hurt and terrified, I could not just abandon him. Is that what you are really suggesting?" Then it struck me. *Perhaps this is the awful reality of war.*

Etienne, like me, was exhausted after a very long, tense, tiring night, so I wasn't going to argue, but I needed to be sure help would arrive for the boy as I had, after all, promised Rene someone would come, and I didn't break promises. Etienne sighed, saw my determination, and softening a little, agreed to help.

"I will see he is collected and taken to one of our doctors, but you need to get back, it's a school day tomorrow, everything must be as normal. Go now, please before it is light, take my bicycle I will collect it later."

But I hesitated, I needed to be certain help would arrive for Rene.

"He is in the ochre cave where equipment was left for me, I have hidden it again with bushes, I can show you." Etienne shook his head firmly.

"Cecile, you did what you thought was right, we'll sort it out now. I'm sorry if you think I'm hard but we need to think ahead here. So many important operations to come, for the good of everyone we need to keep you safe."

Pushing the cycle over the rough ground, then just about managing to ride it, I reached the school as dawn was breaking. Quietly letting myself in, I had a good wash, dressed in my school clothes and sat in the worn armchair drinking what passed as coffee. I couldn't help wondering how Rene was, what the future was to bring, and realised with a feeling of disquiet, I really didn't understand Etienne at all.

It was going to be a long day, I felt very tired when the adrenaline of the previous night had worn away, but I had no time to sleep. It was after all Friday, so I just needed to get through today then I could have a long, and hopefully, restful night.

Returning to the empty classroom during lunchtime that day, I found a single red rose garnished with a satin ribbon left on my desk. It had to be from Otto, a reminder of our meeting to come on Sunday, no doubt. I sighed, playing the attentive, amusing girlfriend seemingly impossible at this precise moment, but it would have to be done. Maybe, just maybe, the red rose was his way of saying sorry for the argument last time, I could only hope so. I hurried up to my room and put the rose in a glass of water, thoughtfully rolling the red ribbon into a loop in my hands, which I carried it back downstairs. One of the older girls was helping to tidy up after lunch, I called her over and gave her the red satin ribbon. The joy on her face considerably brightened my day, as the ribbon was immediately wound round her ponytail of straggly hair, with the girl continuing to wear a smile all afternoon.

Later as the children left for home, I stood exhausted, in the playground and looked for Etienne. He was there and looked directly at me, and clearly nodded his head, which I took to be as a signal that Rene must be safe. At least that is what I wanted it to be.

Chapter 15

Walking up the narrow main street on Sunday morning, shaded by the tall three storey buildings, I did at the very least, feel refreshed with plenty of sleep and a quiet Saturday. The ancient plane tree in the small square by the church and the Marie was now almost in full leaf, providing copious shade for those villagers chatting before entering the big stone church for Mass. By now I was recognised by a good number of people, and I acknowledged their greetings with a nod and smile, then I entered the church by the big carved wooden doors thrown right back each Sunday to allow light into the previously gloomy interior. I took my usual place in a side pew and opened the worn prayer book that had been handed to me, being surprised to find a small, folded note inside. Involuntarily I looked around, how on earth did anyone know I would get this prayer book? Everything seemed as normal in the hushed atmosphere of the church, with Etienne and family nowhere to be seen today, I surreptitiously opened the note which contained a simple message, 'here nine o'clock tonight'. It seemed activity was increasing.

But of course, and I could hardly forget, first there was my afternoon out with Otto. Though in many ways I was looking forward to spending time with him for which, as ever I felt guilt, I was also determined this time that there had to be no disagreement or confrontation. I really didn't like the expression I had seen on his face during our last outing. I had planned, and I had always done a lot of planning, to make the afternoon as light-hearted and filled with fun as I possibly could, so I needed to keep the conversation away from current events.

Taking extra care with my appearance, though my wardrobe was, to say the least, limited, I was waiting in the trees at our usual meeting place in plenty of time, with a fixed smile, but a small, but ever-present, feeling of dread.

Otto pulled the car slightly into the trees as normal and I ran up as he leant over to open the door. The sun shone on his unruly curly blonde hair, and a matching sunny smile radiated from his face. Thankfully it all appeared positive so far, and once seated in the car he moved immediately to kiss me.

"Herr Kaufman, taking advantage of a young lady as soon as she steps into your car, how could you!" For a split-second Otto looked confused, perhaps angry, then saw the sparkle in my eyes and recognised the teasing tone in my voice. He laughed, taking my hand formally and kissing it gently, allowing his lips to linger on each of my delicate fingers. He then replaced my hand and let his linger meaningfully on my knee.

"Forgiven?" He asked.

"Completely." I replied with a soft kiss to his cheek and a playful stroke at the nape of his neck with my fingers. "But today is going to be all about enjoyment, right? No talk of anything that isn't happy, or else!" Otto laughed again, and set off along the road, a beaming smile on his face.

"Cecile you are so good for me," and again a lingering kiss to my hand.

Watch your step, don't overplay this into something you can't get out of.

Stopping in our usual place and setting off along the deserted track, I tried hard to keep everything as light-hearted as possible, playing silly hide and seek games with a kiss as the forfeit for being found. We laughed and giggled like two love struck teenagers all the way to the top and our usual vantage point, where we sat down still laughing and quite out of breath. Then I felt him take a deep breath ready to speak.

"Cecile."

"No Otto, no, remember, today nothing serious, you can only tell me amusing things."

"But Cecile."

"No, Otto, please." I managed to silence him with a kiss, but it only worked for a few seconds.

"Cecile, I have to say this." He put his finger to my lips to stop me talking. "I have never felt like this about anyone, I love you so much, I want to ask you an important question." I had to stop him, this was getting out of hand and becoming far too serious.

"Ask me anything you like Otto, my love, but today you are not going to get a serious answer, please just let's enjoy today as today. I love you too, you know that."

There, I have said it, but am I really lying to him?

Otto slumped back against the rock, the important moment for him had passed and there was obvious disappointment in his eyes. I had to defuse the situation, so turned to him, stroked his face, laid my head on his chest, taking his hand in mine whilst caressing his fingers.

"Otto, please, just let's be happy today, there is too much sadness all around. Please enjoy the here and the now because neither of us knows what will happen tomorrow".

He gently turned my head and kissed with intense passion, so I could feel the tension release from his body, then he hugged me hard, almost taking my breath away.

"Otto, I am not going anywhere, don't worry. I am here, you know that".

"No, but I might be," was his unexpected reply. I was stunned for a moment.

"Going away, not coming back?" My voice betraying an anxiety and disappointment I could not hide.

"I don't really know yet. Some important people in the High Command are coming tomorrow for meetings and to make decisions. Everything is changing, perhaps moving north, or maybe further south. I honestly don't know, but I don't expect I'll be here much longer. So, you see I have to make plans for you, I can't lose you now."

Alarm bells rang in my head, as no amount of planning had prepared me for this. There was a silence between us, I had to stop him in his tracks somehow, so I carefully said,

"My Papa always said,´ face your problems when they arrive, you can't solve the future till it comes´ so please Otto, lets enjoy today for today and let tomorrow take care of itself." Another long silence, but I seemed to have interrupted his train of thoughts. Eventually he turned to me saying,

"Your Papa was very wise, and he has a very clever daughter, who I love very much." He stroked my face and gently kissed me with increasing passion, which my body responded to even though I was trying to stop. With reluctance in his voice he pulled away from me and said "Come on, it's getting late, we should go back to the car now. I have a picnic, brought especially for you."

Otto watched me with a smile of indulgence, as I rather inelegantly licked my fingers, after eating the foie gras he had brought, and I wiped my hands on the napkin whilst eyeing up the big ruby red cherries in the picnic basket.

"So, you are going to be busy for the next few days?" asking as casually as I could, taking the stalk off a cherry and feeding it to him.

"I am merely the note taker in the meetings for my Commandant, so it's not that interesting, but it means I am included in all the plans. There is a big reception planned for tomorrow night, with lots of important people going, and many pretty ladies will be there."

"Prettier than me?" I teased. He took my hand and looked straight into my eyes.

"No one is prettier than you, I just wish I could take you".

"Why not then?" I was still teasing really but stupidly realised too late I had cast caution to the winds.

Otto was silent for just a moment, then a big smile spread over his face.

"You'll come with me, Cecile? That would make me so happy."

Now get out of this. How could I have been so silly. I thought quickly and then spoke as determinedly as I could.

"I'd love to go with you, but don't you realise it's impossible, for one thing I just don't have the right kind of clothes to wear, everyone will be very dressed up, and anyway how are you going to explain who I am." I resolutely shook my head. "It really can't be, but I am so sorry my love."

But Otto wasn't going to be thwarted by minor detail.

"I'll fix the clothes, yes honestly, and you can be a friend from Paris. It's over at the Chateau at Lourmarin, a long way from here, so no-one will know who you are."

I shook my head again, but it seemed that once this particular cat was out of the bag, I realised it was going to be very difficult to replace it. I tried very hard, my anxiety levels racing, but it became apparent that no amount of reasoning would make him change his mind. He was determined that I was coming as his guest, no argument. So, taking a deep breath, realising this was a huge risk, and against my better judgement I gave in to what seemed the inevitable, and agreed.

"All right Otto, I will be your guest for the evening, but please explain how you are going to fix all this. I have to look the part, or people will wonder what is going on."

Otto just smiled, looking happier than I could remember, telling me that all I had to do is be ready at six o´clock tomorrow evening. If I walked out of the village along the road to Apt, he would collect me.

"But what am I to wear?" I was persistent with this question as I knew that nothing would mark me out as different more than my clothes, or rather lack of suitable ones.

Smiling, and this time teasing me, he just replied "Wait and see what I will have in the car, we will stop somewhere for you to change, but don't worry you will be the prettiest girl there."

Chapter 16

Sunday Evening

A shadow slipped out from a side alley, taking my arm and falling in step with me as I walked up the narrow main street from the school to the church. Murmured greetings, I knew it was Etienne, by now I knew his touch, and the way he wrapped his arm around mine holding it tight. I hadn't seen him to speak to since turning up in the early hours at his home after hiding the inured boy Rene, last week, though I had glimpsed him collect Jean from school. I was eager for news.

"Is he alright, is he safe?"

Silence followed, Etienne sometimes did this when he didn't know what to say, but I needed to know.

"Rene, is he safe?"

"Yes". I let out a sigh of relief, but I wanted more information.

"Where is he, how is his leg?"

"You don't need to know." He was trying to shut down the topic, that much was obvious.

"Etienne," I could hardly contain my frustration, and recklessly raised my voice. "I left him a cold dark cave with a damaged leg, for goodness' sake, I want to know."

"SHHHHH, don't speak so loudly." He glanced around, then lowered his voice. "It's safer for everyone if you don't know details. But yes, he is at a safe place and his leg is treated."

"Broken?"

"Yes"

"Thought so, it was my fault I should have warned him to keep clear."

"It was not your fault, you rescued him risking yourself and he did say he wanted to thank you when I saw you again."

We walked on, in relaxed silence, along an even narrower road, round the curved back of the big stone church toward the medieval walls leading to the chateau on the ridge. Etienne glanced behind him and took a sharp turn down some steps and into a cellar which led to another dimly lit room. Tonight, he stayed, taking the chair next to me and nodding greetings to the five other men sitting at the table in the room. Some I had seen before but, not all.

This must be important with so many of us here and Etienne included for the first time.

Without introduction, we were not here for niceties, the man, who I recognised from previous meetings at the head of the table began to outline the plan. He was the one who always had the smell of pipe tobacco around him.

By now, end of April 1944, everyone hoped the longed-for invasion and liberation of their country was not too far away. General de Gaulle kept promising so in his Free French radio addresses. Even the occupying forces knew something was coming, but as yet, due to bluff and counter bluff, they had no real knowledge of where the invasion would strike. The Nazi forces were still spread around the continent ready for action not knowing if it would come across the channel or from the south and the Mediterranean. Surprise, and the advantage this would give the liberators, was crucial to establishing a bridgehead on landing. Reinforcements from the enemy army needed to be held up from reaching the invasion front too soon. A solid foothold had to be established before further liberation forces could move on into France, and this is where the Resistance would show its importance.

The 'French Forces of the Interior' as General de Gaulle was to call them would, in a unified effort, engage and delay occupying troops, launching attacks at the same time, if all the groups could all work together. Targets had been decided for each area, working in a cohesive plan to halt troop and equipment movements across the nation as a whole. When the coded messages came via the BBC, the Resistance would rise together, and the Nazis would be forced into fighting on multiple fronts.

One significant problem was that the individual groups of fighters had no overall leadership. Most were headed by a figure from their own area, and co-operation between groups was not easy, and in some cases non-existent. Some groups were aligned to the communist 'Partisans' others to the Gaullist 'L'Armee Secrete', and there was little love lost between them, though both did agree on wanting to drive the German forces out of France.

The group sat in silence in the dimly lit room as the plans were revealed. Major communications links were our targets, and we all guessed those would be the most likely, but as yet, we didn't know when. The main railway line from Apt to Cavaillon was to be one target, it ran down from Digne and Sisteron in the high Alps to the Rhone Valley and from there north and south and was used frequently to move troops and heavy equipment. Already it was a common target, as it was easy to unbolt the rails and move one slightly to disrupt the next day's traffic. But a more permanent disruption would mean more men, and some means of transport to completely remove sections of track, which would be much slower, though far more effective. Removing bolts was a 'hit and run' job, it was easy not to get caught, but removing complete lengths of track would take more time. They would need to be an awareness of night-time patrols and implement a system of lookouts, but it could be done and would be extremely disruptive. I listened intently but knew this was not going to be my task. Various nods from the other listening men confirmed my thoughts. It was for them to undertake not me.

When my task was revealed, I was completely taken aback. I already knew that the major road link into the Rhone valley at Cavaillon depended on a single bridge as there were no other bridges for miles up or down stream. The task given to the Resistance was to make that bridge unusable for the enemy. There were of course any number of ways this could be achieved including the obvious attack with our somewhat meagre firepower at each end which could delay convoys on the bridge, but we all realised that it would only be for a short time. To effectively stop the troop and armaments movements the bridge had to be destroyed, or at least made impassable for heavy traffic for a significant length of time. This bridge was an old, but substantial stone structure consisting of arches spanning the width of the Durance as it meandered toward the Rhone at Avignon. It would be quite a task to destroy if you had easy access and time, but nigh on impossible with the two ends guarded round the clock and any access onto the bridge strictly controlled.

"We have a consignment of explosives," one of the older men explained, "and we can expect help from the people in Cavaillon, but they don't have the expertise. A radio message from London suggests you, Cecile, should lead that part of the operation."

All eyes turned to look at me in the room, and despite feeling overwhelmed by the task, I knew I had to carefully hide my feelings.

"I can manage that I feel sure," I replied with a confidence I really didn't feel. "But I need to see the bridge and meet the leaders of the others involved to be able to finalise the plan".

"Of course, that will be arranged". The meeting concluded very soon after that with the participants leaving at carefully timed intervals, as a group of men on the street after dark would cause suspicion. As I got ready to go, the older man called me over for a private word.

"I need to explain," he spoke quietly so anyone left in the room could not overhear. "The Resistance in Cavaillon are not pleased that they aren't going to lead operation on the bridge, so you must produce a plan to convince them or the whole operation could go wrong. This part of the overall strategy must succeed. Do you understand?" I nodded but there were details that had to be sorted if this was to be successful, as blowing up solid stone bridges needed considerable planning.

"I can put ideas together, but I really need to see the bridge and the area around it before I can finalise any plan." I explained.

"That can be arranged, tomorrow evening, I will fix some transport."

"No, not tomorrow. I can't." I firmly stated.

He looked quizzically at me. What was more important than this?

I felt the need to explain, "I'm sorry but I have agreed to attend a reception, and it would cause suspicion if I didn't go as it is all planned and agreed."

"Ah, I see, your 'Nazi Boy', well see you bring us some useful information then. I hear he is more German than Nazi, and that he isn't an enthusiastic soldier. If it wasn't for the influence his

82

father, he wouldn't be where he is." I could hear the sarcasm and scorn in his voice.

"His mother is French, and anyway he is a gentleman." I retorted without thinking, though I managed to stop myself from further comment. I knew I ought not to be so involved with him, and I should not give away my feelings.

Again, another quizzical look.

"Just take care Cecile, I am told he is clever, perhaps too much for his own good, you must not arouse any suspicion. They know we have someone good with explosives, but not much more, so you should not take any risks. I'll set up the visit for Tuesday evening, and the meeting for Wednesday, as we don't have a lot of time."

I nodded, and left the room to find Etienne waiting who, of course, did not ask me what had been said, he was much too well trained for that. He walked me back to the school in silence, but it was a companionable silence. Holding tightly onto his arm and feeling a strong sense of security, I relaxed as I didn't need to pretend with Etienne, to act a character, I felt he was the only person who really knew who I was. I desperately wanted to get closer to him but felt the invisible barrier of his dead Resistance girlfriend between us every time I tried.

I would like to have discussed the coming operation with him but knew I shouldn't, Etienne would get to know the details if he needed. I also knew telling him about my concerns over the proposed evening out with Otto would bring little sympathy, for if there was one thing on which Etienne and I were never going agree, it was Otto.

Chapter 17

Monday Evening

The mirror was old, tarnished at the bottom with a small crack in the corner, however it gave a clear reflection, and I studied myself in silence. Who was this person staring back at me? A resistance fighter, a dedicated enthusiastic schoolteacher, an aristocratic young lady, or a collaborator with the enemy being seen in public on the arm of a German officer? The problem was I didn't really know as I was trying to be so many different people, and I was beginning to wonder how long I could maintain the charade. *Who was I convincing?* Some of the people some of the time? The trouble was it had to be all of the people all of the time, and for not just my safety. For the umpteenth time since I had agreed to this, I chided myself about the evening ahead. What was I doing accepting Otto's invitation? I must be mad, as up until now we had been so careful not to be seen together, and now I was going to a formal function on his arm as his guest. The idea was incredible and perhaps so stupid that I began to think I might get away with it.

Anyway, there was no going back now, it was time to leave to meet him. With my hair, painstakingly rolled and pinned around my face in the most fashionable way, and my normally fresh-faced look enhanced with makeup, I knew I looked elegant and aristocratic, certainly not a village schoolteacher, I only hoped Otto would approve.

Strolling out along the road to Apt I heard a car pull up behind me and glancing round noticed immediately it was not Otto's usual car, the back door opened, and I was suddenly struck with terror. What if this was a trap? Should I try to run now while I had time? However, Otto's voice called out to me and reassured, I climbed in the back to find him resplendent in full dress uniform. At his signal the driver sped off, with Otto in the back seat, smiling from ear to ear. He gave me a large brown paper parcel, and an enthusiastic kiss on the cheek. I peeped inside to see silky black material, and felt shoes in the lumpy parcel, it seemed Otto had kept his word. We stopped quite soon at some houses on the approach to Apt, where Otto led me inside and upstairs to a room devoid of people but basically furnished.

"I'll wait out here, or if you want, I can help you dress?" His voice was teasing me, and I smiled but firmly closed the door. I really could not believe the dress that emerged from the brown paper. How had he done it ? It fitted so perfectly, sleeveless with a low neckline the bodice fitted snuggly with sophisticated folds of black crepe. The full-length skirt, gathered from the waist moved classically as I walked. I also found a pair of silk stockings, he really had thought of everything, and black swede leather shoes with open toes, an ankle strap and a substantial heel, they too were exactly my size. The look was completed by an elegant pair of long black evening gloves.

Opening the door I glanced shyly at Otto seeking approval, as he took my hand and kissed it formally.

"And now to complement your natural beauty." Otto took a small velvet case from his pocket, opening it to reveal a string of pure white tiny pearls with a diamanté clasp. He expertly fastened these around my slim neck and stood back to admire his handiwork.

"What can I say, you look more beautiful than ever, Cecile my darling, I can't wait to show you to the world. Come on now we mustn't be late." I really didn't know how to answer that comment, being shown to the world was exactly what I did not want but there was no way out of this now, so I just smiled and followed him back to the car.

We set off across the Luberon Mountains toward Lourmarin where the Chateau sat proudly on the ridge to the north. Setting us down close to the huge entrance doors I glanced around at the fine military uniforms and the sophisticated dresses of the ladies. There were obviously some very important military men, some local dignitaries and wives who were happy to socialise with the enemy, or were not given much option, and a fair sprinkling of the kind of women I despised most, collaborators. But surely this was what I was doing? This was a world away from my village life and the schoolroom, but however not from my upbringing. I knew exactly how to behave in such company, which was useful as I certainly did not want to draw any more attention than necessary to myself. Otto, of course had other ideas, and determined to show off his beautiful Cecile, he clutched my arm under his and strode forward through the waiting guests.

Once inside the Chateau, we emerged into a huge hall with ancient portraits on the walls and full-length doors at the end onto a terrace overlooking the magnificent gardens. Otto steered me straight to a group of senior officers who were standing together deep in conversation. My knowledge of the German language was almost nil, as Otto and I spoke only in French, so any conversation with other guests was going to be limited which, I thought, may well be a good thing.

An older officer with grey receding hair, numerous medal ribbons on his chest and a considerable girth, turned to Otto, who formally introduced me as his 'friend from Paris'. I caught the word 'Commandant', and realised this must be the officer for whom Otto worked. I smiled and let him take my gloved hand and formally kiss it. He seemed to hold onto to it just too long for comfort, but maybe I was being oversensitive. The Commandant made some remarks to Otto which clearly didn't need translation and were obviously about me. I pretended not to notice but concluded that they must think I was unable to read body language or just be too dim to notice, probably the latter. I wondered if Otto would translate the comments for me later. Smiling to the other officers as we moved on into the crowds and I began to wonder if I could really keep this up until it was time to go, as it was certainly testing my acting skills.

"So that was your superior officer?" I enquired as we moved toward a waiter with glasses of champagne. "What was it he said about me?"

"All complimentary my love, I assure you." But I really didn't believe him.

The champagne was good, it being a very long time since I had tasted any, and the food circulating on huge platters carried by very formally dressed waiters was delicious. However, I couldn't stop myself thinking of the children not so far away who would be going to bed hungry that night, and this made me angry and defiant. I held myself up straight, and looking around the room, saw I was being noticed by a number of the assembled guests. We made a fine couple, for I knew I carried myself well and the cut of the dress enhanced my petite figure, and Otto looked splendid in his full-dress uniform. But with Otto carrying a smile so wide and holding onto me so tightly that it was pretty obvious that I was more than just with an 'old friend from Paris'. We circulated the groups of people, all conversing in German, with Otto pointing out a group of high-ranking military officers.

"Are they all staying in Apt?" I asked casually. I hadn't forgotten the need to collect any information that might help the local Maquis. I would at least feel marginally better about the evening if I could find some snippet to pass on.

"Oh no, that's not good enough for them, they are staying here at the chateau so, they travel each day to meetings with us." Interesting, they would be travelling the only direct route over the Grand Luberon from Lourmarin to Apt each day, along the narrow combe that cut through towards Bonnieux.

We made our way outside onto the large terrace overlooking the gardens, where the sun was just setting. It was quiet and the air was fresh.

"Enjoying yourself, my love," Otto inquired carefully. "You look so wonderful, everyone is saying so, I am so lucky to have you." He kissed me gently on the lips and I smiled as genuinely as I could.

"It's wonderful Otto." But I was lying through my teeth and wishing so hard that I had never agreed to come. I was just not part of this world, of his world, and it made me all the more certain that these people who flaunted their superiority in this way while others suffered needed to be removed, sooner rather than later. I suddenly revelled in the thought I was helping in this task. Otto found us an empty table on the terrace and returned quickly with more champagne and a plate of ridiculously ostentatious food, which I picked at it, drinking the champagne and ensuring Otto ate the lions share.

I could hear music from the hall now, so food finished, Otto steered me back inside and toward the centre of the room where some couples were dancing a waltz. Taking me in his arms we spun around in perfect harmony, drawing the attention of some of the onlookers. I was well aware again that we made a very handsome couple, but worried about drawing so much attention to ourselves.

Sometime later I retreated to the terrace where the air was cool, while Otto dutifully danced with some of the older lady guests, and I leaned against the wall of the Chateau, enjoying the cool of the stone on my back. Otto's Commandant appeared on the terrace alone, looked around and spied me in the corner. He walked purposely toward me, stopping just that bit too close for my liking.

"Ah," he said in correct but thickly accented French. "Otto's young lady. Now where did he really find you? And where has he been hiding you all this time?" I didn't reply but tried to look innocent, however he took one of my hands and held it firmly, beginning to stroke my face with his other, gradually getting closer with his not inconsiderable bulk, pressing hard against me. I felt trapped, with his podgy, clammy hand beginning to travel down my neck toward the low-cut front of my dress. I tried to wriggle away but he just leaned a little more heavily against me making any movement impossible. My instinct was to knee him sharply in the groin and complete the task with a chop to his windpipe which would considerably slow him down, as I guessed he had no idea I had been trained in unarmed combat. Stopping my natural reaction to this repulsive attention was requiring a lot of effort, but I realised assaulting Otto's commanding officer was about the worst thing I could do, however right it might feel at that moment.

"Cecile." Otto's voice came from the doorway, and he began to come along the terrace towards us, causing my assailant to drop my hand and step back hurriedly with a somewhat fixed smile.

"Ah Otto, we were just getting to know each other a little better. What a splendid girl." He moved away, patted Otto on his shoulder and left quickly. Otto could guess from my face what had taken place and taking me by the arm walked away from the melee of the party to the peace of the garden. I was seething and could hardly contain my feelings and turned to confront Otto.

"Is that the way he behaves with all women or just ones he thinks he can manhandle as he wants? It is because I am French that he treats me this way? After all we all throw ourselves at you wonderful handsome invaders." I broke free from his grip and stalked off toward the edge of the lawned gardens, with Otto following.

"Cecile, please, listen I am so sorry. I should not have left you alone, I know what he can be like but presumed he would not try to take advantage of you. Please forgive me."

Silence. He stood behind me, put his arms around me, leaving me facing away from him and the gathering of people. He could feel I was shaking, but concluded it was fear, when in reality it was overwhelming anger however, I knew I had to control myself, so I turned to him.

"Please take me home Otto, I don't belong here."

"Of course, if that is what you want my love, but first will you come and meet someone I need to speak to, then I promise we will go. Look I won't let go of your hand until we reach the car. Alright?"

Nodding I looked at him and thought, not for the first time, what on earth was I doing to get entwined in this whole situation. Passing through the guests milling around on the terrace and in the hall, I was relieved to see the Commandant deep in conversation not noticing us walk quickly by. Otto only stopped when they reached a group of high-ranking officers and spoke to one, insisting on introducing me. Again, a kiss on the hand, but this time it was a much more considerate, refined gesture.

"So, you are the young lady I have been hearing about. I saw Otto's father just a few days ago. Now I can reassure him he is keeping delightful company." All said by a tall, older, but very upright man, in perfect French with a benign twinkle in his eye. I relaxed a little but thought I was not so sure the news of 'Otto's girl' should be reaching his father quite so soon.

Sitting close to Otto in the rear seat of the car as it swung its way along the Combe de Lourmarin back toward Apt, I relaxed and fell asleep, enjoying the security of his arm around me. He roused me just as we entered St Saturnin, and as it was late and dark, risky as it was, he delivered me to the schoolhouse. I was greatly relieved to be back to my normality.

"I'll return the clothes next time I see you." I whispered as I got out of the car.

"Cecile, no, they are yours, my present to you."

"But the necklace, you must take that back, please unfasten it for me."

"My gift to the one I love, wear the pearls for me Cecile, please". I realised that I wasn't going to win this, so accepted with dignity, kissed Otto and disappeared into the shadows at the back of the school.

Chapter 18

Tuesday

I didn't get much sleep that night, as the events at the reception kept churning round in my head. Perhaps I had gleaned some useful information, I wasn't sure but just by passing on the content of conversations, as I had previously done, felt as good a reason for continuing to see with Otto as any. At least that is what I kept telling myself.

Waking to a normal school day after a short and fitful sleep put yet more pressure on me but, thankfully, I was now more skilled at managing the class. I so much enjoyed the interaction with the children that my energy came back very soon. After lunch, a note appeared on my desk, I never fully understood from where and how but accepted it without question. I was to be ready for an evening trip to Cavaillon at 5pm so, it seemed, the reconnaissance was on for tonight as had been suggested. It didn't leave me much time to consider the task before I was going to meet the others tomorrow, Wednesday, but I would have at least seen the bridge and be able to make some basic plans.

At 5pm exactly, I left the school building to find Etienne standing in the shadows by the front gate. A smile from him, which was a nice surprise, and an improvement on my usual greeting. I followed him round the corner to find an old motorcycle leaning against a tree. I had wondered how we were going to get to Cavaillon and if the horse and cart might have been the mode of transport, but for that distance it would have taken a fair amount of time. I had never ridden a motorcycle before, let alone as a pillion passenger, but with a thirst for adventure I smiled at Etienne.

"This looks fun, but is it going to get us there and back?"

"Of course, but we will take the back roads so as not to meet any patrols. We have just about the right amount of petrol." He was teasing me, I could tell and was pleased at his much happier mood than usual.

"Well, we will just have to push it back if we run out then won't we." I replied light-heartedly, hoping the evening would continue to be as pleasant.

Climbing up behind Etienne, he instructed me to hold him tight round his waist, and we clattered out of St Saturnin with the engine making a vast amount of noise. Gradually this lessened, but there was going to be no chance of conversation. I clasped my arms tightly round Etienne's waist and hung on as he sped along the narrow back roads to Cavaillon. I loved the wind rushing in my hair and, I had to admit, the close contact with Etienne. Taking advantage, I leaned my head forward against his, allowing my lips to brush the back of his neck, and I thought I felt his body tense then relax back into me, or maybe I just imagined it.

We slowed down to enter Cavaillon and drove through the wide streets by the station lined with plane trees, their extravagant foliage now shading the pavements and the roadway. The old town with its narrow streets dated back to Roman times, and would have been fun to explore, but the reason for our evening out was just outside the town, heading toward St Remy de Provence. Etienne drove past the entrance to the bridge as slowly as he dare without drawing any unwanted attention. This could have been difficult with the noise the old motorcycle was making, but the two soldiers on duty completely ignored us, continuing their check on vehicles before being allowed onto the solid stone structure.

Etienne kept the motorcycle going alongside the river until there was a patch of grass and trees away from the road where we had a clear view of the entire bridge. Almost transfixed by this huge, solid structure, I dismounted and stood staring at this magnificent, grey stone bridge that spanned this wide section of the Durance. There were eight arches in total to completely cross the river, each supported by a massive stone pillar that rose from the riverbed. It would need an impossible amount of explosive to destroy the whole bridge, but perhaps we could weaken the structure at one point and thus make it impassable. I noted that the river made two different courses in the middle and one of the stone pillars was surrounded by a small sandy island covered in storm debris from the winter's floods. Etienne parked the motorbike and came up quietly behind me.

"This isn't going to be easy," I explained. "But it may just about be possible." There followed silence between us as I was thinking, trying to plan scenarios in my head while Etienne slipped his arms around my shoulders, and I leant into him. He sighed and spoke.

"If you can't do it tell them, don't risk your life for something that won't work."

"I have to try Etienne, after all, that's what I am here for. It's my job, my contribution to the success of the invasion and the liberation we are all waiting for." He seemed to pull me closer, wrapping me in his arms trying to protect me from something that wasn't even visible. I needed to run some basic ideas past him, so I stayed staring at the bridge, but I was also enjoying being in his arms. I asked a question.

"How many men would it take to capture and hold each end of the bridge for say 15 minutes?" He thought for a moment.

"If we surprise them, probably three or four at each end would do."

"We need a big truck, or maybe an old tractor, to send across the bridge. Do you think that's possible too?" I needed his thoughts on my plan. This time I distinctly felt Etienne shrug his shoulders.

"I think so, but what are you going to do with the tractor?" I turned in his arms, looked directly at him, playfully placed a quick kiss on his lips, and whispered,

"Wait and see."

Etienne, who could tell I was teasing him now, smiled back, and at first hesitantly, but then gaining confidence he returned a more lingering kiss. He looked directly into my eyes before he broke away.

"I think I'd better take you home before, well … Come on, climb on, it's getting dark, and this bike doesn't have good lights."

The ride back was as exhilarating to me as the outward journey. I just loved the sense of speed with the wind rushing past, and also I conceded, I loved having my arms around Etienne, and frequently nuzzled his neck. We seemed to get on so well this evening, I was pleased and hoped it would continue. It felt so good not to have to keep up a pretence with Etienne, I could just be myself, not having to concentrate and pre plan every word I was going to say for fear of giving something, however small, away. It seemed also Etienne was much happier than previously to be in my company. Perhaps, I concluded, we just needed more time to really get to know each other, but that just didn't seem to happen.

I had important events to plan for, with a number of ideas spinning in my head, that I hoped would be good enough to convince the Resistance from Cavaillon the following evening, as I realised I couldn't do it without their co-operation. In the back of my mind, I remembered the reaction of the local fighters when I was first introduced, being petite and female was a good way to hide from the enemy but didn't necessarily correspond to confidence in my abilities. I would just have to try very hard to convince them my plan would work and hope for their cooperation.

Chapter 19

Wednesday

There was only one way from Chateau at Lourmarin to cross the mountains to the barracks in Apt, up the Combe de Lourmarin to the col between the Grande and Petit Luberon, over past the hilltop stone village of Bonnieux and down into the Calavon valley. The sniper knew this and just had to bide his time, they had to come this way.

From his hidden vantage point on the cliff, he had a clear view of the road running up the combe nestled deeply below. Here the road wound in a series of tight bends following the course of the river below on the far side. Mostly a dry riverbed, it only came to life when the turbulent storms of autumn and winter brought flash floods carrying huge amounts of debris along the narrow valley.

Silence, only broken by the cries of the buzzards circling overhead in the cloudless azure, blue sky. It was early but he knew the cars could be coming at any time and had to listen carefully for their approach. He would only get one chance of the necessary clear shot. It was imperative the bullet landed on target, because then, and only then could the next part of the deadly action take place. Faintly at first but then more definitely, he could hear car engines approaching, and taking up position, finger on trigger, he waited until the first car appeared round the bend.

Not even one outrider. He smiled to himself, these military personnel were arrogant. Did they think they could ride around completely unprotected in this kind of territory? Perhaps they just did not heed local advice, even if they inquired. He didn't know and simply didn't care, as it made things easier for him. His first shot rang out and hit the desired target and, as the front tyre burst, the lead car skewed toward the cliff face, completely blocking the road, causing the second car to skid to a halt, colliding with the first. The noise of skidding tyres and crunching metal echoed brutally round the enclosed valley. Then shockingly silence, but he kept a close direct aim on the cars in case of any activity. A head popped up to road level from the sunken riverbed opposite and rolled two primed grenades toward the stricken vehicles. Seconds later two massive explosions upturned the cars and set them alight, and with their job done, the sniper and accomplice melted away into the mountains. There was no further movement within the burning cars.

Retribution was swift and vicious. That same morning ten men chosen at random were put against a wall and shot in Lourmarin, with the same atrocity ten miles to the south in Lauris. Possible suspects were rounded up for brutal questioning, but no-one knew or if they did, revealed who the perpetrators were, or how the Resistance could possibly have known that those important military personnel would be traveling that particular route at that time. The local German Militia were under significant pressure from Berlin, for answers were needed fast as to why six of the military top brass were now dead and two more severely injured. Someone would have to pay for this.

I heard about the ambush and the reprisals that followed from Monsieur Foix over lunch the same day, as he always had all the local news, but I was never sure how. He was shocked as was the whole village, as who knew if the troops would arrive that afternoon and take ten of our own men to shoot?

Later that day, when alone, I tried to reconcile the news with the bigger picture. I was deeply upset by the atrocities happening to the south of the Luberon, as I felt I had caused all this, with my information which, I was sure must have precipitated the attack. Everyone knew assassinations of high-ranking military personnel were known to bring disproportionate revenge killings in the local area. Who decided what action was to be taken and if all this was worthwhile when the civilian population was to bear the brunt of the retribution? It was not up to me, I did not make the decisions, but I could not help but feel responsible. How many children would now be without a father, or wives without a husband, for what gain? If the Resistance wanted the support

96

of the population as a whole surely this must be a factor in their planning. Of course, the loss of leading military personnel was bound to hamper the occupying forces, that I had to agree, but the cost to the local population was however, heavy.

It had all seemed so simple when I had volunteered, all very 'black and white'. There was 'us 'and the 'enemy', with no need to consider anything different. But here, on the ground it was just not so straight forward. Spending time with Otto had convinced me that not every German was bad, nor indeed every French man good, as I knew Otto's feelings about the brutal repression of the local population. I also knew Resistance fighters who cared little for their own people and saw them as pawns in the fight for power with their idea of a liberated France which was not that of the Allies. However, I kept coming back to the simple fact that it was probably me, and my information alone had precipitated these assassinations and the horrible consequences for the people of the villages in the southern Luberon. Had I passed on the information just to make me feel better about attending the reception with Otto? Sitting in the old leather armchair I shed tears for the ones who had lost their menfolk that morning, those tears joined by tears of frustration at the entire situation, which just seemed to get more and more difficult for me to accept.

Time passed slowly. I realised I had to be less emotional, more professional and prepare for the meeting that evening with the Resistance from Cavaillon. It was up to me to get their approval and co-operation for the action at the bridge, and I had to be calculating and convincing, whatever I was feeling inside. I just had to accept that war was a dirty business, and I needed to distance my feelings as I had an important role to play, after all that is what I had volunteered for.

There were two older men I had not seen before at the meeting that evening in the village and I guessed they were from Cavaillon. Not at all smartly dressed, they had lined, sun darkened faces from years of work out in the fields. They were, I suspected 'Partisans' who were on the communist wing of the resistance, whose vision of France post liberation was not mine, or those of the local St Saturnin Maquis. But for this operation we needed to work together for the common good. The local Resistance was represented by the usual two well-dressed gentlemen, I had begun to expect to see. They made no introductions, but a gesture invited me to speak.

I outlined my plan, then filled in the detail with a sketch plan of the bridge and the surrounding area I had drawn. I explained exactly what needed to happen and what ammunition and explosives I would require, including how many men were needed to help. I would have to take a prominent role, as the timings were crucial if we were to at least weaken the bridge, and at best, destroy part of it. I was brief as I could be and delivered the plan succinctly, and all that was needed was their agreement and a date. But what did they think? I finished talking and waited with somewhat bated breath, as I felt my plan was a very practical idea and had very good chance of working. There was a long silence in the room. Who was going to speak first?

The men from Cavaillon muttered to each other in strong guttural Provençal accents, then turned to the local men.

"Its fine by us, we can do what is asked and supply men and arms, but we don't have much explosive, we don't use it." Adding thoughtfully afterwards, "If we had someone like this then, well, who knows what we might do?"

The explosives would be supplied by the Ventoux Resistance it was agreed and a Cavaillon contact would engage with me when I thought it was needed. It all now depended on an agreed date, that was yet to be decided but it was bound to be soon. I left the meeting first and presumed some talk about me would go on when I was not there. But in the end, I didn't mind, the Cavaillon Resistance seemed to be happy, in fact impressed by the plan, now all I had to do was make it work.

As I left Etienne darted out from the shadows by the church, I was surprised and delighted as I hadn't seen him en route to the meeting. I greeted him with a smile and a kiss to his cheek and felt the security of his arm around mine as we walked, a longer way than usual, back to the school. I knew and accepted that we shouldn't talk about future operations, but I told him that it was all going ahead as planned, after all he was in on the recognisance. I also asked if there was any more information about the atrocities to the south of the Luberon, as I feared more reprisals would have occurred, but Etienne had heard nothing more. I felt, very strongly, as if I wanted to share my guilt over the killings, but decided this had to be kept to myself, it was, after all, my burden to bear. Sharing was not going to help my conscience feel any better anytime soon.

Chapter 20

Thursday

The next day some sort of calm had returned in the village. It seemed the reprisals were aimed at the villages to the South of the Luberon where the assassinations had taken place. More soldiers than usual were passing through the village, people watched with fear in case a truck stopped, but it appeared these soldiers were off to cause trouble somewhere else, and St Saturnin seemed safe for now.

I immersed myself in teaching to try to forget my troubled conscience, and it mostly worked, with the end of the day coming quickly. The children straggled across the playground as usual leaving the classroom empty. Tidying up, I was deep in thought planning the next day. It was the last day at school before the long summer break, and I intended it to be a day of fun with games, hoping the classroom would be filled with laughter for one last time. Secretly, I had made lots of small prizes over the last week so everyone would win something, hopefully making happy memories, as this was so important with everything else that was happening around the village.

I sensed the presence of another person and, looking up, saw Otto in uniform standing quietly in the doorway watching me. He was the last person I had expected to see, and it was impossible to contain the genuine smile on my face, and the rush of enthusiasm and happiness at seeing him. I hurried across the classroom into his arms and looked up for a welcoming kiss. Otto however, looked distant, considerably troubled, and though he hugged me in return, he made no move to smile or kiss . He then moved determinedly into the classroom and closed the door.

"Otto my love what is it? You look worried, it's so lovely to see you but what are you doing here at school? You know we agreed not to meet in the village where we could be seen." I took a few paces back, looking questioningly at him.

"Cecile," he paused, obviously having great difficulty choosing his words. "Cecile," he began again, "I know." That was all he managed to say before stopping. I looked puzzled, and this was genuine as I had no idea what he was trying to say, then he went on slowly as if he didn't really want to have to say anymore.

"I know about you and have worked out what you are doing." He stopped again, appearing to have run out of words to express himself. I still kept the puzzled expression, but a distinct feeling of dread began to seep into my veins. I opened my mouth to say something, anything, to find out more, but he stopped me with a definite gesture of his hand.

"No, please don't say a word. I don't want to hear more lies." Another silence as he struggled to keep his composure, then he looked directly at me for the first time that afternoon and I could see the anguish in his eyes, as he eventually spoke again.

"Quite simply I love you, whoever you really are, more than anyone else I have ever known, and I can't imagine life without you. I really don't know if this is all a charade for you, I don't think so and I very much hope not, for that I couldn't bear." Another pause. I opened my mouth trying to respond with something to reassure him, but not a sound came out.

"Cecile listen, the net is closing around you. Please don't deny, don't lie to me, just listen. I can help, I want to help you, but we only have a matter of days to get you away. They don't know exactly who you are but, believe me, they will put the rest of the pieces together very soon."

"Otto, I...." He put his finger on my lips to stop my words.

"I don't want to hear you, just listen. With my contacts I can get a travel permit to get you away from here. You can go to my grandmother in Bavaria; she lives on a farm, it is far away from this awful war, and it is where you will be safe until I can join you. Then Cecile, meine Liebling, we can be together." He paused again, and gathered himself to continue, but this time the tone of his voice changed.

"Or you can choose to stay here and take a chance that you are not arrested, but I would not count on that. The choice, my

101

Cecile, is yours, but we don't have much time. I won't, I haven't said anything about you, simply because I love you too much. But Cecile do you love me? Or is this all part of your game? Do I, or did I ever mean anything to you?"

I stared at him trying to take this all in and trying to decide what on earth was I going to say.

"Otto, Otto," I felt tears rising and I spoke quickly, telling him, of course what he wanted to hear, all the time wondering if I was actually telling the truth.

"I love you. I adore you; I can't imagine life without you. But I don't know what to do. You must give me time to decide, please, my darling, give me some time." He stepped back towards the closed door and keeping the distant expression on his face, explained again.

"We don't have much time. It's entirely up to you. It's your decision." He turned to go with no kiss of farewell, and looking back, reminded me. "You have perhaps only a day or two to decide." Then he was gone as silently as he had arrived.

I stood in complete shock, the tears I had been holding back now streaming down my cheeks. Nothing could have prepared me for this, but one thing I immediately knew for certain was that I would never see Otto again. Only now did I really realise exactly how much I foolishly had let myself grow to love him.

I must have stood rigid for fully five minutes with so many conflicting thoughts travelling through my mind. I didn't understand my feelings, but I felt a great sense of loss, of what might have been, but I couldn't follow his plan however much I might have wanted to, that was simply out of the question. I had arrived here to do a job, not get romantically involved with one of the people I had come to help defeat. Thinking rationally in extreme circumstances had been part of our training, but affairs of the heart had not been taken into account.

Eventually I began to think more sensibly getting my emotions under control, realising that there was a much more pressing question. How to remain safe? If, as Otto had suggested, and I had no reason to doubt him, my identity was at the point of being revealed, I knew I had to get that message to the local Maquis as fast as possible. Running upstairs with a tear-stained face I dreaded meeting Monsieur Foix but managed to reach the sanctuary of my room unobserved. Turning the key in the lock, I began to breathe deeply, trying to control my tears and emotions. I washed my face and made myself as presentable as possible knowing I had to act as if nothing had happened. Then I ran down the stairs and left the school by the back entrance, walking the short distance to the café on the corner where trade was slow in the afternoon, as most of their regulars were out in the fields.

I strolled up to the bar as normally as I could manage, and spoke to the proprietor, giving him a coded message before ordering a coffee and retreating to a small table in the shade at the back of the terrace. I guessed one of the younger sons was a messenger for the Maquis, as I had been given this means of contact to use in an emergency. I felt I had no other option at this moment, and though the afternoon sun was warm I shivered as I waited for a reply.

The local Resistance moved swiftly with a hastily arranged meeting a few hours later wanting me to move to a safe location immediately. Not only was I important in their future planning, particularly the bridge attack, but I knew too much about the local organisation and people involved to allow any chance of arrest and interrogation. They were adamant that there must not be any risk at all of me being picked up and questioned. I, however, was equally determined that I could not just disappear, after all I had lived in full view of everyone, including the occupying forces, so if I unexpectedly vanished then surely that would fuel suspicion and prove my guilt.

"The villagers who have become my friends will be in danger. Monsieur Foix knows nothing of my true task but will be guilty of harbouring me. No. I have to leave in public view as I arrived." I was determined that they were not going to change my mind. The two older men frowned and muttered but agreed I had a valid point, as a disappearing schoolteacher could cause unwanted attention.

"I feel sure Otto will say nothing, remember the information I passed on would not put him in a good light, so I do have a suggestion, and I hope you can agree." I went on to outline the plan I had been formulating since Otto's visit. It was quite simple, tomorrow Friday was the last day of the school term, and

103

everything would go ahead as planned. However a 'message' would arrive from my 'mother in Paris' needing me to return urgently due to illness, so then Monsieur Foix could legitimately drive me to Apt in the afternoon to catch a train to Cavaillon where there would be a connection to Paris. My departure would therefore not in any way be suspicious.

There seemed to be a long silence before agreement was reached. However risky it was, Otto had suggested I had a day or two to make up my mind, so it should just about work. One of the two Resistance leaders eventually nodded in agreement but added.

"We will need to inform London of the developments, they may well have their own suggestions, but that will take some time. In the meantime, we will follow your plan, but you must not take any risks. If you suspect at any time you are in imminent danger leave the village, go into the hills and wait for us to help you." In many ways I hoped any orders from London would take a long time, as I needed, and very much wanted to be here for the bridge operation to proceed. Whatever happened, it was going to be a long, anxious twenty-four hours for everyone but especially me.

Chapter 21

Friday Morning

I had hardly slept, a total mix of emotions keeping me tossing and turning and very much wide awake. Did I love Otto? There were times I thought I did, but I knew I had a very sheltered upbringing and realised now that I had never talked to my mother about men or love in any meaningful way. Any encounter with the opposite sex had been very stilted with social contact supervised and limited. I accepted I had never before been attracted to another human being as I was to Otto and, as realisation dawned, also to Etienne.

I had allowed the relationship with Otto to flourish under false pretences, stupidly thinking I was capable of acting a part and not getting emotionally involved. The trouble was Otto was very likable, completely engaging, and I had so enjoyed our times together responding eagerly to his advances. If anyone held back it was him, thankfully always the gentleman, unwilling to force his wishes on me, calming my overtly passionate advances. Realising I was deeply attracted to him, he could have taken advantage of me, and I would have willing participated, but yet he didn't. However, was I actually in love or was it just my body responding in a frenzy of lust? Did I even know the difference? I knew I couldn't even contemplate his offer of a safe passage to Bavaria to wait out the rest of the war for his homecoming. However, the fact that he had even made the offer allowed me to think fondly of him, and to desperately seek a solution that would not hurt him anymore than I had already done.

I honestly felt I had, or I ought, to let Otto know what was happening. Perhaps then he could let go of his feelings for me, and not end up hating me for ever, as that, I realised I just could not bear. My feelings for him were so immediate and raw, but however I rationalized these, I had to admit I had thought I loved him, well perhaps I did. In another time or another place, but how many times had I already been through that, it had no relevance, for this was here and this was now I needed to remind myself. What was more important, my feelings or the liberation of my home country? The answer was easy to say but wasn't going to be simple to actually undertake. We all had to make sacrifices, how many times had I heard that, but simply put I had never made one so difficult before.

I decided to write him a note to explain my position, which I could post at the station as I left Apt that coming afternoon. A brilliant idea, but what was I going to write? I accepted he would see through the probably ill thought-out excuse, about my mother being unwell in Paris, but at least, he would think I was gone from St Saturnin and, hopefully in his eyes at least, out of immediate danger.

The sun was now rising making a rosy glow as I eventually and thoughtfully put pen to paper.

My darling Otto
Please don't think badly of me. My mother is ill in Paris, and I must go to be with her.

I want you to know how much I love you and just wish, as you said so early on in our friendship, that all this was happening in another time and another place where our special love for each other could flourish.

You will always be in my heart, and I hope you can forgive and keep me in yours.
With all my love,
Cecile

I placed this in an envelope and addressed it to him at the barracks in Apt. Then I sighed, hoping that I had closed that particular chapter, because now I needed to concentrate on getting through the day.

The children were excited and boisterous that morning as we all had great fun playing games, singing, and reading stories. By lunchtime everyone had a small gift, and there was laughter along with a lingering sense of happiness throughout the schoolroom. I was going to miss all this I sadly realised, as being with the children each day had been one of the happiest parts of my time in St Saturnin. Over lunch I explained the sudden arrival that morning of a 'message from my mother' to Monsieur Foix who was greatly concerned for her, and immediately offered to take me to the station in Apt so I could return to Paris, as soon as the children had gone home that afternoon.

"I do so hope you can return soon," he confided. "The children love you and so many of the parents have told me how pleased they are with their child's progress this term. You have made such a difference. I do hope you realise that."

I smiled, it was good to be appreciated, and quite simply there was nothing I would have liked more than to return to the school for the autumn term, but sadly I knew that was never going to happen. As the children left that afternoon each shook me by the hand and many hugged, kissing my cheek. I found it difficult to hold back tears and stood thoughtfully watching them skip across the playground towards the gate, out of my life forever.

I looked for Etienne, not knowing quite what I would do if I saw him, but he did not collect Jean that day, perhaps that was for the best after all. I had wondered if I should have sent a note with Jean, explaining my departure, but as ever did not wish to implicate anyone in my disappearance. It was better to keep this to myself as much as possible, anyway surely Etienne would get to know what had happened.

Up in my room in the attic for the last time I gathered just a few things in a small worn leather bag, as I decided I must not raise suspicion at the station with a suitcase. Taking one last look around the room my eyes rested on the beautiful long black evening dress hung on its hook, it was not even a week since I had worn it, and yet so much had changed. I had the string of pearls safe in my leather bag, a last-minute decision as I felt needed something to remind me of Otto, remembering he had suggested I wore them to think of him. After all, as I was supposed to be coming back, so most of my meagre belongings were being left behind.

Monsieur Foix chattered in his usual way as we travelled across the plain toward Apt with my nodding and making appropriate noises, trying to control my emotions on leaving somewhere that had very much become home over the past months. We travelled south with the Luberon Mountains directly ahead, changing hour by hour with different light playing on the landscape. They had become an important feature in my life I admitted, with the hilltop villages standing out as scattered stones seemingly flung onto the mountain side. The Luberon ridge was defined sharply against the skyline, the air so clear you could see the individual trees of the forest that clothed the summit. Behind me, equally impressive were the Mountains of the Vaucluse with the white stone top of Mount Ventoux dominating the locality. The Provencal people were proud of their heritage, and as I had discovered, willing to fight fiercely to protect it.

I carefully asked Monsieur Foix to drop me just before the station and promised to keep him informed as to the health of my mother. I shook him warmly be the hand, thanked him for all his help over the past few months, and got out of his battered old Citroen.

Now, clutching my bag tightly, and not looking back, I walked toward the station, with my apprehension growing. There could already be an alert out to arrest me, I quite simply did not know, but I understood I had to show my identity card to buy a ticket and access the platform so that could single me out, yet I had no choice. I slipped the letter to Otto in the yellow post box on the side of the building and tried to be calm as I walked into the station.

Two soldiers were standing by the entrance to the platform checking papers. As calmly as I could, but with my heart racing, I bought a ticket to Cavaillon, and copying the demeanour of the other women passengers stood in line to reach the platform. Keeping my hat pulled down and my eyes downcast, I showed my identity papers and ticket, and my tactic seemed to work, with thankfully, the soldier uninterested in yet another dowdy woman traveller. I moved out onto the platform breathing a little more easily, however time seemed to stand still, and the minutes felt like hours. Where was the train?

At last it arrived in a flurry of noise and steam, allowing me to climb aboard with the other passengers, deliberately choosing a carriage with three other women, positioning myself away from the windows. The train took a long time to depart, with soldiers constantly walking up and down the platform, but eventually a whistle blew, the wheels started to grind, and the station disappeared in a cloud of steam.

Apt was left behind.

Chapter 22

Friday Afternoon

The train stopped twice before it reached Cavaillon, each time there were soldiers on the platform, and each time it felt the train was stationary for a very long time. When it eventually pulled out of the stations, I breathed a little easier. Eventually, on arrival in Cavaillon everyone had to leave the train, most exiting the station immediately passing two bored looking soldiers checking identity cards. However, I went straight to the ticket office in the entrance hall and, making sure the clerk got a good view of my identity card, I enquired and bought a ticket on the next train to Paris, which would depart in two hours. Turning to leave the station in the meantime, and stupidly not thinking clearly, I made my way toward the side exit, where there were no soldiers on guard.

"Wait! Where are you going?" I had been spotted by one of the soldiers who was, by then, marching across the entrance hall toward me. *Try not to act as if nothing is out of the ordinary. Keep your head down. Don't react.* I stopped, and stood head bowed in submission.

"Identity card, now, and ticket." Without speaking I handed over my identity card and both my used ticket from Apt and my new ticket to Paris, saying nothing, keeping my eyes downcast, but my heart beating so strongly I felt it could be heard by everyone in the station. The soldier slowly read and reread the tickets and looked at the identity card very carefully. I could feel my legs start to shake, my breathing had turned to shallow with almost non-existent breaths, but I knew I had to control my fear.

Breathe deeply, concentrate, and don't arouse any suspicion.

Eventually the scrutiny of the tickets and card was complete, and they were handed back to me, with the soldier deliberately dropping them on the floor. Relief flooded through me, and without thinking, bent to pick them up, giving the soldier the opportunity to use his booted foot to send me sprawling across the hard tiled floor, grazing my knees. As I lay shocked on the floor, I heard him laughing and walking away, at least I was not going to be subjected to a further assault.

Slowly, and as unobtrusively as I could I got to my feet, knowing I must not draw any more attention to myself. What had happened was an almost daily occurrence to the local population, and though I felt anger rising, I was aware I must manage to hide my feelings. Collecting my bag, tickets and card from the floor I walked cautiously towards the main entrance. The soldier was back on duty at the exit, however this time he was busy with another traveller, so his compatriot waved me through without any further check of my papers. I walked away across the road and onto the wide, tree lined boulevard that led toward the town centre as calmly as I could. Thankfully there was no further interference from the soldiers.

I kept on walking down the street each step making me feel safer, grateful for the shade from the plane trees in full leaf while shaking internally. The station entrance and the presence of the military was gradually disappearing from sight, and the immediate danger it seemed, was passed. At the furthest corner of the wide boulevard, I walked into a small cafe, ordered a coffee giving a coded message, and took a seat in the corner of the shaded terrace outside, watching people passing on the street. I eventually began to breathe more easily, glanced at my grazed knees which had stopped bleeding and realised that I had probably been very lucky to leave the station at all. That had been too close a call, I needed to remain even more alert.

A waiter appeared and placed a small cup of dark liquid in front of me, slipping a brown envelope under the saucer. Giving him a sunny smile with my thanks, I slipped the brown envelope into my bag, and gratefully sipped the coffee, feeling more optimistic all the time. After gathering my thoughts, I left the cafe and crossed the road ahead into the old part of the town where the streets were narrow, the buildings close together, and more people were going about their daily business. I checked twice to see if I had been followed, as I had deliberately not taken a direct route, but nothing seemed out of the ordinary. Soon I turned down a quiet side street and found the rather shabby entrance to the Hotel les Deux Etoiles.

Inside in a dark brown painted reception area a bored young woman was behind the reception desk, her brassy blonde hair loose over her shoulders, reading the local paper. Happily, she was completely disinterested in me, as I was disturbing her quiet afternoon, but slowly looked up as I approached her desk.

"I need a room for three nights, my father is in hospital, I am here to visit him." My excuse tumbled easily out of my mouth. The receptionist gave me an irritated look and eventually put down the paper and checked the hotel register.

"Third floor, room six, breakfast, 8am in the bar. Identity card?" She held out her hand, so I gave her a creased worn card that I had already taken from the brown envelope given to me at the café.

"Madame Besson? Pierrette Besson? From Cereste?" I nodded. The details were entered in the register, and a large metal key handed over. Walking quietly up the stairs I breathed yet another sigh of relief that day, as the new identity card had been accepted without hesitation. It might well buy me some crucial time for the future, as I had no idea if Mademoiselle Andre was on any list to be arrested, but the risk was certainly there. Now I had a new identity and hopefully it would be remembered at the station that Mademoiselle Andre had actually bought a ticket to Paris, though I knew only too well I would not have been seen getting on the train. Perhaps I very much hoped, in the confusion of the station, no-one would remember if I had or had not caught that train to Paris.

Room six was hot, shabby and airless. I opened the window and threw back the shutters allowing the cooler late afternoon air to invade the room. I had a good view of the roofs of the old town and the square opposite the hotel, thankfully all was quiet and seemingly peaceful. Exhaustion swept over me with the tension of the day having become too much, and glancing at my watch I realised I had time to regain some strength before my evening rendezvous with the Cavaillon Resistance. I lay down on the bed and fell into a dreamless sleep waking with a start some two hours later, convinced I had overslept and missed the vital meeting.

But with plenty of time to spare, I quietly left the hotel, though I needn't have worried as the receptionist didn't even look up from her current reading material, such was her interest. Again, making sure I wasn't followed, and keeping my head down, I took a long route round the old town. When convinced I was alone, I headed back to the cafe on the wide Boulevard where I had drunk the coffee and collected the new identity card that afternoon. Taking the same corner table, I ordered a glass of wine this time and watched the world go by from my half-hidden seat in the corner.

A shadow fell over the table, and looking up I felt my heart jump as Etienne stood in front of me. The safety and security I had felt in St Saturnin had fallen away so quickly that day but now, just seeing Etienne helped me regain some of my composure. I stood to greet him with the Provençal greeting of three kisses to alternate cheeks, feeling good about his strong arms around me, however briefly. I really hadn't known how much he would know about my hurried departure but realised, as ever, little had been missed by Etienne. He sat down ordered a glass of wine and looked directly at me.

"Are you alright Cecile? You look very pale and anxious." I knew he was a man of few words, but I needed to realise he really did care about me, he was just more reticent in showing it. I nodded and smiled to reassure him realising there was no point in recounting the difficult episodes of the day as that was now behind me and we needed to look forward. Etienne took a sip of wine and continued.

"It's quiet in the village, it seems as yet no move has been made against you or the school. Luckily Monsieur Foix accepted our suggestion without question and has gone to his sister near Marseille, so the school is empty. This all bodes well for our operation, so let's hope it continues." He raised his glass to mine hoping to bring us both luck. I was relieved and smiled and felt the touch of his hand over mine on the table, with the familiar feeling of reassurance.

"That's good." I replied, "I am so pleased to see you. I didn't know who would contact me, this way it makes working together

113

much simpler." Etienne returned my smile and didn't move his hand away.

"Has everything worked out here? Are you somewhere safe?" I nodded and began to relax for the first time that day, continuing to sit in the late afternoon sun in companiable silence.

"Are you ready to go now," he eventually asked. "The meeting starts soon, and we need take care arriving, then afterwards we can talk more."

Setting off as usual, arm in arm, we must have looked like any other young couple enjoying each other's company, trying to banish the hostile environment around us. Taking a circuitous route, we arrived at an undistinguished house on the edge of the old town, where we were hastily bundled into a back room with three men already seated, each with a glass in hand. Rough red wine was presented to us and again glasses were raised. I recognised one of the men from our previous meeting in Apt, and with greetings exchanged, the business of the evening was quickly discussed. I quickly outlined the plan, what part I would play and what I needed from the local volunteers.

Essentially the bridge needed to be in the hands of the Resistance for sufficient time to allow the planned explosive placement work to take place. We knew the ends of the bridge were guarded by just two soldiers at night as traffic did not usually cross after dark.

"That's not difficult." One of the three men declared.

"But we need to make sure neither end is alerted or anyone in the surrounding area, so it must be done in silence." I had to be sure that once the bridge was under our control we would not be disturbed by reinforcements.

"Leave that to us, no noise, both ends I can assure you. Just a couple of dead Nazis." He spat the words out with relish.

"We also must have a precise time to work to." The guard change was 9.30pm, so 9.45pm was agreed for the takeover.

"I also need two reliable men and a small rowing boat standing by just upstream, before then. People who will follow orders quickly and can get away easily afterwards. There will be a lot of attention on the bridge once the operation is complete." A glance between the three, a nod and that was agreed. Etienne spoke up for the first time, he had been keeping his usual silence.

114

"We must complete the operation tomorrow night, our message from London has already come through. Our actions will be part of a sustained campaign to disrupt transport links across southern France, we must all realise there is no room for delay or failure."

The rest of the room considered his words, everyone taking a sip of red wine as if to mull over the implications of what had just been shared with them. We all knew the risks and now, the importance of our actions, as tomorrow would be part of the decisive plan that could help liberate our county from the long years of oppression. Our contribution was vital, and no one needed to remind us.

Chapter 23

Saturday

The sun filtered through the shutters waking me early the next morning. I had slept soundly and dreamlessly which was good, as recently vivid portrayals of the operation to come had haunted me, disturbing my sleep over the preceding nights. There was still a lot that could go wrong, and the responsibility for the flawless execution of the plan was mine, that I much I understood, there was to be no room for error. By this time tomorrow....... no, I mustn't think that way, as I had no idea where I would be.

I obviously could not return to the hotel, as there would be a high security alert throughout the town. The occupying forces wouldn't take long to guess who was behind the operation, and therefore I was still in the locality, so widespread searches would be swift and brutal. I hadn't asked what would happen after that night, where I would go, as I didn't 'need to know,' for now anyway. First things first, the bridge must be breached, the main road route needed to be disrupted, and this was primarily up to me.

But that wasn't until this evening, the whole day stretched ahead, and I needed to fill it and keep my worries at bay. After a meagre breakfast, I left the hotel and spent an enjoyable few hours walking round the main Saturday market held in the streets of the old town. I began to relax just a little, being inconspicuous among the other shoppers, wandering and losing myself in the hustle and bustle of the vibrant, busy stalls set in the narrow streets. There were some vegetables, salad crops and local fruits to buy, with other household items and many second-hand stalls as the local people tried to subsist under the occupation. Only those who were happy to collaborate or work without a choice for the occupying forces had any cash to spend, others got by as best they could. However the market, whether there was any produce to sell or money to purchase items, was a social gathering, and I felt at home and secure, as I had done in St Saturnin, among the local people smiling and exchanging greetings with stall holders and passers-by.

Purchasing some rough baked bread, a slab of hard ewe's milk cheese and a handful of small tomatoes, I walked out of the town in the direction of the bridge over the Durance River. Passing the entrance to the bridge, guarded by three soldiers, I swiftly walked on, arriving at the riverbank further upstream. There I sat quietly, back against an old, gnarled oak tree eating my picnic thoughtfully studying the bridge, with particular attention to the stone pillar and arch surrounded by a small island about halfway across the river. I went over and over the plan in my head as I ate the bread, cheese and tomatoes, hardly tasting them in my concentration. I felt pretty confident my plan would work but knew luck would need to be on our side. Then looking around and finding a safe place under the bushes at the edge of the river, I hid the dark clothing I would wear that night. I needed to arrive in good time but must not to arouse suspicion as I walked through Cavaillon to the river that evening. The heat of the afternoon eventually drove me back to the cool of the hotel so I could rest.

A warm dusk was falling as I made my way back to my place on the riverbank, with the full realisation of the responsibility that fell on me that night beginning to weigh heavily on my shoulders. I had no control over certain actions and could only assume the Cavaillon Resistance group would have their plans well in hand. They needed to send their two helpers to the riverbank and also successfully take control of each end of the bridge, but the actual operation to disable the bridge was my plan and mine to execute more or less alone. I knew it had to work, and this continued to play on my mind, as this bridge was a vital communication link with the north of France. Vehicle and troop movements would use this means to enter the Rhône Valley and move north, so the loss of the bridge would cause major disruption, and thereby give the allies important extra time to create a bridgehead in northern France. In previous operations I had planned and helped in the preliminaries, but then been sent away before the execution.

Tonight, for the first time I was leading the team with myself in the front of the operation.

Taking deep breaths to try to remain calm, I went over the plan in my head yet again. There was every reason it would work perfectly, however I was also painfully aware that all eventualities just could not be covered. Having changed into my dark men's clothing, a cap pulled down on my head and with the time now ticking quickly away, I knew there was no turning back.

I heard the gentle muffled splashes of the small rowing boat coming down the side of the river. In it were two young volunteers who knew the river well and lived locally enough to get away when the operation was underway. Waving them into the bank I stepped into the boat, and they continued downstream heading for the island in the middle of the river surrounding one of the stone arches. This was a dangerous manoeuvre for although it was by now dusk, the bridge still remained under enemy control, as the guards at each end would not be removed by the Resistance for some time yet, so any vehicle crossing the bridge could see us. However, there was preparatory work to be done, this would take time, so the risk just had to be taken, as the boat was carrying the boxes of explosives and all the necessary equipment for this part of the operation. I knew it was vital to position these explosives correctly and set the fuses carefully before the ends of the bridge were taken under our control.

Quickly and as silently as possible, I worked with the two men positioning the boxes of explosive materials around the side of the pillar under the landward arch. I had accepted early on that there was no chance of demolishing the broad stone pillar, but the point at which the arch left the pillar to span to the next one was the target. Synchronised explosions below and above on the bridge should weaken that point and hopefully allow part of the heavy stone structure to fall away into the river. At the very least it would be severely weakened, but I was aiming for far more, I really wanted the bridge to be breached, ensuring the link across the Durance would be disrupted for many weeks to come.

I connected the fuses to the explosive material but knew that in order for the timing to be as near perfect as possible, someone would have to return nearer the precise time of the planned explosion, and that couldn't be me. A hurried whispered conference and I showed one of the two men how to set off the primed fuse, as he had agreed to be the one who would come back later. We left as quietly as we had arrived, safely reaching the riverbank back up stream and pulling the wooden boat into the reeds out of sight. The young men happy to wait in the shadows until they were needed again.

Now the next step. I consulted my watch, half an hour to go until the guards were removed from the access points to the bridge. I needed to work quickly, so clambering back up to the road I spotted an old tractor at the edge of the field opposite. Crossing the quiet road unseen, I reached the machine and glanced up and down the deserted road, we had guessed that no one would have any suspicions about a farm tractor left in the fields overnight, but I knew I had always to double check everything. From the shadows created by the profusion of leaves on the vines a figure emerged, Etienne had arrived. After a hurried greeting, I assured him all was as arranged under the bridge, but we needed to work now on the second explosion. Hidden under the tractor was more explosive, and knowing these were precious supplies, it made me all the more determined to make the whole operation work. We set about attaching the explosives under and inside the tractor, then attached the fuse.

When complete, a check of watches told us that the bridge should now be under our control, and as promised, the takeover had been silent. We could not be sure but just had to rely on the professionalism of the local Resistance fighters and continue with the next part of the plan.

With just five minutes till the time I had given to the man in the boat to light the fuses under the arch, I started the tractor, slowly lumbered off the field and drove up the road toward the bridge. The noise of the ancient engine filled the night air, but that could not be helped, and I pressed on as quickly as possible. Reaching the entrance to the bridge I saw no guards and the barrier was standing open, so I turned the tractor onto the roadway across the bridge checking my watch again in the moonlight, thankfully still on time. I trundled slowly across the stone bridge aiming to stop just above where the stone arch met the side of the pillar we had previously primed with explosives.

One problem immediately became obvious, I could not see over the sides of the bridge to know exactly where I was in relation to the stone arches that supported the bridge. I had researched the bridge as diligently as I could but had not been able to physically cross it to see how high the side parapets were. I was just going to have to make an intelligent guess and be ready to reposition the tractor, but I knew time was not on my side. Stopping the tractor in what I guessed was the correct position and leaving the noisy engine running I jumped off and looked over the stone walled parapet. I was almost in the correct position, and I caught sight of the rowing boat going back upstream, so the fuses under the bridge had already been primed. That left me very little time if, as they needed to be, the explosions were to be simultaneous. Climbing back on the tractor I inched it forward to the best guess of the right position, shortened the already very short fuse to hasten the explosion, lit it, leapt off, and began to run as fast as I could back across the bridge.

Seconds later a huge blast of air and an ear-splitting explosive boom lifted me off my feet, throwing me headfirst into the solid stone wall at the side of the bridge. Everything went black, and with the splashes of the first stone blocks falling into the river below heralding the success of the operation, I lay motionless, crumpled against the parapet.

Chapter 24

Saturday night

Etienne was waiting by the entrance to the bridge for the explosion, deciding that he needed to make sure I returned safely from the structure. In the past two days he had begun to realise how vulnerable I really was. When in St Saturnin I had always seemed full of self-confidence, I didn't seem to need anyone, especially him he had concluded. However with my sudden departure from the village, with the threats so openly made against me he knew they had taken their toll. Etienne had long ago accepted I was fiercely independent with my own strongly held views about how operations should be undertaken with an outward aura of not needing anyone. However, he had seen the obvious relief on my face when he had arrived at the café after I had made my escape to Cavaillon, a clear sign that I needed him. Knowing all this, he was determined not to let me down. He hated with a vengeance the officer who had so openly courted me in the last months, wishing for just five minutes alone with him to get even for all his threatening behaviour.

He had watched as the tractor made its way across the bridge, and a quick check had revealed two soldiers lying inert with broken necks tucked away at edge of the road. He knew that no one would disturb them for a short while but, once the explosion had ripped through the quiet of the night, every patrol of the occupying forces within a five-mile radius would be bearing down upon them.

Etienne had made a decision when he met me in Cavaillon, not to immediately pass on some information which he knew I would find unsettling. Time for that later, he had decided, only later had never arrived, and the message had yet to be delivered, there just hadn't seemed to be a right moment. After the events of the night would be soon enough he thought, as the success of the operation was of prime importance, and Etienne knew I would not want to be distracted.

He felt and heard the explosion, as it rocked the buildings around the entrance, with the ground shaking under his feet. Staring at the bridge where a huge cloud of dust now hung in the renewed silence of the night, he realised I should have come off the bridge by now. He expected to see me emerging from the gloom at any moment, but when I didn't appear, Etienne couldn't hesitate any longer, and he ran onto the bridge scanning through the settling dust, calling my name. When he saw the figure lying so still, crumpled against the stone parapet, his heart plummeted. Darting forward, he scooped up my petite, seemingly lifeless frame in his arms hoisting me onto his shoulder and ran back across the bridge as if the entire occupying forces were at his heels. I came to sufficiently feeling the movement under my body and groaned. Etienne was relieved but unable to say anything as he used all his available breath and strength to move as quickly as he could off the bridge, along the side of the road and away from the town. His motorcycle was hidden down toward the river, and he just needed to get there and away before soldiers arrived if we were to stand a chance of survival. Arriving where the machine was hidden, I felt him place me carefully on the grass before he brought the motorcycle out from the bushes.

"Cecile, Cecile," he spoke quietly and urgently close to my face. "Wake up. You have to help me get you away." I moaned softly and this time half opened my eyes, with a large angry bruise continuing to grow above my right eye.

"You need to hang on behind me, please try to help." He lifted me astride the seat behind him and using the belt from his trousers, he looped it around me and then himself to try to secure me as a pillion passenger. Then, as swiftly as he dared, he roared off down the road putting as much distance as he could between the bridge and us. By now a large gap was appearing by the arch of the bridge, with stone bocks continuing to fall noisily into the river.

He got to Cheval Blanc on the main road without meeting any traffic, then decided to take the back roads and tracks along the base of the Luberon. It would be slower, as the surfaces were poor, but safer as he was unlikely to meet any patrols in the woods. Gradually, I began to regain consciousness as we bumped along the rough stony surfaces with my grip round Etienne's waist strengthening all the time.

There was no question in his mind about our destination, though he had specifically been told not to bring me back to the area around St Saturnin, as it was far too dangerous. Soldiers had raided the schoolhouse early yesterday and anyone who had known me, which was probably most of the population of the village were liable for raids on their houses and further questioning. However, in his mind he had no choice, dangerous, probably foolhardy, but he was making his way to his home outside the village, this being the only place he could think of where he could keep me safe and ensure recovery.

Leaving the motorbike hidden in a circular stone store in the corner of a field some way from the house, he held me tightly as I stumbled alongside him still dazed and incoherent. Once inside the house he bathed my bruised head and tried to keep me awake knowing sleep and a head injury were not good bedfellows.

"Cecile, come on drink this." He offered some strong-smelling liquor. I wrinkled my nose and tried to push it away. "No, try it please, it will help." Giving in I drank a little, coughed and spluttered, but opened my eyes more fully. Another sip went down a little better.

"What happened? Where are we? Has the bridge been breached?" I was definitely coming round though my brain was hammering in my skull. Typical, Etienne thought, my concern was for the success of the operation not myself, as he sat beside me and held me upright on the sofa, arms tightly round my waist.

"Yes, the arch was falling into the river as we left, it looked like the bridge was collapsing at that point, so you have done all you can. We now need to think about you." I tentatively felt my forehead and the huge emerging bruise. It then all came back to me, I had been too close to the explosion, that was a stupid mistake and could have killed me.

"It won't happen next time." I replied grimly, my head ponding, but now sipping water I was certainly starting to feel altogether much better. A poignant silence fell between us, and I knew him well enough by now, to understand it meant something, so I turned my head to look directly into his eyes. I felt Etienne take a deep breath, because he realised, and I guessed, I wasn't going to like this at all.

"There isn't going to be a next time, Cecile. London has called for you to return. A light aircraft is coming tomorrow night to pick you up from the plateau near Sault." This was the news he had known all the time since my departure from the village but had dare not relay to me. It had been decided that I was in too much danger and knew far too much to even think of being taken by the enemy. I had to accept that I was to be recalled for everyone's safety, however my reaction was entirely predictable.

"No, no there is still so much to do here, I can't go now, I won't leave.

"But you are not safe. They know exactly who you are now, and the schoolhouse has been raided. You cannot be hidden successfully without considerable danger to other members of the local Maquis. I'm sorry Cecile, I am only passing on the decision made in London. The time has come for you to go before we are all put in danger if you are captured."

I shook my head, I couldn't quite believe it, and tears began to roll down my cheek, I just didn't want to believe him. It was obvious to everyone including me that I could not come back to live in the village, but I had imagined I would hide out with the rest of the fighters in the hills and continue to use my skills in future operations until the area was liberated. Etienne fully understood the depth of my disappointment and, holding me in his arms gently kissed away the tears from my cheeks. I looked up into his dark brown eyes and kissed him with a passion that came from deep within me, a passion that had been waiting for weeks to finally surface. The kiss was returned, and he slowly stroked my hair, all the time looking straight into my eyes.

"Cecile?" An unspoken question hung in the air which he felt I would understand, and I knew exactly what he was suggesting, as we had so little time left together.

"Yes," was my simple reply, but really my eyes had already answered him. Taking me by the hand and leading me out of the kitchen and up the simple wooden staircase, we both knew this would be our last chance to be together. Neither of us wanted to waste any more time.

Chapter 25

Sunday morning

Etienne woke me with a gentle kiss. I had slept soundly in his arms with a feeling of safety and security that I had not felt for a very long time, and although a dull thud restarted in my head, the large lump of a bruise had mostly receded.

"Wake up, Cecile my love, it's early but we must get you out of the house before the rest of the family wakes." I understood immediately as my presence in the farmhouse was putting all the family, Etienne's sister-in-law, his mother and his nephew, Jean, at great risk. The occupying forces now knew my identity, and they would be checking all those who had ever been seen with me. I had come to Etienne's house to Jean´s birthday party, someone could remember, and the house might be raided at any time. The demolition of part of the bridge in Cavaillon would very likely be attributed to me, so they would know I was still in the area. I had to leave, and quickly, then at least if the soldiers came no-one needed lie about having seen me.

We crept down the stairs and went out into the courtyard with Etienne whistling softy to the two hunting spaniels. Opening the large door, letting the dogs bound out first, we left and turned across the fields of vines toward a tree covered knoll in the distance. Stopping in the cherry fields to gather the last of the full red ripe cherry crop for breakfast, we walked on hand in hand, the dogs quartering the ground around us. The silence that comes with early morning filled our ears, but already the sun was up, and the summer warmth began to take hold of the day. Crossing two more fields we reached the substantial mound which was covered in small oak trees. It was ideal as a hiding place as it had a clear view of the land around all the way back to the farmhouse, with the small, dense oak trees, more like overgrown bushes, giving shade and cover. Etienne spread a blanket on the ground, and we sat close together in silence eating the cherries. I didn't want to break the spell but eventually I spoke first.

"I will be perfectly safe here until we can leave, I mustn't cause any problems for your family."

"I don't want to leave you alone Cecile, but I have to act normally, so that means the usual work routine. I'll come back with some lunch later, and I'll try to get Jean and the rest of the family to go to see some friends to get them out of the house and away for the day. Listen, if you see any activity that seems suspicious go straight to the Ochre Caves, they won't find you there, but I will know where you are." I listened carefully, nodded and looked him straight in the eye taking his hand and holding it tight.

"I haven't thanked you for getting me off the bridge. If you had not risked your life to come back, I would have been captured, or dead. Now you are putting your family at risk for me, I really don't know what to say." His response was simple, he moved closer, took me in his arms and kissed me slowly.

"I don't think I really have to explain Cecile, do I? Too many misunderstandings have kept us apart, mostly my fault I know, but now I want to make sure you are safe because quite simply I love you. I have done for a long time but, just somehow sent you all the wrong messages, said all the wrong things and drove you away." I smiled at him, pleased to hear his explanation, but knowing I must not delay him.

"Go on, go and act normally I am safe here, but I'll look forward to seeing you at lunchtime, as a chance to sleep this morning is going to help me later on the day. I hope some rest will help this headache finally disappear." I reached up gave him a quick kiss and pushed him away. "Go on, go now before.........." Etienne laughed, knowing what I was suggesting, stroked my hair, whistled to the dogs and set off back across the fields.

I watched him go, resting my back against one of the mature trees. I had also felt an emotional bound with him for much of my time in St Saturnin, but was unaware he had felt the same, as his behaviour towards me had sent out conflicting messages. His determined opposition to my liaison with Otto was born out of

126

his instinct that it was a dangerous way for me to behave, and I felt sure, jealousy that I was with another man. Since our recent reunion in Cavaillon the basis of our relationship had changed, and his feelings for me were clearly visible. Feelings which I was only too eager to return, and the urgency of taking the chances that love brings during times of war had intensified our feelings. Now of course I had to leave, I knew I had no choice in the matter, but it seemed we were both destined to be fated in matters of the heart. Perhaps one day, when all this was over we would find a way be together, I could only cling to that hope.

I looked around at the view and could easily see the village of St Saturnin from my vantage point, with the cluster of stone buildings and the big, tall octagonal church tower in the centre standing out highlighted by the sun. Now I had time to reflect on my life there over the past three short months.

I had come to do a job and, in many ways, had been successful, but it was bitterly disappointing to be leaving. I felt I could do so much more for the Resistance and, of course now more than ever, I longed to stay to be with Etienne. Without the turmoil of war, I realised we would not have met, and it was my fervent wish to be able somehow, to stay together. I realised I had to have some optimism, or I was just not going to get through today. The heat of the late morning sun made my eyelids droop as I recalled the enjoyment that teaching the children had brought. Picturing each child, I smiled and drifted into a relaxing sleep, remembering amusing episodes in the classroom, thinking that perhaps when all this was over, I would become a teacher, as shaping and changing young lives was a challenging but rewarding ambition.

My senses were dulled by sleep, so it took the second round of noisy barking to alert me. Sitting up with a jolt I could hear plainly now the excited, expectant noises of approaching tracker dogs. I scanned the view from my hideout, and in the distance, but not far enough for safety, were soldiers strung out in lines searching through the fields of vines, the dogs leading the advance.

There was not much time to decide or choose my actions. Grabbing the blanket, I left the tree covered mound as noiselessly as possible, setting off south, at right angles to the direction of the search party, who were headed across the plain towards the hilltop village of Gordes. Hurrying through more overgrown vine fields I frantically tried to remember the suggestions given, seemingly a long time ago now about losing, or at least making it hard for those tracking you. I zigzagged through the fields, scuffed up the earth in places where it was soft, and crossed a number of stone surfaced roads. Roussillon, the orange and deep red ochre cliffs standing out in the direct sunlight, was on the hilltop ahead, with the disused, ochre mine workings lying around the base of the hill. Small tunnels ran in many directions and the loose sandy surface would make tracking a scent difficult, as I vividly remembered leaving Rene securely in one of these caves. I needed to find it again quickly, but for safety I ought not take a direct route or leave any obvious signs of my passage.

All the time I had been running I had not heard the barking getting any louder, in fact the search appeared to have continued on across the vineyards not turning south following my path, but I could not be sure or risk returning to my previous hiding place. Having found the tunnel and using a branch to agitate the sand to cover my footprints I backed into the hidden entrance of the cave. Replacing the bushes as cover I crawled along the narrow entrance shaft until it opened to the wide cavern. Only then did I dare stop to allow my breathing to return to normal hoping that, as Rene had been, I would be safe here.

Cold and in complete darkness I huddled in the blanket I had carried from the hideout in the trees. Etienne had told me where to go if danger appeared, but I wasn't to know if he was safe, what if he didn't come for me? The search party could have been to the farm and arrested him, but I had to stop these thoughts as the only thing I could do now was wait, hope and I unashamedly admitted, pray.

Time had little meaning in the dank, blackness of the cave. I recalled how quickly I had prised Rene's hand from mine when I had left him that night alone, in the darkness and in pain. Could I have provided more comfort for him? It was easy in hindsight, but at least he had been rescued and taken to safety. What if no one came for me? The question played on my mind constantly, despite moving my thoughts conspicuously elsewhere.

The cold began to eat into my bones, with the feeling in my toes and feet long gone. I felt as if I fell asleep, I might never wake as the numbing damp, cold took hold of my body, and I began to fantasise about sleep and warmth which lulled me into a half-conscious state.

Scrabbling at the entrance to the cave brought me rapidly to my senses, and with flight not an option, I knew I was trapped, so fight it had to be, and I scurried into a corner, picking up a large stone and waited.

"Cecile, are you there?" It was Etienne. I was so overwhelmed I couldn't put words together but made a crying noise to let him know I was inside the cave.

"Etienne, Etienne," I eventually croaked, the dust of the cave having invaded my lungs. In the darkness he found me, held me, kissed, and reassured me, warming me with his body as he hugged me in his arms.

I had spent so much time in the last few months being brave, being unemotional, being the S.O.E. person I was trained to be, but the events of the last twenty-four hours had just been too much. I sobbed and cried on his shoulder until my raw emotion had passed with Etienne holding me tight until the hysterical crying had ceased.

"We must go soon." He eventually said softly. "If we don't reach the rendezvous on time the plane won't land. Listen, it's all going to be fine. They didn't come to the farm this time but continued on through the vines toward Gordes. I have got my motorcycle nearby, come on the warmth of the sun is still in the air, you will feel better when we get outside."

We crawled through the narrow entrance into the late afternoon sun shine, with the sun's heat allowing much needed warmth to return to my body. Etienne passed some bread, cheese and much needed water

"Go on eat you must be starving; you will need all your strength tonight." I readily ate the food and greedily drank the water, feeling my body gradually revive. We retrieved the motorcycle hidden in some bushes and Etienne passed me a small leather satchel which I strapped across my body.

"This contains important documents you need to take with you to help the next people who will come to help us," he explained. I understood, as having the correct identity papers, travel permits, even food coupons would ensure an operative could remain hidden among the population. Those who prepared such items in London needed updated originals with greater frequency now more people were on the ground in occupied territory. A wry smile, it seemed I had my part to play even in departure.

Sitting pillion behind him, I clung on as we left the caves behind and began to travel north to the plateau and the makeshift landing strip where the single engine aircraft would land in just a few hours' time.

Chapter 26

Sunday Afternoon

The route to the Plateau d'Albion, a huge barren landscape lying at over a thousand meters above sea level, in the shadow of Mount Ventoux, was through the gorges of the Nesque. The road was narrow and winding following the path of the river far below, with a sheer stone cliff face on one side, and an abrupt drop to the steeply wooded valley opposite.

We rounded one of the blind corners on the motorcycle at speed, travelling much too fast to take any action to avoid a roadblock placed just a few hundred meters ahead. Without any warning there were gunshots fired directly at us, and the motorcycle slewed across the road with Etienne and I rolling clear. Our choice was limited, the cliff face on one side, or the drop to the valley on the other. Decisively, Etienne grabbed my hand and pulled me over the edge toward the gorge falling into the trees, where we tumbled down a short steep slope. Getting up on our feet, we began to run further into the trees fleeing from the gunshots behind us. The bullets ricocheted off the trees, and after another burst of fire, Etienne cried out grasping his arm. He had been hit.

"Go on." He shouted. "Go up the gorge towards the road, then the village is just a few miles further on. I will go back down and lead them the other way." I hesitated; I didn't want to leave him.

"Go now Cecile, please, it's your only chance." He was pleading with me, and I could see the urgency in his eyes, so this time I went up the gorge as fast as I could scramble over the fallen branches and through the maze of thickly growing trees. More gunshots, the sound breaking the silence in the forest, but further away now. Etienne was uppermost in my thoughts; had he been shot again, or had they caught him? I wanted to turn back to help but my head told me I had to keep going.

Then there were voices shouting not too far behind me, which made me decide I had to find somewhere to hide as I couldn't outrun the soldiers or their bullets, so I dropped over another sharp edge and pressed myself against the overhanging cliff. No one could see me now from this side of the gorge, but I could hear voices and crashing through undergrowth very close now. I stood rigid pressing against the stone and earth cliff and holding my breath.

The soldiers seemed to be right above me, as I could hear their guttural conversation and smell the tobacco on their clothes. After what seemed an unbearable length of time, they finally turned and left, noisily moving away, returning through the trees. I began to breathe quietly again and waited, making myself count to sixty slowly, five times after which I could hear no sounds in the trees above and I reasoned they must be far away by now. I could hear nothing at all, so slowly climbed back up onto the bank, stood still and tried to work out which way to go.

It was then that I saw him, standing not five meters away, he was waiting silently and watching. He raised his handgun; it was pointing directly at me.

"Otto." The word was barely a whisper.

"Cecile." There was an unpleasant sarcasm in his voice, as I tried not to let the panic in my eyes show. I moved a small pace toward him, but his face was set rigid, his blue eyes steely staring at me. I decided to speak first.

"Otto, please, just let me go. You don't have to do this. Please, my love."

"Don't use those words, you don't love me, you never did, you're just a liar, and a murderer."

"Otto, please, you don't understand." I tried to keep my voice steady, thinking that if I engaged him in conversation I might, just might, be able to get away somehow.

"Oh, but I think I do. You think you are so clever, you played me for all you could. You led me on just to get information, all the time proclaiming you felt love for me. You must have thought what a fool I was." He raised the gun, and I heard the preliminary click of the trigger mechanism.

"No Otto, please, I did, I do love you. I adore you. But what was between us could never have a future. The happiest times of the past few months for me were when we were together." I had to sound as if I was telling the truth, and in so many ways I was, I just needed to make him believe me, I had to play for time.

Thankfully, he hesitated, but his expression did not change, as I began to realise that killing me would in fact solve all his problems and no doubt get him a medal for catching the notorious explosives expert. After all, a dead Resistance agent couldn't reveal any secrets that could implicate him. I made a decision; however foolhardy it might seem. I drew myself up to my full five foot three inches and tossed my head confidently, almost arrogantly, looking directly into his eyes. If I was going to die here and now, then I certainly wasn't going to show him any fear.

"If you don't accept what I am saying then just go ahead and shoot me. After all I am only the women you proclaim to love."

Otto didn't move or speak but kept the gun pointed at me. It felt as if the silence between us continued for an eternity, then abruptly he lowered the gun, stepped forward toward me and slapped me hard across my cheek, causing me to stumble away from him. Then immediately dropping his gun and grasping me in his arms, he kissed and stroked my hair while murmuring, "Meine Liebling," over and over again. I hugged him in return and looking up into his now softened eyes, kissed him on the lips. The kiss was returned with violent, passionate urgency, then he threw me roughly to one side.

"Go, just go Cecile, go now." I hesitated, then saw him turn away, his whole body shaking and a low animal like groan, almost a howl, emitting from his lips. It was hard to suppress the overwhelming desire of my heart to run to him, to hold him in my arms, to comfort him, however my training took over. I turned and ran, fleeing along the bank of the gorge stumbling over the tree roots, tears streaming down my face.

I was running, blindly, gasping for breath, all the time going uphill as Etienne had said towards the road.

Etienne, what had become of him? Would he get away? How badly was he hurt?

I tried hard not to think about him, or the confrontation with Otto, but to concentrate on getting back to the road and on to the meeting point. I must not let emotional feelings overwhelm my senses, as I still had a job to do, but I found it impossible to blot out the simultaneous images of Etienne running with blood streaming down his arm and Otto on his knees, weeping, a broken man. This wasn't how it was supposed to end.

At last ahead some brightness, the trees were thinning out, the horizon descending, a narrow road came into view, and stopping cautiously in the trees alongside the road, I controlled my hysterical breathing and listened intently.

Silence. I waited. Silence. No engine noises, no voices, no gunshots, just silence. By now darkness was falling, so I decided the risk had to be taken, as this road led to St Christol, the village on the plateau en route to Sault, where the rendezvous was planned. As I knew no other way; I would just have to follow the road.

Glancing at my watch I realised I had just less than an hour to make the rendezvous, which would be enough time if I hurried as, in the growing moonlight, I could make out the outline of the cluster of houses, with the church at its centre. Keeping close to the edge of the road, ready to hide in the fields at any noise, I made my way as quickly as I could, focussing on the church spire. Miraculously I realised, I still had the small leather shoulder bag containing the documents, as I had looped it across my body for safety and somehow had kept it attached as I had stumbled and fallen through the forest.

Without the need to stop and hide I made good time and entered the shuttered, darkened village with five minutes to spare. Carefully I made my way in the shadows to the main square, where the church with the tall spire stood.

Now what? I slipped over to the darkest shadow at the side of the building and waited, where almost immediately a hand touched me on the shoulder, noiselessly from behind.

"Follow me but keep to the shadows till we reach the edge of the village. We don't have much time." My guide disappeared quickly behind the church, and I followed at a safe distance, keeping to the deep shadows thrown by the tall buildings set close together. Soon we crossed the road at the edge of the village and, lit only by moonlight, plunged into a field of lavender, running up the space between the rows.

The plants were almost in full bloom, their scented foliage passing above my waist, and as we brushed past the stems we created an explosion of lavender scent. The field seemed never ending, then we ran through another just as huge, and just as I began to wonder how long I could keep up this pace, the second field came to an end, giving way to open rough grassland. We moved rapidly to a single stunted tree beside which two other helpers were hidden.

"Now we wait," whispered my guide. I got a good look at him for the first time, and saw he was much older than I had thought from the pace at which he moved, his sun-darkened, lined face, giving me a reassuring smile.

"The weather's good tonight, they will come soon, you will see."

Gradually the sound of the light aircraft could be heard approaching, and waiting until they could see it, the two helpers ran out of the cover of the tree. Running in opposite directions, they arrived at prepared mounds of vegetation which they set alight. Two mounds as beacons lit the start of the runway, the single mound would be the stopping point. The small aircraft swooped low, touching down just past the two fires and rolled up to the single light, turning ready for take-off before stopping, keeping the engine running. The door was flung open from the inside, with a large package for the local Resistance lobbed to the ground. I was ready and waiting, and after a hurried, but heartfelt 'thank you' was mouthed to my guide, I climbed aboard, as the engine noise increased. Almost before the cockpit door was closed, we were racing across the bumpy field heading for the two lighted beacons, the single fire behind now had been extinguished, with the two in front dying quickly.

The plane took off level with them and climbed rapidly toward Mount Ventoux which was directly ahead, and as we climbed above the white stones that made up the distinctive peak, the pilot turned to me with a broad smile.

"Welcome aboard." He pointed to a leather sheepskin lined flying jacket in the foot well.

"Put that on. It's going to be cold up here, but we'll be safely back to England before dawn."

135

I heard none of his words, staring out of the plane at the fast-disappearing landscape, with at first silent tears of relief and, then of overwhelming loss, rolling down my cheeks, as I realised I had left behind the only man I knew I would ever truly love.

Part Two

Stephanie

Chapter 1

Stephanie, 1963 aged 18

"You have done what?" She looked incredulously at me, after all previously I had always accepted her decisions.

"I've accepted the offer of a place from York to read English. I got the grades I needed."

"But we agreed. You were going to Goldsmith's College here in London so you could live at home."

"No. You agreed with yourself and didn't take any notice of me. I am going to university in York this September, I have accepted their offer in writing today." My mother got up from her chair, walked over to the tall sash window that looked across the street and stared out. She was petite, immaculately dressed as ever, backlit by the evening sun filtering through the window panes. I really do think she was lost for words, or perhaps thinking carefully about what she ought to say. I had never defied her in such an enormous way before.

"You can go," she simply said. I didn't know what she was referring to, York or a simple dismissal, but dare not ask. "I don't wish to talk to you at the moment." Silence and a deep breath from me.

"I am going out this evening, round to Paula's house, her parents have asked me to join them for a meal. Is that OK?"

"You know the rules, home by 9pm." All this said as she stared, expressionless out of the window not meeting my anxious gaze. I could smell the lingering scent of boats burnt and left her study resisting, only just, the temptation to slam the door.

I climbed the stairs to my room with the all too familiar deep feeling of having disappointed my mother yet again. Somehow she could make me feel as if it was always my fault, and it was my problems that caused our rifts and tensions, never hers. How many times, over how many years had I climbed these stairs after some kind of admonishment from her, feeling the same unhappiness. I could go and slump on my bed as usual or start afresh now, after all she could not control me when I had gone to university, so I wasn't going to let her spoil my evening.

All the same I felt empty, unsettled and unhappy deep inside as she was my mother, all I had, and I had upset her, I could not help wanting her approval, the bond between us was so deeply embedded. As I let myself out of the front door soon afterward, I could hear her talking quietly on the telephone, it would be work of course, her life blood, her total commitment without thought for anyone else, least of all for me.

As soon as I was out of sight, I undid my neatly tied up hair, scrunched it so it looked even more unruly, and opened my coat to reveal a shorter than I was allowed mini skirt and a tie dyed, nearly see through, cheese cloth cotton top. Makeup went on expertly at the bus stop, so by the time I arrived at Paula's house I looked very much like the other celebrating girls, as far from a family dinner, we were having a full-blown party. Subterfuge had become, in my later teenage years, the way I coped with the outdated 'expectations' it was assumed I would follow. Mostly I got away with the plausible untruths, rarely caught out since my mother didn't watch very carefully.

She had been lulled into a false sense of security by my younger self who, wanting to please and retain her approval, had rarely stepped out of line. The few rebellious moments had been quickly and harshly stamped out, so she thought I wouldn't dare to push, never mind, break her boundaries, but this was the beginning of the 'swinging 60's' for goodness' sake. There was more to life than her outdated expectations, so I walked a tightrope, keeping Mamma happy at one end and myself and friends at the other. The very idea of staying in London to study had filled me with horror. It was her way of keeping control, though to be fair, from her point of view, she was protecting me.

It hadn't always been like this, as my earliest memories are of love and kindness. Long days spent in her company, playing and talking, with her quiet voice singing songs in her own language as I drifted off to sleep in her arms. I felt very much wanted and loved, enveloped in a cocoon of protection. She wasn't always there, and I spent time with my live-in Nanny who, at the time, was far stricter. But most days I remembered, I had time with my mother alone, when I was the centre of her attention and could reciprocate her love. We had our own secret language that Nanny didn't understand, and by the time I was to start school aged five, I was fluent in French and English, and now I realise, a smattering of German endearments, which I soon learnt, were best kept to myself.

It was by no means unusual in 1950 for children to be without a father at home. Many soldiers had sadly not returned from the war, living on in their children conceived in brief, intense moments, snatched during the last year of conflict. I just presumed, as I grew up with no information to the contrary, that I was one of these, for as a young child my father was never mentioned. My mother called herself 'Mrs' and no difficult questions were asked, certainly not in my hearing.

Once at school my mother's absences with her work began to grow. I was left for longer periods of time with 'Nanny', but still had the close, loving and very much wanted relationship each time she returned. I never fully understood what work she did, even now I am unsure.

"I can't talk about it," was her stock reply. "I work with people in the Government, that's all you need to know. I need to go away sometimes, but I will always come home to you don't worry." The conversation usually concluded with a hug and kiss to the top of my head accompanied by one of her whispered Germanic endearments so special between us. However, I did learn that there was a line drawn, which I was not to cross, between her work life and her time spent with me. When not with her in the drawing room I was expected to stay with Nanny well out of the way, on the top floor of the three-storey large Victorian terraced house where we all lived.

As I grew older, I realised sometimes exciting happenings seemed to occur downstairs in the evenings. People came to the house and there were the sounds of animated voices and music from the dining room. Fascinated, I would sneak out of my bed and peer down though the banisters on the stairs catching a glimpse of the finely dressed ladies and gentlemen in black suits with white ties at their throats. Casting caution to the winds one evening, as only a 6-year-old can do, I carefully descended the stairs in my nightdress, as Nanny sat in her room with the radio on. There were people talking and the sounds of a meal being eaten in the grand dining room which I was not allowed, ever to enter. Pushing the door with all my weight I appeared suddenly in the room and the conversation round the table came to an abrupt halt. There must have been a dozen or so adults all seated at the magnificent polished mahogany table.

"Now who have we here?" said a tall smiling man seated close to the door. I could see my mother at the head of the table opposite. Before I had a chance to say anything she had swept me off my feet, taken me out of the room, and closed the door. Looking angrily at me, she pushed me in the direction of the stairs.

"Get back up those stairs to bed," she whispered fiercely in my ear, "I will deal with you in the morning." Nanny appeared, flustered, at the top of the stairs full of apologies, and took my hand squeezing my wrist hard so it hurt, as she hurried me back upstairs. Nanny, equally, was not pleased, I found that out with a wallop to my bottom when out of sight of my mother. I cried myself to sleep that night so sure my mother didn't want me anymore. I had never cried myself to sleep before.

Nanny was first to be dealt with in the morning. If she was anything to go by, I was not going to get off lightly with this transgression. She left my mother's study ashen faced and glowered at me with real hatred as I passed her by in the hall. I then stood before my mother; head hung down as she scolded me for the actions of the previous night. She crouched down to my eye level and whispered,

"You see, my darling, you are 'my little secret'. Just you and I, we need no one else. I love you so much it breaks my heart to see you cry, but my work needs me as different person, without you. Do you understand? You must never, ever, do anything like that again."

I nodded, not really knowing what she meant. I knew what a secret was, but how was I one? She kissed my cheeks wet with tears, hugged me with an intensity that was almost alarming, and explained that a new nanny would be arriving this afternoon and until then I was to behave very well for our housekeeper who would look after me. Remembering this now I think I got off lightly, no wonder nanny had given me that look.

Chapter 2

Five days had passed without any direct communication with my mother since I had announced my intention to go to university in York. Avoidance was easy, I just waited till she had gone to work, then made sure I wasn't around in the evenings, but made every effort to conform to her expectations. It couldn't go on, of course, we had to communicate, if about nothing else my departure to York was growing ever nearer, but I had decided to wait this one out. Let her come to me this time, I had enough of apologies for things that were not really my fault. I knew, deep down, that all this was about protecting me, in her eyes at least, and I did try to understand her point of view.

She had grown up in a different era and had never really accepted that the world had moved on. It was impossible to get her to talk much about her childhood, I had tried. I knew she had left Paris with her mother before the outbreak of the second world war on the insistence of her father who had Jewish connections. There had been aristocracy and wealth in Paris, as she once described to me the elite circles in which they moved in society, the expectations placed upon the young ladies of that era, with ´marrying well´ all her mother was concerned about. Strikingly pretty with huge brown eyes and a petite figure that suited the fashion of the '30's she had attracted a lot of attention, and always accompanied by her elegant young mother, they were a sought-after couple.

However, London had come as a shock to them both, and while my mother set about learning the language and making a new circle of suitable friends, her mother, who was always seen as 'delicate', went into what was known at that time as a 'decline'. She kept away from any social contact, refusing to come out of her room, pining for her husband and her home country. Things went from bad to worse when the war actually started, and they felt compelled to leave London to stay with some vague friends deep in the Dorset countryside.

Once Paris had fallen to the Germans there was no more of the sporadic communication with her father. Her mother just could not cope, caught pneumonia in the damp, cold conditions, and died very suddenly, leaving my mother all alone, aged 20 in a foreign country. Little wonder then, that she became a strong character, able to control her emotions and manipulate those around her. So it was not surprising that she wanted to protect me, her only child, indeed her only family, from the outside world. I think if she could have stopped me growing up, keeping me hidden away as a precious young child for ever she would have taken that option.

However, that couldn't happen, so I grew up and became someone different, a person in my own right, someone else, not just an extension of herself. Now I had disappointed her greatly, going directly against her wishes, and even worse was about to leave her in London when I started university in York. I really didn't know how she was going to come to terms with this.

At breakfast on the sixth day of silence our housekeeper passed on a message,

"Madame will see you at 6 o'clock today." She always used that outdated term, presumably my mother preferred it. So, she was first to blink.

At six o'clock precisely, I knocked on the door of her study and let myself in. I had no intention of backing down, but I did need to know where I stood financially, as if, and I really did not know what she was thinking, she refused to support me at York, I had to think again about my plans. Writing quickly with her usual back and gold fountain pen, she looked up from some weighty document and actually smiled. I felt a little more confident but was very much on my guard.

"Come and sit on the sofa with me and have some coffee," she pointed to the perfectly set out tray with matching cups set at right angles to each other. I sat half turned towards her on the velvet upholstered seat and accepted a cup.

Silence, I had no intention of beginning this conversation.

"Stephanie, I have thought a lot about your decision. It would have been so much better had you actually come to me so we

143

could talk it through before you accepted the place at York. No, no. Please let me finish. I am very proud of you achieving a university place and of course you must go. It is an opportunity I never had. If York is your choice, then you will go, not exactly with my blessing, but my love. I will, of course, support you financially, I want you to have time to devote to your studies not have to work in some tiresome job. Is this what you want to hear? Can we be friends again now? I have such little time left with you." She looked directly into my eyes.

I didn't expect a complete capitulation, this was not how these interviews normally went. I opened my mouth to say something, anything, and unsuccessfully tried to hold back tears welling up in my eyes as big round droplets rolled down my cheeks. I put my arms round her neck and sobbed into her shoulder. Tender Germanic whisperings I had not heard since childhood were spoken softly as she stroked my hair and held me close. This was the Mamma I remembered, I had wanted so often, and now I was leaving her.

"Come on now. Why the tears?" I sat up and looked directly into her huge dark eyes.

"I'm sorry, so sorry. It's just....."

"Shhh, the less said the better. Just remember whatever happens you are my daughter, and I love you more than you can ever realise. You are a strong person like me, and I am pleased to see that, but please remember the world is a harsh place, I want you to take great care and make me proud." I dried my tears, smiled, and gave her a kiss to both cheeks.

"Now, here is a little something to get you some new clothes for your new life at university." She handed me an envelope that clearly contained a bundle of notes. Thank you seemed inadequate but that was all I managed before the phone rang and her attention was elsewhere. I left the room quietly, with a smile which was returned as she started to speak on the telephone. But as I climbed the stairs, a fleeting thought crossed my mind. Had this actually been a supreme piece of manipulation, after all, who was the one who said sorry?

Shopping with the unexpected windfall was great fun the next day with Paula and her big sister, who had just completed her degree at university. I had plenty of advice and being sensible, well I was going to the ´north country´, I first bought a bright yellow raincoat with hood and quilted inner, then a couple of soft polo neck jumpers and a pair of rather expensive but beautifully cut black velvet trousers. These put a substantial hole in the cash, but there was plenty left for more frivolous items.

On returning to the house, I heard my mother in her study and after ditching some of the clothes upstairs I took my yellow raincoat, the jumpers and the velvet trousers to show her. Her mood was as welcoming as yesterday, she admired the clothes and laughed at my reasoning for the heavy-duty raincoat.

"Stephanie, would you like to join me for drinks this evening with a very old friend of mine? Not for long, he will only be here about an hour, but I would like you to meet him." The shock must have registered on my face. I had never been invited to meet any of my mother's friends before, as it was always assumed I would keep well out of the way, upstairs. The pause caused my mother to jump in.

"If you are already doing something this evening that's OK".

"Actually, I had said I might go round to Paula's house, but no time was fixed, so Mamma that would be lovely, thank you."

"Good, he is coming for six o´clock. Why not wear your beautiful new velvet trousers, you will look splendid, I am sure." Slightly confused by this sudden change of direction, I agreed and ran up to my room to get ready. What was going on? What significance did this man have? The first thought, as ever with my position, was the unknown 'father' figure. Fathers were never discussed, any reference or questions firmly refused and resisted, and I had learnt quickly not to go down that line of questioning. No, that would be too obvious of course. But the question remained in my head.

Chapter 3

New velvet trousers, big white full sleeved blouse with lace at the neck and cuffs, and my unruly brown curly hair semi neatly clasped in a bun at the back of my head, I carefully applied minimal makeup. I knew make up was frowned upon, we had had plenty of spats about that, but I wanted to seem sophisticated for whoever this man was.

I arrived in the drawing room to find my mother looking out of the window. She had changed from her elegant work attire and looked, if it were possible, even more immaculate in a simple green dress that enhanced her petite figure.

"Very nice Stephanie, you look so grown up. Not my baby anymore." Before I could reply the doorbell sounded and a tall, broad shouldered gentleman was ushered into the room. Obviously older than my mother, he had a full head of greying wavy hair, intense blue eyes, a square jaw and a wide smile on his face. Perfectly dressed in a well-cut pinstripe suit, he sported what looked like the colours of an old school tie. He went straight to my mother and kissed her on the cheeks, and gave her a small, but meaningful, hug.

"So lovely to see you, my dear." Turning to me he stopped and took my proffered hand, lifted it and barely but significantly touched it with his lips, such an old fashioned but delightful gesture, then he looked me directly in the eye.

"Now who have we here, Cecile, not your daughter? You are much too young to have a daughter of this age."

"Julien, you old flatterer, of course she is my daughter. Stephanie, this is Julien Grant, a very dear friend of mine. I am so pleased you can eventually meet." I was uncertain how to reply as 'hello' somehow felt inadequate. But I smiled, and the situation was rescued by my mother asking Julien if he wanted his usual drink. Soon he had a whisky in a cut-glass tumbler in

146

his hand and I had been passed a small glass of sherry. I suppose I would have to learn to drink the sweet, strong, sickly stuff if I was to progress in society. Conversation easily followed, mostly between Julien and my mother who, it was patently clear, were very close friends. Only when she had to slip out to take an important phone call did I become the centre of attention. His face was familiar, but I just couldn't place it, so it was my turn to delve.

"Have you known my mother a long time?" Stupid question really, that much was obvious, but I had to start somewhere.

"We have worked together for many years. One might say we have a 'mutual admiration society'". He chuckled, then continued. "There is no one quite like your mother. But I want to know more about you, she has been hiding you away for years, her best kept secret. I think she felt people would think the less of her if your existence was common knowledge. But tell me, she says you are off to university, she is so proud. Where? And what to study?"

So, the conversation flowed easily again as I could talk for England about my love of English literature and my excitement at spending the next three years immersed in books. I was probably in full flow about the romantic English poets when my mother returned.

"Getting along well without me I see."

"You have a very interesting, intelligent young lady here, not forgetting a very pretty one as well. I can quite see where it comes from." Was my mother actually blushing?

"But unfortunately, I must dash now, dinner at my club with, well you don't need to know, but someone you don't keep waiting! We must all meet again very soon, and Cecile, stop hiding this young lady. She is a great credit to you." He took my hand, barely touching but kissed it again, kissed my mother on her cheeks and gave her a farewell hug and was gone. The room seemed empty without him.

I collected the glasses and put them the highly polished silver tray.

"Mrs Miller has left us some supper in the dining room, will you join me?" We rarely ate together, most times I sat in the kitchen with 'Mrs M' as I called her, while my mother was late from work, or away. So, we sat down in convivial silence to cold ham salad with cool new potatoes that had obviously been waiting for us for some time. Perhaps this was the time to gain some information.

"Julien, a lovely man, you have known him a long time?" casual question.

"Sir Julien, actually, and yes probably almost 20 years. He has always been so supportive and helpful, because it's not easy for a woman alone, you need to understand that. There are not many women working with me, it's very much a man's world."

"I see, so does he work with you at the moment, only I seem to recognise his face?"

"Julien, no he's in the foreign office now, something important, you may have seen his picture in the newspaper I suppose." Silence followed; she wasn't giving much away. I needed to press further if I was going to make the most of the opportunity.

"So, he helped you some time ago?"

"Stephanie," my mother paused, but not in an irritated sort of way. "The world was a very different place just after the war. A woman's place, especially if she had a child was in the home, she simply did not go out to work. But I had to support you, and anyway I was young, and wanted to continue to use my skills. Julien needed a good translator who could speak French and English and manage his negotiations, he soon realised I was discrete and able to fulfil the task. He knew about you, but very few people did, as it would have been unacceptable for me to continue working with a young baby. So, I kept you a secret from most people, and at first, I only worked when he needed me then, at his suggestion, took German lessons so I could offer two languages to translate. Later when you were a little older, I worked for him all the time. In meetings I was able to translate as people were speaking, not everyone could do that, it's not just translating really but interpreting. He trusted me completely, then I began to travel with him to many important international conferences."

"But you knew him before the war?"

"During the war, but I can't speak about that".

"Why not?"

"I just can't, I don't. That's just how it is." She gave me a look that I knew meant I needed to tread carefully and remember the boundaries I had been set.

"But Stephanie you were always well cared for," she continued, "I saw to that. I didn't hide you because I didn't love you, you must never think that. I did what was best for both of us. Things are so different now; it is difficult to explain what the society was like 18 years ago."

"I know you love me Mamma, it's just that there is so much I don't know. I really want to find out more." A pause.

"Sometime perhaps, but now we have more important things to discuss. When are you planning to go to York? Have you got everything you need?" She had cleverly steered the subject away from herself. I would just have to be patient.

Chapter 4

York was everything I had anticipated and more. I was entranced by the lectures, varying from my favourite romantic poets to learning to decipher medieval English, and readily set about the hard work of continued reading and writing essay after essay for my tutorial group. I made so many new friends, from many differing backgrounds, all with the same desire to talk and debate obscure issues into the small hours of the morning, usually over instant coffee and cheap biscuits sitting on the floor of someone's room. I had never had so much freedom before to choose what I did and when I did it, all within the company of likeminded people. I felt I had landed in heaven.

The weeks flew by. My bright yellow raincoat became my trademark wear, and I was thankful for it in November when the darkness claimed the streets and the rain and cold tried to eat into my southern bones. I telephoned my mother each week, dutifully at a time agreed and talked about my activities for the majority of the time my coins gave me in the phone box in my hall of residence. She quietly listened, seemingly content I was happy, but I think, sad in the realisation that her daughter had spread her wings and would never be her baby again.

Christmas 1963 came all too fast – my first term completed. Where had the time gone? My first set of exams successfully taken; I spent a weekend with a new girlfriend before I returned home to celebrate the festive season with my mother. She seemed genuinely pleased to see me, there were hugs and nonstop talking between us for the first two days. She actually sought out my company, returning home from work early so we could eat a meal together and encouraging me to tell her about my life in York. She had even taken some holiday from work so we could spend time together shopping and visiting art galleries. We went to a play on stage at a West End Theatre, and although we lived in

London, this had never happened before. There was no mention of 'house rules' and expectations, but I was careful and made sure I was home before 10pm if I went out in the evening. Rocking the boat had never been a good idea, and I wanted to try, at least to keep this harmonious atmosphere, it was so much more pleasurable for us both.

My mother always gave a huge party on the Saturday before Christmas. It had become a tradition though, in previous years I had arranged, at her suggestion, to stay at Paula's house that night to keep out of the way. However, this year she had made it clear she expected me to attend and mingle with her guests. Part of me just didn't want to be involved, making small talk with strangers was not really my idea of fun, and a night out with Paula would be far more to my taste. But curiosity got the better of me and, anyway I felt very much that I did not want to upset my Mamma.

The house was lavishly dressed for Christmas, it had always been this way. As a child I had my own tree in the nursery that Nanny and I hung with treasured baubles saved from year to year. I suppose I previously just hadn't taken any notice of the rest of the house, it just happened each year, but now realised Mamma had the whole house decorated by a professional firm so that it looked spectacular and, of course, perfect for her guests to see. No family traditions of hanging lights on the Christmas tree together in this house, but what you have never known you never miss I supposed.

I took great care with my appearance that evening as I felt very much as if I didn't want to let her down. Mamma had bought me a beautiful glittery red dress which was rather expensive and fitted very well, even I thought I looked sophisticated wearing it. She obviously wanted me to impress her friends, which considering she used to hide my existence this was a huge change of behaviour. I took some deep breaths to try to calm myself, I was obviously expected to make a good impression at this party.

There must have been fifty or sixty people at the soiree, with the drawing room, hall and dining room full of chattering people as I descended the stairs. All wore expensive, elegant clothes, the gentlemen in velvet jackets or suits with dress shirts and bow ties, the ladies often in long gowns of silk or taffeta with ostentatious jewellery on show. I was pleased Mamma had bought me this red

151

dress, as my usual party attire of a pair of velvet trousers, however well cut, would not have done the job.

I circulated with trays of delicious looking finger food as a way of avoiding lengthy social contact. What was I going to say to these people anyway? My mother seemed in her element, a side to her I had not seen before, laughing and smiling and then deep in conversation, quite the socialite. Perhaps she was accustomed to this? I wasn't to know. I was grateful to see a friendly face in Julien arrive, quickly got him a drink, and greeted him enthusiastically. He immediately gave me a kiss on each cheek and a hug and walked with me to a corner of the hall where it was quieter.

"Stephanie, you look so well and so grown up. University must be agreeing with you."

"Yes, yes I love it, and it is so good to see someone here I know. All these other people look so important and self-contained, I was beginning to think I would creep away upstairs soon."

"Don't be silly, you look so grown up and elegant tonight. I expect your mother is pleased to see you, as she has seemed quiet and a little downcast when I have seen her. I know she was so hoping you would go to university in London and not be so far away."

I bristled a little, taking this as a criticism. I hadn't really expected Julien to so openly take sides on this issue, which I had hoped was dead and buried now.

"Julien, if you know my mother well, which I think you do, then you will accept she can be very controlling. If I had stayed in London she would have wanted to have a say in everything I was doing. It would not have been a good position for either of us. She may not agree, but I know I have done the right thing." Julien gave a knowing smile.

"Of course, I do see your point of view, I am not taking sides honestly. I just don't like to see your mother unhappy, as I have known her a long time and seen her cope with the perceived social stigma when you were a baby. Unmarried mothers in 1945 were not so uncommon but it didn't make them any the more acceptable to society." The words hit me like a bombshell.

'Unmarried Mother', I had not expected this, after all she wore a ring and called herself 'Mrs'.

"My mother was never married!" the words came out in a sort of squeak and Julien could tell from my face that this was news to me.

"Goodness, I think I have really put my foot in it. I thought you knew. Just please forget what I said, and don't mention it to your mother. It will only upset her." But this cat was well and truly out of the bag. As I tried to compose myself, a little voice inside me tried, unsuccessfully, to say it really didn't matter at all.

"Julien, please, you have to tell me more. You see she won't talk to me about anything like this. She just changes the subject and then gets angry if I continue. You knew her during the war didn't you? What did she do, who was my father and what happen to him?" Julien paused and looked thoughtful.

"Now, it's not for me to interfere here. Your mother will talk to you when she is ready, and it seems I have already said too much. I really do wish I had not said anything." He paused but decided to go on. "Your mother overcame her problems with great resolve. Stephanie, her only concern was for you, you do need to understand that." I just didn't know what to say. Julien's revelation had brought back all the early teenage obsessions I had with identity. The brief antagonistic challenges I regularly had with my Mamma always ended in days of subdued silence on my part, with no further knowledge gained, as I was told in no uncertain terms to stop raising the subject if I knew what was good for me. Not that I did, my resolve and will being very much like that of Mamma, but I learnt very little except how to create a bad atmosphere between us. I looked straight at Julien willing him to continue.

"Your mother, I daresay you realise is a very attractive, intelligent woman, I asked her to marry me many years ago when you were still a baby, in fact I kept on asking her at regular intervals, but the reply was always the same. She was having none of it. I know there were other admirers who have tried over the years, but they all got the same reply. When one day I pressed her on the subject, she revealed that there was only one man she could ever truly love and that, sadly, she had lost him. She

153

claimed would not be fair to marry when her heart would always be elsewhere." As Julien said these words he looked suddenly lost and very sad, it was obvious he had been deeply in love with my mother for many years, and I now felt responsible for upsetting him. I took his hand in mine, looked into his eyes, and tried to smile.

"I am so sorry, I didn't mean to upset anyone. I won't repeat a word of our conversation to my mother, but I do want to thank you for being so frank with me, it has put some things into perspective. Please come and join the party with me, perhaps you can introduce me to some of these interesting people." Julien smiled and we went into the drawing room where he led me toward a young man standing in the corner.

A kindred spirit I noticed, obvious by his standing back to the wall, scanning the assembled people hoping to find a friendly face but not able, or willing, to break into the clusters of chatting guests. I knew just how he felt. Much younger and of slimmer built than Julien he had a full head of wavy black hair, falling untidily onto his forehead and fashionably long onto his collar. Sporting a black velvet jacket, pristine white shirt and dark trousers he had obviously taken great care over his appearance, but he had a rather worried look, which instantly changed when Julien approached.

"Matthew, this is Stephanie, Cecile's daughter." Julien simply said by way of introduction.

"Stephanie, Matthew works with your mother. Now you must excuse me, I can see someone I need to talk to." Instantly he was gone, and Mathew smiled very encouragingly at me, no doubt with relief that he eventually had someone to talk to. A brief embarrassed silence then we both started to speak at the same time.

"Sorry, sorry, yes I work with your mother, just started a couple of months ago," he informed me.

"So, what do you actually do?"

"Well, can't say really Official Secrets Act sort of thing but I am really just acting as an assistant, her 'bag man' I suppose you could call me. There to do exactly what she wants."

"I am sure she enjoys that," I interjected. I think he missed or failed to understand the sarcasm.

154

"She is so amazing; she can think and speak in three different languages at what seems the same time. Everyone in the department tells me how lucky so am to be with her. But I didn't know she had a daughter, no one told me that."

Mostly because no one knows, I thought.

"Look you don't have a drink," he said, "let's get you a glass of wine and I can top mine up, then we can have a good chat. I don't really know anyone here."

"Neither do I," was my response, "except Julien." We made our way through the crowded room, Mathew guiding me gently with his hand on my back to the dining room, where a large glass of white wine appeared in my hand, and he filled his with a rich, dark red. We then moved to the hall where it was less crowded. The wine tasted good, I really didn't drink alcohol, apart from odd glasses of cheap student plonk bought in for celebrations at university. This was different, smooth, and dry without a nasty aftertaste, so I suppose I drank half the glass in one gulp.

The conversation flowed easily, as we exchanged stories about university. Mathew had just completed a degree in French and German at Oxford and was very interested in my thoughts about York, he had found Oxford rather stuffy and old fashioned, but his father had wanted him to follow in his footsteps. Gradually, I began to feel a little lightheaded, probably from the rather large glass of wine and nothing to eat.

Out of the corner of my eye, I glimpsed my mother standing at the drawing room door her eyes fixed on us, her expression was one I had seen many times before, and it was clear she wasn't pleased. She appeared at my shoulder, the expression unchanged.

"Matthew, how nice you could make it. Now Stephanie, I need you to come with me to meet someone." She swept me away, without a chance to say anything, her hand firmly on my wrist. I knew better than to protest and create a scene, and dutifully followed her to a middle-aged couple standing by the fireplace in the drawing room, where my mother introduced me and promptly left the room. Was she going back to Mathew? What did she imagine was going on? The couple were totally disinterested in me, and obviously did not want interrupted, so I left them as quickly as I politely could and made my way back to the hall. Mathew was nowhere to be seen, either in the hall or the

155

other rooms. I realised he must have already left, and was that of his own volition I wondered? What on earth was wrong with me chatting to a young man? How could my mother surmise that this was a problem? Just how controlling did she want to be? My decision to go to York seemed now all the more important and justified.

I had had enough and the effect of the large glass of wine on an empty stomach, along with the behaviour of my mother had given me a thumping headache. I looked for Julien, not wanting to sneak away without first saying goodbye to him. He was chatting to a lady in the drawing room, and I hovered just in his sight, hoping he would get the hint I wanted to speak to him. He very soon excused himself and came over to me.

"Julien, I just want to say, 'Goodbye and Happy Christmas'. I really have had enough of this party and just want some peace and quiet in my room."

"Has Matthew gone? I thought you two were getting on so well."

"Well, let's say someone else thought that too and wasn't at all pleased for some unknown reason, and she made sure our conversation came to an abrupt end." Julien looked surprised, and then realised what I was saying, and shook his head gently.

"That's a pity, I think I am beginning to understand the reasoning for your choice of university in York."

"Exactly, but it's not your problem. I do hope I see you again soon, but I must say one thing, my mother was a fool not to accept your marriage proposal all those years ago, though you may have had a lucky escape." I quickly kissed him on both cheeks, hugged him close, and then left the room before he had time to think of a reply.

Chapter 5

Stephanie. Eight years later, 1971 aged 26

My three years at university passed far too quickly. My life was filled with friends and social gatherings, simulating lectures and tutorials, and quite honestly hard work, but I thrived on it. Gradually my contact with Mamma lessened as I didn't tell her much about what was really happening in my life, or rather the important things to me. She seemed content to know that academically I was doing well, and I seemed happy. Yes, I spent some time back in London with her and sometimes she made an effort to spend time with me, but these occasions dwindled as I spent more vacation time with university friends. She appeared proud enough at my graduation and we had a great celebratory lunch afterwards with Julien, but by now she had accepted I suppose, that I was never coming to live back in the house in London that she called home. It never once occurred to me to return to London, as my life and my new friends were in York now.

I had never had a problem with making friends, as from first starting infant school I seemed able to gather like-minded souls and sustain their friendship. Perhaps I was interesting or different or just easy to get on with, I never really knew, as I valued friends making up for my lonely sibling-less, single parent childhood. They were at least normal, as nothing else in my life seemed quite to fit in with the lives of everyone else. Once at university there was an instant pool of new friends, those in the hall of residence, people on my course and other students I met in my rather hectic social life. Most weekends were taken up at parties. The 'disco' party where I would spend my time at the furthest point from the noise that was called music, chatting, as I danced only when really pressurised. My preference was for the 'Stand up and Talk Politely' party, as they became know in my circle. Food and drink, usually bring a bottle, so I developed a liking for cheap cider, were provided and we all stood around talking and talking until late into the night.

I stayed in York to do a Post Graduate Teacher Training course so I could go on continuing to spend my time immersed in English language and literature and pass my enthusiasm on to others. I enjoyed the whole concept of teaching, and it seemed I was good at it. After the one-year course I accepted a place at a well renowned secondary school in York and began my working life.

I had boyfriends but nothing in the least bit serious, as I didn't want any commitments, I had spent enough of my life considering another person all the time, and I valued my freedom. This unwillingness to enter a long-term relationship continued after I had been awarded my degree and when I began teaching. I watched as other friends paired off, coming back with a broken heart or an engagement ring on their finger. My best friend from home Paula, with whom I exchanged long letters each week, soon after university took the 'normal' step and got engaged to a fellow accountancy trainee. Their marriage followed quickly after they had both qualified, and she was expecting their first child before two years of marriage were gone. She hadn't changed, we still wrote intimate letters, I visited when in London, we remained very close friends, but I just couldn't understand her thinking. This was certainly not how I saw my life developing.

Then I met Greg. He joined our walking group, a convivial loose grouping of friends from university and teaching who enjoyed a good five mile walk in the Yorkshire Dales at the weekends and an enjoyable two hours in the pub afterwards. I enjoyed the social contact, and it was a great way to keep up with old friends and make new ones. What was it about Greg? I had no idea, but I suddenly had feelings coursing through my veins I had never before experienced. A PhD student from the States, he was like nothing I had previously encountered, he was so different. Was that what attracted me? He was eccentrically dressed, even among other students, with incongruously short, tidy hair and a well-trimmed dark beard, topped off by a large pair of tortoiseshell framed glasses, for which I think he had no real need. We became a 'couple' very quickly, and life began to revolve around being with him, I couldn't think of anything else all day, as love had hit me with a force I didn't understand, and I didn't know what to do. He appeared equally smitten, spending all his free time with me, telling me how much he loved and wanted me. We ended up in bed within the first week and I was blissfully happy, especially when he moved into my small flat in York.

So, the early summer of 1971 passed in a haze of emotion I really didn't know how to control. I was 26, for goodness' sake, not a love-struck teenager, but I had no previous experience of falling so head over heels in love or sustaining a relationship, so I just assumed this was for ever and began to plan taking Greg to London to meet my mother who knew nothing about this intense relationship. She actually knew very little about my life now, but I dutifully wrote a letter once a month talking mainly about my job and she replied. We continued to communicate on a very superficial level, though I knew, deep down however, she would be horrified if she knew what I was doing. But, of course, it never came to that.

One afternoon in late June Greg and I were enjoying a drink outside at a pub by the river. It was a warm sunlit evening with the rowing boats passing lazily on the calm water. There was a pause, I think I sensed something important was going to be said but totally misread the signals. He looked straight at me and said,

"I have had a good job offer from a publisher in New York, a well-respected literary journal. It's what I have always wanted." My imagination went into overdrive, as I saw myself living in one of those grand apartments you see in New York on the television. I would have a teaching post, but only part time, so I could be the perfect wife with a delicious meal on the table each night. We would be so happy, but then I heard his next sentence.

"I am leaving this weekend actually, they want me to start right away. My parents have lined me up somewhere to stay in New York till I get my own place." A pause, I will at least give him that before he dealt the earthshattering blow,

"We've had great fun Stephanie, sweetie," he said in his New England drawl. "But this was never going anywhere, was it?" I felt my world shatter as I took in those words. Was he actually telling me he was going to New York alone? Then the realisation dawned, he must have been planning this for weeks, all the time sharing my bed and declaring his undying love, when in reality, I wasn't wanted anymore. I was being cast aside like some used paper handkerchief. He had taken me for a complete fool and in that moment, I thought I would never, ever, trust a man again. I really couldn't speak, but I managed not to burst into tears, controlling my emotions fiercely, something I had learnt in the numerous fraught teenage confrontations with my mother. Tears had meant she had won, so I made sure she never saw any. I stood up, inwardly shaking, but taking great pleasure in pouring the rest of my half pint of cider all over his loud checked shirt and corduroy trousers before I walked away, ignoring his protests. The next day, I left his belongings in a cardboard box outside my flat and didn't care who took them. I never saw or heard from him again.

Somehow, I got through the rest of the school term. My friends were very supportive, and they revealed they didn't really like Greg very much, no-one owned up to inviting him to join our group in the beginning, it seemed he had just latched on himself. Why didn't they warn me? But I know I wouldn't have listened, as I was so besotted, not willing to hear anything said against him. At least I had heeded the advice of a close girlfriend and started 'the pill' very soon in the doomed relationship, so I didn't have that worry about, however, Greg had given me a jolt that made me look at my life.

I was moving toward thirty years old, with no plans except more of the same, and I needed to realise there was a big wide world out there that I was yet to experience. So, before I had the chance to really consider what I was doing, I applied and was accepted into the British Forces Teaching Service, resigned my job in York, and by the New Year had arrived at an army base in Cyprus to take up a teaching post. Everything was very different, but it was just what I needed. Any lingering thoughts of Greg became a thing of the past.

Chapter 6

Stephanie. Seven years later, 1978 aged 33

The paving stone was only a little out of line, but enough for me to catch the toe of my silly, but very fashionable new sandals, and send me sprawling forwards. My school bag of third year essays on the plot of Midsummer Night's Dream landed ahead of me, with the papers spilling out. I went down heavily on my right knee, grazing my hands as I tried to stop the fall.

"Goodness, are you all right?" Strong, well-muscled arms lifted me back to vertical, and I could see they belonged to a tall, broad shouldered soldier dressed in the usual combat fatigues. I felt very foolish, falling like that but also rather shaky, and sensed blood running down my leg.

"You've made a right mess of your knee. Come on I´ll take you to the medics to have it looked at." He sounded concerned.

"No, no it will be OK, I just live round the corner I'll sort it at home. Thank you anyway, you are very kind." At least I was remembering my manners.

"I'll come with you, just to make sure you get safely home, you look a bit unsteady, can't have you falling over again, can we?" Ignoring my protestations, he gathered my errant essays into the bag, carried it and supported me as I hobbled round the corner to the door of my flat. I still felt very silly, but actually thankful of his support, as my knee had gone very stiff and was quite painful. Reaching my front door, I got a better look at my 'knight in shining armour'. A youthful square jawed face, thick black curly hair cut regulation short, huge dark eyes still radiating concern, and a slightly lopsided wide mouth that fell easily into a smile. I noted the captain's rank on his uniform, as I scrabbled in my bag and eventually managed to find my keys to unlock the door.

"Look." I said, not quite sure what to say , "Would you like to come in for a cup of tea or something, you have been so kind." I had managed to pull myself together, but glancing at his wristwatch, he shook his head.

"Sorry can't right now, I am already running a bit late, but if you would like, I'll come back this evening and take you out for a restorative drink. How's that for an idea?" The lopsided smile spread across his face, almost ear to ear. It was infectious, I smiled back.

"I'd like that, thank you, but you really must let me buy you a drink."

"Back here 7.30 then? Its Philip by the way, see you soon." He turned and jogged off quickly toward the main buildings, leaving me standing on the doorstep wondering what I had let myself in for. As I cleaned up my knee and scraped hands, I considered telling him I wasn't well enough to go out, just to get out of the arrangement. I had steered clear of close encounters with men since the awful Greg affair, even though it was such a long time ago. I still made friends easily but made sure I moved in groups when men were involved. Any attempt to establish a relationship, however casual, was resisted. I told myself I was never going down that particular route again, but how could I refuse Philip? He had been so kind, and anyway I was over thinking this, he looked five or six years my junior. Just go out for a drink and enjoy it, after all, why on earth would he want to start a relationship with me? When I look back at the naivety of that final statement I still smile.

7.30pm on the dot my doorbell rang. Wearing one of my 'trademark' cotton printed, shirtwaist summer dresses that I knew complimented my figure, and a pastel coloured cotton cardigan over my arm, I opened the door, smiling before I had turned the handle. There was Philip, in casual civilian wear, the lopsided ear to ear grin already on his face. Without any hesitation, he leaned forward and kissed my cheek.

"Are you OK now, you do look a lot better, I did think you were about to faint this afternoon, it was a nasty cut on your knee." His smile had changed to a look of genuine concern.

162

"Oh, I can assure you I am not the fainting kind" I replied light heartedly. "Anyway, I'm Stephanie and very grateful for your help, I don't normally go throwing myself on the ground, honestly."

"Well, I am taking your arm to get you to my car, just in case, no arguments, OK?" His car, somehow the inevitable open top, small sports model in red, was sitting just round the corner, and he steered me gently into the passenger seat.

"I know a nice quiet bar down by the river, nothing rowdy. Great for a drink, it's really not far," he announced as we set off. Conversation was difficult due to the engine noise and the wind rushing past the open top.

"Is the knee really alright," he shouted against the noise, "I thought afterwards I should have insisted and taken you to the medics, it was a nasty tumble."

"Its fine, honestly, I am quite capable of looking after myself." He glanced across with a more suggestive grin this time.

"Oh, I am quite sure you are."

Arrival at the bar took away the need for an instant reply. Watching him depart to get the drinks I thought I had better take care here, I was enjoying his company, and the feeling appeared mutual. Over a pint of shandy for him and a glass of white wine for me the conversation flowed freely, as he talked easily about himself, with that lopsided smile ever present. A second son of a farming family from Sussex, he had enjoyed all outdoor activities, but especially sport at school rather than studying, rugby being his great passion. So, the army seemed a natural choice, and with a few strings pulled by his fathers 'old boy' network, he gained a place at Sandhurst. Since then, some active service and now a stint at this base in Germany helping train the young officer recruits.

"Loads of time for rugby," he assured me. He then looked straight at me. I felt those intense dark eyes almost looking straight into my soul, so thought I would keep my story simple.

"I actually just arrived here last September in time for the academic year. I had been at another base in the south of Germany and before that in Cyprus. I teach English at the secondary school, hence the essays." I held back from telling him

163

I was really the new head of the English department, not wanting to push my academic background.

"I ended up teaching overseas for the army on a sudden whim, and well, I enjoy it." I certainly wasn't going to tell him about Greg and my broken heart, or I suddenly decided that I didn't 'do' relationships with men, which I normally did if cornered by a prospective suitor. What held me back? I have thought about this in the years that followed. Something between Philip and I just felt right, even then, on the first time together, and I just didn't want to push him away. I glossed over my childhood and relationship or lack of it with my mother, and talk between us flowed easily, with lots of laughter. I had not enjoyed myself so much for a very long time.

A glance at my watch and I realised it was 10.30pm and I had school the next day.

"Goodness Philip I must be getting back, I have a full timetable tomorrow and a drama club rehearsal after school. It's been such fun this evening, thank you so much." Taking my hand in his he held it tight.

"Stephanie, I have to ask. Is there someone you are seeing, a 'significant other' as it is politely put, I don't want to tread on any toes?" I smiled and shook my head. How old fashioned and gentlemanly, and of course this was my opening to say 'I don't do relationships', but for some reason I didn't. So he rapidly continued, "I would love to see you again very soon. What about Sunday? We could spend the day out and have a meal, I know a great place, and if you are up to it, a walk. What do you think?" I probably agreed far too readily, but I did want to spend more time in his company so why pretend otherwise? We agreed 10 o'clock Sunday and as we arrived at the door of my flat, I wasn't at all surprised by the very pleasant kiss on the lips before he disappeared into the darkness.

Chapter 7

When I reflect on the summer of 1978, I can remember so much of it in sharp focus. Senses were heightened, feelings intensified, the world was a brighter clearer place, it was as if I had emerged from a cocoon to a realisation of what life could really be.

The cause, well of course, Philip. I knew then I had never before experienced the stomach lurching, head over heels, dizziness of real unadulterated love. Greg, I realised was an obsession, a crush, a whim, but Philip was my soulmate, the only person I wanted to be with. As if by magic he felt the same and constantly demonstrated this to me by simple actions of an arm protectively around my shoulders, a whispered endearment or a kiss and an equally overwhelming desire to be in each other's company.

I quickly became part of Philip's life, introduced to his wide circle of friends, included in formal Army occasions and accepted by the world, at the base in Germany at least, as his partner. His lopsided grin was now ever present. I had raised, on our second outing, the anxiety I had over my being older than him, it was actually only 3 years, and Philip looked astounded. I honestly don't think it had occurred to him, or he had not noticed. Perhaps women are much more aware of age, he just looked me straight in the eye and said,

"Do I look as though I care about anything except being with you," disposing of that particular problem with a kiss. If anyone else noticed, the remarks never got back to me. Cathy, my friend, fellow teacher, and next-door neighbour said I was oversensitive and overreacting.

"Goodness," she exclaimed when I told her of my worry, "If he asked me out, I wouldn't start looking for excuses not to go!"

"I've never seen Philip so happy", confided one of his close friends." Of course, there have been girls before, but not like you.

He is so totally committed to you, and the focus of his life seems to have shifted. I hope it is the same for you as I don't want to see a valued friend hurt." I was able to reassure that friend, for Philip had changed my life as well, and I had no intention of walking away.

My memories are clear of a warm, dry, sunny summer where a lot of time was spent out of doors playing tennis, walking, eating and drinking in the fresh air, taking from life as much as we could. We were both busy people, so time together became a precious commodity each day, each minute to be savoured.

Our great plan was a two-week holiday to Lake Constance, Bodensee, as the Germans refer to the great elongated stretch of water that borders three countries to the south of the Black Forest. In the summer, it was a magical playground for walking, swimming, sailing and sightseeing.

We stayed at a small hotel on the north shore of the lake. Built in a traditional wooden style we had a room on the top floor with a small balcony that overlooked the lake and the Swiss mountains beyond. I know that hindsight has a way of making everything seem perfect, but I knew even then it was going to be the most wonderful two weeks I would ever spend. Away from his Army responsibilities Philip was completely relaxed, we took each day as it came and included as many opportunities to see and experience the area as we could. We also had the quiet intimate quality time together that we had never had before. Just to lie in bed, be close and feel so secure was a revelation to us both. We wanted to enjoy the moment, but of course talked about the future, our future and set about planning the rest of our lives together.

Philip had to go on manoeuvres with his officer recruits for three weeks early in September, but on his return we were determined to announce to the world our total commitment, until then it was our secret. A secret like that felt the most wonderful thing in the world, and so difficult to keep that I wanted to shout from the rooftops about how much I loved Philip and how I was going to spend the rest of my life with him. But it had to be a secret, because we wanted to tell our families first, then announce to everyone our engagement. I had some misgivings about the

166

reaction of my mother, but Philip was so reassuring, and in the end, I didn't care what anyone said, we knew what we wanted,

"Just a little longer, then we can tell the whole world." he whispered "If I could keep you for myself all the time, I would! But we can look forward to the rest of our lives together." Any reply was silenced with a kiss that left my heart lurching and head spinning. Thinking back even now I can feel the overflowing happiness that consumed my senses.

We didn't want to leave our paradise of the lakeside hotel, but I had to return to a new term at school and Philip was to leave with his officer recruits on the 7th of September. He promised to phone as often as he could and left me holding back my tears as he drove away to join the regiment.

He kept his promise and most evenings that first week he managed a brief conversation, but he warned me that they would be away from telephone communication soon and I was just to wait. He would telephone as soon as he could, and it was only two more weeks then we would be together again.

So, that afternoon two days later when I had not heard from him, I wasn't at all concerned. I had just arrived home from a hectic school day when there was knock at the door. The sight of the family liaison officer filled me with dread, because they only ever bring bad news, but even then, I didn't think of Philip.

"Come in. Come in," I managed to say. "Is it my mother you have come about? I haven't been in touch for some time, but she wasn't ill when she last wrote."

The lady officer slowly shook her head.

"I am really sorry, but I have come to tell you the Captain Philip Deveraux was killed in a mortar explosion during a live firing exercise yesterday. One of his friends said you and he were close and that I should let you know immediately." It was as if time stood still, and I had become detached from the real world. I could not comprehend the news, just standing unable to speak or listen to the rest of what the officer was saying.

"Miss Legrand, Stephanie, is there someone I can get to be with you. Please sit down." She gently led me to the sofa, the one Philip and I always sat on together and sat beside me.

"What about a friend I could call, or a neighbour? I can't leave you like this." Being left was exactly what I did want, but I

167

managed to suggest she get Cathy, my friend, another teacher at school, from next door. Soon she was passing the news to Cathy in the hallway in hushed tones, and I heard the front door close. Cathy came back into the room and looked shell shocked, sitting beside me on the sofa without any idea what she should say.

The news just reverberated round the silence. Philip, my Philip was gone, that was all I could think but not take in. The mind starts to play tricks, they must have got the wrong man, because in one minute, the telephone would ring, and he would be there as usual, larger than life itself. Or this was a dream, a very bad dream and I would wake up soon and it would all be back to normal.

Of course, neither of those two options was true. Cathy eventually started talking, but I couldn't understand or hear her. I was just numb to the world, I could not cry, or scream or shout, all the things I wanted to do, so I just sat and stared with dry, unblinking, unseeing eyes.

I lost track of time, Cathy let a man into the room, a doctor I presume, and he gave me some kind of injection that quickly made me very drowsy, and I fell into a deep sleep of oblivion.

Chapter 8

I remember clearly oblivion becoming my best friend during those days. When I came round to a world without Philip, I took some pills, and the world went away. Cathy came and went bringing food I didn't want and wouldn't eat, I communicated only if really necessary and then in monosyllables. Loosing track of days and nights, I just wanted to sleep, a dreamless sleep of nothingness, beginning to hope I would not wake up. The world and reality, of course had different ideas.

I think it was four days after the news had arrived that Cathy came into my bedroom late one morning, pulled the curtains open and told me to get up as I had a visitor. I just groaned, rolled over and covered my head with the sheets. Cathy sat on the side of the bed.

"You are not going to like what I am about to say, but you need to stop wallowing in grief. What would Philip think? Your life must go on and the sooner you try, the better it will be. One of Philip's friends is here to see you, so get out of bed and make yourself presentable." She left the room with an audible door slam.

Of course, she was right, if a bit harsh. The last thing I wanted was to see a friend of Philip, but I knew I would have to face a visitor sooner or later, so throwing on some clothes and dragging a comb through my hair I stumbled into the lounge blinking in the bright sunlight. It was Luke one of Philip's closest friends, a fellow rugby player and comrade in arms in his platoon. He stood up, obviously searching for the right words, understandably not easy in the circumstances. He stepped forward as if to take me in his arms, but alarmed, I moved sharply back, I didn't want anyone, except Philip to touch me.

"Stephanie, what can I say, we are all so sorry and at a complete loss. I know Philip was the world to you. I cannot try to imagine how you are feeling, but I had to come to see you. I felt it was only right you knew what happened. That is, if you are ready to listen. I can come back whenever you want." I managed to nod and shocked myself by my quiet, indistinct voice replying.

"Please stay and talk. I just don't understand anything at the moment."

"Perhaps a little walk outside. The sun is shining, and some fresh air may help you to feel a bit better." I nodded again. This time he took my arm in his and I didn't have the strength to resist, and we walked out of the front door into the sunshine. He was right, it did make me feel a little better.

"There's a bench under the trees just over there." He pointed. "Why don't we sit, and I can talk to you." As we sat side by side, I stared unseeing into the distance, Luke put his hand over mine on the bench and with great difficulty, I resisted the urge to snatch it away. He was just being kind and thoughtful, so I had to stop overreacting, but it was all so raw and painful.

"Philip loved you very much." He started, then stopped as if unsure how to go on. "He let me into your secret because he was so excited he couldn't keep the news to himself. He asked me to start planning a big party for when he returned, to announce your engagement, because he wanted to surprise you, to please you. It's so so sad. Everyone can't quite believe the awful news. Philip was such a huge character he will leave a great void in all our lives."

Luke went on to explain the details of the accident for which I was grateful, however hard it was to hear. Apparently two of his officer recruits had strayed into a live fire zone on an exercise, with their radios not receiving their message to evacuate. Despite the danger to himself, Philip set out on foot to alert them, but as he got there, a live mortar shell landed close by instantly killing all three soldiers. A dreadful accident it seemed, though of course there would be an inquiry later, but for now, the Army was closing ranks and concentrating on burying its dead.

"That's part of why I have come. The funeral, with full military honours, will be next week, on Thursday in his home village in Sussex. A good number of us will be there and I could ask for you to be included in the travel party as you were, in all intents and purposes, his fiancé." I shook my head determinedly.

170

"No, no I don't want to be included. I know I could not cope, for lots of reasons, I don't know his family, they don't know me, and I would just feel as if I was intruding. My Philip was a soldier in Germany not a farmer in Sussex, so it would be all wrong. Thank you, but I don't want to go." Luke was silent for a moment but quietly replied,

"It has to be up to you Stephanie, of course. Please think about it, you can change your mind at any time." But I knew I wouldn't.

"And please Luke, don't mention the engagement to anyone. There is no point now, I can't marry Philip so why tell anyone. I want that to remain just between Philp and I."

We sat in silence in the sun for some time before Luke walked me back to the house and promised to visit again soon. No doubt he would keep that promise, but continuing friendships with Philip's friends was not going to be a priority. It would be much too difficult for me, because if Philip couldn't be there, then I didn't want to be either.

Cathy and Luke had given me the jolt I needed. She was hard but right, I had to get on with life even if my heart was still with Philip. I showered, washed my hair, put on clean clothes, and went to see the Principal of the School where I taught. I wanted to return to work as quickly as possible. I had to take my mind off the numbing grief, and work seemed the obvious way. Some people said I went back too soon, and perhaps they were right, as I doubt my teaching was brilliant during the next few weeks, but it was at least therapeutic for me. Philip was still a huge presence in my life, but teaching gave me a focus for each day

I took a day's leave for the funeral. No, I hadn't changed my mind, the whole pomp and ceremony of a military funeral was never going to be for me, but I needed to be there in spirit. At the appointed hour I sat alone in the small Catholic Church in the nearby village, where Philip and I had gone that very first evening for a drink. In the silence I just let my thoughts wander to remember the time we had together, remembering our deep affection, committed love, and the pleasure of just being together. I sensed a presence at the back of the church and turning, saw Philip standing in the shadows. I stared but didn't move, as he raised his hand in a final acknowledgment and slipped silently away, into the shadows. Though his presence remained with me and still does, even now for fleeting moments, I finally acknowledged I would never see him again.

The weeks turned to months, Summer to Autumn. I immersed myself in work, politely but firmly, resisting all invitations from Philip's friends to join them for a drink, a meal, or even to watch a game of rugby. Eventually the invitations dried up and thankfully, I needed no more excuses. Drama clubs after school and even one on a Saturday morning for the Primary age children successfully filled my spare time. Cathy came by about twice a week, to check on me, and she always brought a pie or a cake, but I ate very little, lost weight and didn't care about my appearance. So long as I was clean, tidy and respectable enough to complete my teaching day who cared if the clothes did not fit, or my hair needed a cut. What did anything really matter if Philip was not there?

After October half term I came down with a sickness bug that just wouldn't go away. Cathy eventually cajoled me to go to the Doctor, as losing weight and being sick was not a good combination she had informed me. The whole story came out to the Doctor as he took my blood pressure, checked my pulse, stood me on the weighing scales, and examined my stomach. He listened carefully to story and my symptoms and gave a half smile.

"I think, my dear, you are actually pregnant, probably around 10 weeks. A test will confirm this, but I am pretty certain it's the case."

"No, that can't be. I was taking the contraceptive pill all the time I was with Philip,"

"Well, the test will give us a definitive answer, but it certainly looks like it to me, remember the pill is not 100% effective. Did you forget to take it one day perhaps? There are lots of reasons why the pill is not fully absorbed by your body. Did you have a tummy upset at all? Missing just one pill can lead to a pregnancy. It's unusual, I agree but it does happen." Then it hit me. On our holiday at Lake Constance, I was dreadfully sick one morning. I blamed the seafood barbeque the previous evening, but I was better by the next day, and thought nothing of it, now it all began to make sense.

The test confirmed two days later that I was carrying Philip's baby. How on earth was I going to cope with this?

Chapter 9

If there was anything that would focus my mind away from the unrelenting sense of loss, then carrying Philip's child was one of them. Being pregnant was still very hard, almost unbelievable, as I felt exactly the same, yet somehow, completely different my body was not my own anymore, I had part of Philip growing inside me.

Walking back from the Doctors I resolved pretty quickly that this accident of nature was going to remain a closely guarded secret. Part of me was thrilled, I would always have Philip with me, the remainder was terrified of what the future would bring, never mind the actual process of having the baby. There was no question of that not happening, as this baby was some kind of miracle, and I was keeping it. Cathy was the only person I confided in, and she was completely taken aback, her diagnosis having had more of a sombre tone.

"That's wonderful news," she exclaimed. "You are happy about it aren't you?"

"I really have no idea what to think," was my truthful reply. "This baby was a complete accident, and I am still trying to work out how it actually happened. But the main thing, Cathy, is that it must remain a secret, please tell no-one. I don't want any rumour or speculation about me or the baby going round the army base and reaching Philip's friends." Thankfully, she fully understood. I trusted her as Cathy was a loyal, longstanding friend and we had always shared secrets, though nothing on this scale.

"So, what are you going to do?"

"If you mean about the baby, keep it. There is no question about that, as it will be a part of Philip that I will always have. But practically I have a lot of thinking and planning to do."

The Doctor thought that it would be May the following year when the baby should arrive, so time was on my side. It was obvious to me I couldn't stay here in Germany on the base, as there were too many of Philip's friends who would surely guess my circumstances, I would have to leave before things became too apparent, but I had time to plan.

I had a considerable nest egg of savings having been with the army teaching for a number of years living in subsidised accommodation. I was good at my job and had no worries about finding a well-paid teaching job back in England once our baby was born, so returning to England had to be the plan.

The sickness went away very soon, and I began eating sensibly if only for the sake of Philip's baby. I still talked to Philip each day, I still felt his presence very strongly and I was reassured I was making the right choices. Even so there were certain difficult decisions that kept rolling round unanswered in my head. My infrequent letters to my mother had said nothing about Philip and now even less about my pregnancy. I just kept on pretending, as I did at school, that everything was normal, and this actually wasn't happening.

However, it haunted me that she really ought to know about her prospective grandchild, most likely her only grandchild. She had been a loving mother to me in my young childhood, and I remembered with affection the special hours spent with her, her arms around me, our secret language whispered into my ear as she stroked my curly unruly hair. Our relationship deteriorated as I met my teenage years as she tried to control me with a suffocating desire to influence my life. I realise now I was, in fact, still am, very much like her, strong in character and resolute in action. The more she tried to exert control the more I rebelled against her. There were endless ugly arguments played out in her study, followed by long weeks of silence, as I served my 'stay at home' punishments, all the time planning my future subterfuge. By the time I left for university we had a semblance of calm, but not much affection between us. There were, of course, faults on both sides, two strong women so sure they were both right, were never going to reconcile their differences easily.

Since leaving home for university our contact had been brief and superficial, but now pregnant and starting to feel maternal surges of feelings, I felt as if I should at least consider telling my mother the news. Writing a letter just seemed too distant and brutal, as I knew I was going to have to explain the whole situation very carefully. Perhaps stupidly, I told myself that, if I explained the circumstances properly, my mother would be so pleased by the news everything would be fine.

With this in mind I planned a visit in December after the schools broke up for Christmas. Maybe I would stay for Christmas with her, I wasn't sure as I had not been home to London for a very long time. Loose clothing had easily hidden my secret thus far, and I had already planned to agree a leaving date of February half term with the school.

I wrote a careful and upbeat letter revealing nothing, asking to visit my mother in December. I kept the date vague to ensure it seemed a casual request, so I would be able to judge from the reply, if there was one, how my mother was feeling. Surprisingly there was a reply almost by return of post saying how delighted she was that I was coming to see her.

Come anytime you can, my darling, she wrote. It has been far too long since I have seen you. Can you stay for Christmas?

This all appeared quite promising, but time would tell, so I wrote back being equally affectionate and saying I would arrive on 21st December but made no commitment after that. I had to get my story straight.

London had not changed very much. I stood outside on the opposite side of the road looking at my mother's house as now I had actually arrived, my nerves had set in. This visit could go either of two ways, but I had a strong foreboding that it wasn't going to be good. The door was answered by a new housekeeper I didn't recognise.

"Please go straight to the study, Madame is waiting." Some things never change it seemed. I left my travel bag and coat by the door and as I walked into the room my mother got to her feet, smiling to greet me. Set on the small table by the same velvet covered sofa, was the same coffee jug with cups and a small plate with my favourite childhood biscuits.

"Stephanie, it's so lovely to see you." I was momentarily taken aback by my mother's appearance. She had aged considerably in the five years since I had last seen her. Still very upright and petite she seemed tired, her face drawn and lined, but impeccably dressed, and as ever, she still managed to dominate the familiar room. She moved to kiss both cheeks, her normal greeting, but followed with an unexpected, uncharacteristic hug. She quickly let go of me and stood back, her expression changing.

"You are expecting a baby?" Not really a question but a statement. The welcome hug had given away my news too soon, with my four months bump clearly being felt under the loose clothing. Her eyes narrowed, her mouth became smaller, and she spat out her next words.

"What have you done? Where is the father? Where is the ring on your finger?" I was shocked into momentary silence, then retaliated before I could stop myself.

"So where is MY father? I know that ring on YOUR finger means nothing." Her face hardened, I should have known better and not spoken to her like that, but I wasn't sixteen anymore, and for goodness' sake, a baby out of wedlock in 1978 wasn't the end of the world. If only she had given me a chance to explain, it wasn't as if this was a result of a drunken one-night stand and I wasn't asking for help. Somehow, I had naively thought I could have explained, and she would have been happy at the thought of a grandchild.

"How dare you," she almost hissed with anger. "You know nothing about your father, or what the circumstances were."

"I know nothing about MY father because you would never talk about him or why he wasn't in our lives. YOU know nothing of my circumstances, but as always, you are so quick to judge."

I couldn't stop myself; I had spoken badly out of turn now, and I knew I was just making things worse. This was exactly how I had feared our meeting would go, in fact it was much worse than I could possibly have imagined.

My mother put her hand on her large mahogany desk as if to steady herself. She looked sad, exhausted and pale.

"Just go Stephanie," she said very quietly but firmly. "Get out of my house. This is exactly what I feared would happen to you. How could you destroy your life so thoughtlessly?"

177

Afterwards I thought of all the things I could have said, how I wanted to tell her about Philip, wanted her to know him as a person, a person I had loved with all my heart. How I wanted to share his child with her, let her know and love her only grandchild. She had adored me as a young child, so why would she not love my baby?

But I just turned, walked from the room, collected my coat and bag in the hall, and quietly let myself out of the house. I was on the train back to Germany the next day.

Chapter 10

Stephanie 1979 aged 34

When I look back at 1979, I wonder now at my resilience. The awful gulf of despair that Philip left, the shock and worry of the unplanned pregnancy, and the estrangement from my mother was a heavy load to carry. The one thing I was determined to complete was leaving the army base in Germany and starting again back in my home country, as the base held too many memories with too many people who would soon guess my situation. I wonder now why I was desperate for people not to know. Did I somehow feel the whole predicament was my fault? I know I certainly did not want sympathy, I just needed to get somewhere to begin a new life with my child, among a population who did not want to know, or care about my past.

A reasonable untruth, I still find it hard to call it a lie, that my mother was not well and as an only child I needed to be with her, allowed me to leave the school quietly at February half term. My communication with my colleagues had been minimal, so my disappearance unremarkable. Only Cathy, who had kept me sane and looked after my health as much as she could knew the real reason, and it was she who helped me pack up my belongings, storing the few articles I decided to keep until I could send for them.

I left early one cold, grey, dark morning in a taxi for the station with one suitcase and a burning desire to get away. After a night in Ostend, I arrived at Waterloo station before midday to be met by my saviour in all this, Paula.

Paula and I had been teenage inseparable friends, with her house and normal family a refuge for me when the battles with my mother grew difficult to stand. We both went to university, York for me and Durham for her. Luckily, Paula was a great correspondent, and we had shared everything, and I mean everything, by letter for years. This had continued after we left university, and even now our monthly letter was a regular item of ' no holes bared' correspondence. So, Paula was one of the few people who knew my predicament.

Paula had sailed through university and her accountancy training with a big firm in London. Very soon after, and uncharacteristically in my eyes anyway, she married a fellow accountant in the same firm. The first baby was on its way soon after followed by a second another couple of years later. Paula happily, it seemed, gave up her career and became a housewife and mother in a suburban semi-detached house. Her letters were still copiously full of fun and happiness, but it had surprised me, I had expected something different from Paula. However, she was there as my friend when most needed and had taken it upon herself to arrange matters back in London for my arrival.

Standing by the ticket barrier she was instantly recognisable. A bit rounder, but by this time she had three children, yet stylishly dressed sporting a fashionable haircut. She was just a grown-up version of the 18-year-old who had left for university all those years ago.

"Stephanie." She shouted above the din of the station." Over here." She enveloped me in a hug and then stood back giving me a distinctly worried look.

"Yes, I know I don't look well." I agreed. My skin was sallow, and my clothes hung from my frame, with the baby bump now pretty visible. "But apparently, according to the Doctors the baby is doing well, it's just pregnancy doesn't seem to suit me, unlike some others."

"It's nothing that some rest and good food can't sort out," she said determinedly. "Come on we will get a taxi, and I will explain on the way." She grabbed my suitcase and set off for the exit, as I remembered there was no stopping Paula when she was in organisational mode. Safely in a taxi she went on to explain she had found me a flat to rent.

"I have had such fun," she explained, dismissing my worries about taking up her time." I have really enjoyed the whole ' flat hunt' task. I do hope you like the one I have chosen. If so, we can pop round to the agent right away and sign up so you can move it immediately."

We pulled up in a quiet street of well-kept three storey terraced houses and entered by a smart blue front door. From the communal hall we took the ground floor door to find a quite spacious, one bedroom flat with a double bedroom to the front and a lovely light living room cum kitchen at the rear with French windows to a small, but private garden.

"It was the garden and the light that sold it to me. You will want peace and quiet with a baby but access to the outside is a great addition. What do you think?"

I looked around and saw a sanctuary from the world, thinking she could not have chosen any better. Perhaps the furniture was a little worn, but the flat had all I needed, and more to begin to get my life on track again.

"Paula you are a miracle worker, however am I going to thank you."

"Don't be silly you are my best friend, and I am enjoying all this so much." We walked back to the high street and Paula left me at the agents to sign all the paperwork while she went home.

"I'll meet you at the flat in half an hour. I'm collecting the car to bring you some things to help settle in."

True to her word she arrived back at the flat with a car full of necessities, sheets and bedding, towels and kitchen equipment, it all got carried into the flat. Once a smart checked tartan rug was thrown over the dowdy sofa I was instructed to sit down and rest as Paula busied herself getting the rest of the flat shipshape. As if by magic a plate of ham sandwiches appeared and for the first time in a long while I actually enjoyed eating.

"Now listen I'll have to go soon, the boys are due back from school, and I need to pick up Gilly from my mother." Gillian, Gilly, was her last child.

"A bit of a surprise really." she had already admitted in her letters. "Ronnie didn't want any more, but he dotes on Gilly now, and well she's a real character. I'll bring her tomorrow if that's OK. Mum is busy and anyway I want you to meet Gilly. Get you into the 'baby mode'." She laughed. "You are going to notice a difference. But still, plenty of time to prepare." I was so tired I felt afterwards I didn't express my gratitude nearly enough, but

Paula shrugged it off with a smile and a promise to return the next morning.

"Oh, nearly forgot, I have arranged for your telephone to be reconnected tomorrow. They said they probably won't need to actually come but just in case they arrive before me you know what it's about."

Once Paula had gone, I looked around the flat and again marvelled at Paula's industry and expertise. There was a beef casserole waiting on the stove with a pan of prepared vegetables, a fridge with all the essentials stacked inside and a small bowl of fruit waiting to be eaten. She was already working on my recuperation, and I realised if I had a friend like Paula, my world ought to begin to improve, so slowly I began to look forward with less anxiety to the future.

True to her word she was back the next morning complete with Gilly. A whirlwind of a two-year-old with pretty blonde curls, stocky legs that carried her around very assuredly, and a natural ability to charm everyone. She did so remind me of Paula. She sat contentedly for all of five minutes on the floor with some bricks then demanded attention until she got it.

"It's Ronnie's fault." Paula declared. "He spoils her, then leaves me to cope. He was much stricter with the boys. She is so determined, you just cannot reason with her."

"Now I wonder where that comes from?" I was all innocence but caught Paula's eye and she laughed.

"OK, I asked for that," she said. "But here you are while I unpack some more things. She's all yours!" Actually, once her mother had disappeared to the car, Gilly was happy to sit on my knee and fiddle with a doll I picked up from the floor.

"Well, you've got the knack already. I'll bring her round more often." Paula had remerged with two shopping bags which she proceeded to unpack into the kitchen cupboards.

"Paula, I don't know how to thank you, but I am not helpless you know."

"No, but you are 6 months pregnant, tired, and not well to boot. So just let me get on with sorting this flat. Then I can tell you my other plans."

Paula had always been the 'planner', and it was she organised our teenage years, so I had to admit I did miss her when first

182

arriving at university, as arranging my own social life was harder than I had anticipated. Finally, the bags were empty and carrying a cup of coffee for me she sat on the small chair opposite, while encouraging Gilly to build a tower on the floor with her multi-coloured bricks.

"Listen, I have a plan of action." So, I listened and was not only grateful but marvelled at the way she had thought of, what seemed like everything. Appointments at the local Doctor and hospital for the ante-natal clinic were already arranged. She had contacted estate agents and produced brochures of possible properties for me to buy, explaining with sensible logic that the sooner I found a house the sooner I could get settled.

"We don't want to be looking at houses when you are nine months pregnant, or worse a newborn baby in tow do we? Anyway, it's going to take about three months to do all the legal work after you have found the house so the sooner we get going the better." Of course, she was right.

So, without further ado we went for a drive in her car around the local areas to see where I might want to live. My criteria were quite simple. A good quiet location with a local primary school for my baby, and within easy travel of local secondary schools where I hoped I would find a job. I knew what I could afford, as living in subsidized Army accommodation for a good number of years had allowed me to save a substantial deposit, however, looking at the brochures Paula had brought; I was going to need every penny.

Later that afternoon we returned to the flat and discussed the day. Paula had ensured I was clearer about what I wanted, but I was beginning to feel tired, as there seemed so much to do and organise. I think that was when it really hit me, because I was, despite Paula, so very much alone and I would just have to learn to cope. I was going to be a single mother, I had no one to share the anxiety and any problems, and this was not going to change. Not for the first time I felt the overwhelming desire to scream at Philip for getting himself killed and leaving me so alone in the world.

Chapter 11

It was Paula who dragged me through those next few weeks, for without her interventions I think I may have become a hermit and ignored the outside world. I met her family at a convivial Sunday lunch, with Ronnie, tall, gangly, mop of red hair, and horn-rimmed glasses who could not have been more welcoming. Her boys were well-mannered, but full of energy, her house was neat and well furnished. Yes, Paula had it all and seemed so content, but of course it just highlighted exactly what I was never going to have. I loved seeing Paula but dodged invitations to her home after that Sunday.

Pregnancy was still not suiting me. The Doctors at the ante-natal clinic were concerned about me but not the baby, who continued to grow and be declared healthy. Lots of rest, I was assured was the remedy, and after all I had little else to do, but I felt nauseous most of the time, alternating with acute indigestion, so sitting still wasn't much of a pleasure. I needed diversion and thankfully Paula and often Gilly provided that. 'House Hunter' Paula had set to work on my behalf and, after initial visits by her, had gathered a short list of potential houses to see.

"It's such fun." she declared." I do really think this is what I want to do. I've talked to Ronnie about setting up a Property Finding Agency, you know renting and purchase. He says there are lots of young professional people moving to London who simply do not have the time, or energy, never mind the knowledge to find their perfect new home. I could work the hours that suit me and be around for the boys and Gilly when needed. In fact, Ronnie says he will pass my name to some new arrivals in the office right now, so who knows?" Her eyes were bright with excitement.

I was delighted to have helped Paula in this roundabout way. I could see her making a great success of the venture and enjoying it, which was more than could be said about her returning to a nine to five office accounting job, even if Ronnie would let her, and I knew he wasn't keen.

Paula also kept arriving with necessary baby equipment that of course I needed but didn't have the strength or will to obtain. When I suggested she may need the baby bath, changing mat, clothes or any of the other paraphernalia that arrived she shook her head.

"No way," she emphatically said. "Three is more than enough." Then in a quiet voice, as if Gilly would understand, "Ronnie's getting ' the snip' next week. Seems the right thing to do, so we definitely won't need them."

We had fun visiting prospective houses even if it was quite an effort for me, in the later stages of pregnancy. She had chosen her short list well and the third house we stepped into felt right. On a quiet street in a good area, it was a modernised mid terrace with a sunny, small back garden, two downstairs rooms with a kitchen extension, and upstairs two bedrooms and a bathroom. It needed some redecoration and a bit of updating, but then that was reflected in the price. Paula had all that in hand with her contacts and promised a clean, updated, freshly painted house for me to move into not long after the baby was born. I realised I would not have found this house anywhere near as easily without her and spoke to the agent right away. Before the day was complete my offer was accepted, the details in the hands of a solicitor, my baby and I were going to have somewhere safe and secure to live, and that was a great weight off my mind.

I struggled to my next ante-natal appointment unusually on my own. Paula had a prospective client to see but had wanted to put them off to accompany me as before.

"Don't be silly." I had protested, "I will be fine, you mustn't put off anyone just for me. You need the house hunter jobs to establish your new agency." She knew I was right but made me promise to phone her with any news that evening.

As I didn't feel any better or worse than normal, I expected a routine appointment, for in theory I still had four weeks of my pregnancy to go, but the Doctors had other ideas. It seemed my blood pressure was too high for their liking, deciding the baby was now at risk so they suggested I stayed there and then for an emergency Caesarean section. It took all my resolve to persuade them to allow me to go back to the flat with a promise to return in the morning prepared for the operation. They even sent me home by ambulance, though I did demand they let me out at the road end so as not to alarm the neighbourhood.

Paula was round to the flat immediately when she heard the news, packing my bag of essentials, which of course I had not got round to doing, thinking I still had lots of time before I would need it.

Philippa Cecile Legrand arrived safely the following morning, and my life had changed for ever. Pippa, as she was to be known, was an 'easy baby' according to Paula, she fed well, slept soundly for quite long periods of time, and seemed content in my company.

"You should have had one like Gilly." She kept reminding me. "Never slept, cried so loudly she woke up the boys each night, with endless colic pains. I was on the verge of sending her back." I suppose she was right but for me it was such a change of circumstances. Suddenly I had someone else who had to come first, and I felt a complete novice at looking after this precious little individual. Again, the burden of being alone with the responsibility weighed heavily, however I was just going to have to get used to it.

The summer of 1979 arrived early and was calm, sunny but not overly hot. The purchase of the house was progressing well and meanwhile the small garden at the flat was a godsend allowing time in the fresh air but without the necessity of getting dressed up to go out. When Pippa was about six weeks old Paula broached a subject that she knew I did not want to discuss.

"Stephanie, I know you don't want to hear this, but I do think you should try to make peace with your mother. She doesn't even know you are in London, does she? Never mind that she is now a grandmother."

"Paula, keep out of this, please."

"No listen, I know what you have told me and of course I remember when you were younger, and you spent lots of time at our house. But don't you think she would want to get to know, what is, after all her only grandchild?" I didn't reply. A silence fell and a certain awkwardness was in the air, that I really couldn't cope with.

"So, what is your suggestion as you are bound to have one, as ever." I tried not to sound as annoyed as I actually felt.

"I'm not suggesting you just turn up on the doorstep if that's what you mean. Why not write a short letter saying you are in London and that your daughter has been born and if she wants to see you to get in touch by letter? Don't give your phone number. Then it's up to her. If she doesn't reply, well then, you have done your bit, extended a hand of reconciliation, and the loss will be hers." This actually seemed a sensible compromise, Paula had obviously been thinking about what I would accept and what seemed reasonable. I knew she had a very close relationship with her mother who lived not far from her and helped with the children. Paula's mum had seemed like a second mother to me during the fraught teenage years, but she had never questioned my mother's actions or criticised them.

"OK, that might be a good idea. Let me think about it and maybe run the letter past you before I send it. Will that shut you up for the moment?" I said light-heartedly, trying to get off the subject. Paula smiled as she was distracted by the faint cries of Pippa who was waking for yet another feed.

"Let me get her, she is such a lovely baby."

"Having second thoughts about the 'snip' are we, wanting another?" I joked; thankful the awkward moment had passed.

Chapter 12

I knew Paula was right, my mother ought to meet her only granddaughter, but as the meeting of last December had been so antagonistic on both our sides, I was very anxious that any further meeting should not go the same way. Surprising me, by return of post her reply had come to my simple letter, and she seemed genuinely enthusiastic to see me and meet Pippa, and signed 'Your loving Mamma' made me wonder what really lay in store. The only love I remember from my mother came very early in my life. Time passed with her each day was full of laughter and enjoyment, as I sat on her lap and she read stories to me, nuzzling my hair and whispering our special secret language. As I grew up, she spent more time away, and when she returned there was usually a disagreement over my behaviour as reported by my Nanny or later the housekeeper/ child minder. Any hugs and close contact disappeared, and we seemed to circle each other in a never-ending battle of wills. Outwardly, it seemed I had all the advantages of a stable family with no money worries, inwardly I was desperate to be shown affection.

I hesitated on the street looking at the familiar house. Part of me wanted so much to rekindle the relationship I had with my mother, but a large part of me knew how hurt I had been and the length of time I had taken to begin to put it behind me. I could not afford emotionally, certainly not as I felt now, to engage in another hostile visit. So I hesitated but having come this far, I had to give Mamma a chance, though I resolved to walk away quickly if the situation proved difficult.

Pippa was sleeping contently as I rang the doorbell and took a deep breath. The same housekeeper as I saw in December opened the door and gestured to go into the drawing room, so leaving the pram and my coat in the hall, and carrying Pippa, I tapped on the door and let myself in. My Mother as sitting reading the newspaper by the window, but came immediately toward me as I came in.

"Stephanie. How wonderful to see you." The emotion appeared genuine enough and she enveloped me in an uncharacteristic and enthusiastic hug as she kissed my cheeks in her usual greeting.

"And this is my granddaughter? Can I?" She was asking to hold her, and I carefully placed Pippa in her arms. I watched as she carried her over to the window engrossed in her tiny face, touching and stroking her strands of hair, smiling all the time.

"She is called Philippa, Mamma, but I call her Pippa. She is just eight weeks old." It was as if my mother couldn't take her eyes of this precious baby, in fact almost as though I wasn't there at all. She continued to hum quietly to Pippa all the time rocking her and stroking her hair.

"She is just so beautiful Stephanie. She is so like you as a baby and you were so like," and she hesitated, continuing in a very quiet voice, "your father." She had said it. The father word that had never been uttered in my presence before.

"So, she looks like my father?" I said very slowly not knowing how to continue the conversation that I had been waiting for all my life.

"She resembles you Stephanie very much, and you were very much like him. You had, and still have your father´s eyes."

"My father," I began, but immediately got a glance from my mother which shut down that part of the conversation. There was an invisible line here I shouldn't cross, well not yet anyway. I thought I could see tears in her eyes highlighted by the sun pouring in through the window, and I knew it was best not to make a comment. My mother did not like any visible display of emotion, because I think she had always felt it was a sign of weakness. Pippa stirred and made faint crying noises.

"Shall I take her back?" I moved toward the window.

"No, no, just let me sit with her, I am sure she will settle" Sitting in a chair still cradling Pippa in her arms I heard her whisper gently to Pippa the same foreign sounding endearments I had heard so many years ago. Pippa seemed fascinated and as she gently returned to sleep, I was determined to tell my side of

189

the story having left in December without telling my mother what had really happened. I wondered if she still felt the same way about my 'indiscretion'.

"Mama, I just wanted to say I was sorry about my last visit. I said many things I most probably shouldn't have said, certainly not in the way I did." There, as ever I was the one to apologise to allow us to move on. From as far back as I could remember it had to be me to admit the transgression, even when it wasn't really my fault.

"No, Stephanie it wasn't all your fault. I have thought so many times after you left that I should not have judged you so harshly. It's just that I was so disappointed for you, not in you. I can never be disappointed in you, as you are my daughter. I wanted for you a loving husband and a happy family, those things that I could never give you." Silence hung in the air.

"After you had gone, I realised I was much too judgemental. It was just I didn't want you to have to cope with all the prejudices and problems I had to deal with when you were a baby. I so wanted you to have the best of everything in life and that, of course included, a loving husband. I know what it is to have loved someone, however briefly, and then lost them for ever. Please believe me Stephanie I do understand, and I really don't want to lose you or my granddaughter." An apology of any kind was rarely forthcoming from my mother, and I could feel the emotional tension in the air. She looked straight at me with direct eye contact that so reminded me of the times as a child I had stood before her desk in her study accepting yet another reprimand.

"Mamma, I did want to tell you what had happened." I stopped myself, if I was not careful this visit was going the same way as the last. I had to move on and just tell her my story. If she judged me harshly after that then so be it. I took a deep breath and slowly and as concisely as possible told her about Philip and his untimely death and my unknown pregnancy. I tried to do all this without emotion but recounting the time we had together, and the shock of his death was difficult without my voice breaking many times. My mother sat in the chair by the window and held Pippa in her arms as I spoke. I noticed she didn't look at me, rather she concentrated on Pippa, stroking her hair and face. When I told her about Philip's death, she glanced at me and again

190

I saw tears in her eyes, perhaps at last she was beginning to understand.

"I know bringing up a child alone won't be easy, but she is the only part of Philip I have." I let the silence hang in the air. "Mamma, Philip loved me. That much I know. We were going to get married, and he would have been that loving husband and father you so wanted for me. It's so sad he never knew about Pippa, so she is all I have of him, and my memories of course. I had never met anyone I loved so much, and I doubt I will again."

Pippa uncannily chose that precise moment to begin to cry loudly. Perhaps she could sense the emotional tension in the room, even at 8 weeks she was very responsive to my moods.

"I'm sorry I expect she is hungry. Can I take her up to my old room and feed her?"

"Of course, and can you stay for some coffee afterwards?" My mother seemed genuinely keen for us to stay longer so I readily agreed.

Sitting on my bed in my childhood room with Pippa happily feeding I looked around to see many of my favourite books still on the bookcase. The room had been decorated and had a new bedspread, but my bedside table remained with the lamp that had illuminated my nocturnal passion for reading.

Returning with a sleepy, well fed and changed Pippa to the drawing room I found my mother waiting with a pot of coffee and some rather delicious looking scones.

"These were always your favourites, weren't they," she asked, as she again gestured to take Pippa back in her arms. "I'll look after Pippa while you have something to eat." Pippa grizzled a little at being disturbed, but Mama expertly rocked her on her shoulder murmuring her mix of French and German phrases. I decided to tread where I knew I was pushing the boundaries but if I didn't ask today then the moment would have passed.

"So, I have my father's eyes" I started. This time I wasn't going to be deterred." Please tell me about my father, Mamma, I would like to know."

Again, a silence, then a heavy sigh and without making eye contact and shaking her head gently my mother replied.

"It was all so long-ago Stephanie. It was in wartime, and everything changes. You know there may well not be a tomorrow, you grasp what you have today. I knew your father for such a short time, but I felt that we were very much in love." She stopped and stared across the room looking into a distance that wasn't there, wrapped in her memories she had kept deeply within her and hidden for so many years. I could see she was struggling to keep her composure and felt it was wrong to continue to push her. Perhaps she was ready to tell me more? Perhaps she would in the future though I knew that once this subject was closed returning to it would cause as much distress if not more. Then taking the control that I had always expected of her, she brought herself back to the present and as if the conversation had not even occurred, began asking me about my plans for the future. The moment had passed. I had to be content with the scrap of information I had gleaned.

I noticed a surreptitious glance at the clock on the wall. No doubt my mother had work to do or an important phone call to make, such as it had always been for as long as I could remember. I started to make my excuses about getting Pippa home for her next feed and sleep, and reluctantly Mama passed the soundly sleeping baby back to me.

"You must come again soon." She seemed genuinely ready to continue our visits.

"Of course, if that's what you would like," I replied, not wanting to tie myself into anything, but pleased that Mamma had suggested it.

"You remember Julien, don't you? I am sure he would love to see you again and meet Pippa. Why don't I invite him for tea at the same time?" I happily nodded my agreement, as Julien I remembered was an important friend of my mothers, in fact he had confided to me that he had long ago asked her to marry him. I was pleased he was still a special friend and inwardly delighted that my mother wished to 'show off' her granddaughter.

"Why not next Saturday? I am sure Julien will be able to come. I will look forward so much to seeing young Pippa again." I readily agreed, as I felt I had nothing to lose and was happy to rekindle my relationship with my mother, though I knew I needed to be realistic about how close we would actually become. I had worked hard for my independence and was certainly not willing to put that in jeopardy now. With Pippa in my arms, my mother suddenly produced a small brown envelope and held it out to me.

"Please take this for Pippa."

"Mamma," I said recognising what the envelope contained, "I don't need money, honestly, I am able to look after her myself."

"I know, but please, she is my granddaughter, and I do so wish to give her a present, so please just take this and buy something nice for her or save it till she needs something special, so it is from me?" My face softened into a smile, and I leant forward to kiss her on both cheeks.

"Of course, if that's what you would like, then I will do that. So 'Thank you' from Pippa."

As I walked away down the tree lined avenue I reflected on my visit. Yes, Paula had been right, not that I was going to tell her, but I also was conversant enough in the ways of the world to know one swallow does not make a summer.

Chapter 13

Julien, he hadn't really changed. I did some quick mental arithmetic and realised that it was probably 20 years since I had seen him. Upright, with his characteristic military style, he remained an impressive figure, though slightly bulkier all round with his fine head of hair was now pure white but still thick and wavy. What had certainly not changed was his twinkling bright blue eyes, now set in a more elderly face, with his engaging broad smile.

"Stephanie!" he exclaimed. "My! You haven't changed at all." Julien always knew how to flatter the ladies, as I knew, certainly at the moment, I didn't look anywhere near my best having yet to fully recover from the difficult pregnancy and having a complete lack of any desire to look after my appearance. He came forward and kissed me lightly on both cheeks, then looked carefully at Pippa.

"She is beautiful, your mother told me, but then I thought she might be a bit biased."

"She is a Legrand, so is bound to be beautiful." interjected my mother, taking Pippa in her arms and smiling all the time.

"Look Julien, doesn't she so remind you of Stephanie as a baby. You must remember seeing her." Nodding in agreement Julien looked over my mother's shoulder and winked at me.

"All the Legrand ladies are wonderful so far as I am concerned." It was so good to see my mother smile, and the convivial conversion continued with Pippa in my mother's arms gurgling and smiling as she stroked her hair and face.

The housekeeper interrupted us with telephone call for my mother, who apologised but said it was important so she must take it. Passing Pippa to me, she left the room closing the door behind her, and Julien wasted no time in changing the subject of the conversation.

"Stephanie, has your mother told you she hasn't been well?" My shocked face easily gave him the answer.

"No Julien, she has said nothing to me. I noticed she is looking pale and somehow older than I remember, and perhaps thinner than she was, but she has always kept herself so perfect in figure and so well dressed it is difficult to tell."

"I guessed she would not tell you, and she will be unhappy that I am doing so, but I think you ought to know, however please don't mention I said anything. I don't wish to upset her." He continued watching the door for any sign of my mother's return. "I only know because I called her at her office and found she wasn't there, then having rung here the housekeeper told me she was in hospital for tests. She hadn't said a word to anyone even me and I see her for dinner at least twice a week." Julien stopped and took a deep breath.

"She can be a difficult woman. She is so independent." I must have unconsciously smiled here, as Julien noticed and nodded.

"Yes, of course, you know her only too well. However, I waited till she was at home again and just asked why she was in hospital. I was expecting her to prevaricate and dismiss my questions. She is such an intensely private person, but she told me she had been diagnosed with a heart condition that cannot be cured but emphasised that taking daily medication will keep her fit and well." Julien paused; it was clear the news had unsettled him.

"I expected her to be annoyed that I had found out, but I think she was pleased to be able to tell me about her problem. However, as usual she asked me not to share the information with others as, and I think you know your Mamma well, she feels illness is a sign of weakness. I did wonder if she had told you. I do so hope I am not interfering in any way?" What Julien had told me had not really surprised me because on refection Mamma did not look well, but I had put this down to age. It, however, did shock me that she had not thought to tell me.

"No Julien, you are very much not interfering. Thank you for telling me. Mamma certainly hadn't done so." Julien put his hand into his inside jacket pocket and passed me his card.

"Look Stephanie, this is how you can get in contact with me. Please keep it safe and if you ever need anything just get in touch.

I think you know how I feel about your mother, and nothing has changed for me. She is a very dear friend."

I was just putting the card safely into my purse when my mother came back through the door.

"Now then." she said. "Let's go through and have some tea, it's all laid out on the dining room table." She appeared not to notice the sudden silence in the room for which we were both grateful.

The summer wore on. I moved into my own house at the end of August, and again without Paula it would have been an almost impossible task. She organised everything, even pressing Ronnie into driving a van full of my possessions to the new house on Saturday when he should have been watching their boys play football. Arranging for the house to be decorated and some plumbing updates before I moved in was a godsend. She even produced a young man to create a usable garden from the 'pretty kind of wilderness' that existed behind the house.

Even so it was going to take some time to get the house to what I wanted, but then that's what I had, time. It seemed to stretch out in front of me like a never-ending road going nowhere, along which I was stumbling. I had to take control back in my life if only for Pippa's sake and make some plans, as I was living on my savings and that could not go on for ever.

I was recommended to a nice lady called Helen who lived just round the corner, she could look after Pippa when I went back to teaching which I planned to do in the autumn. Well-spoken and organised, with two youngsters of her own, one already at school, she would be just what Pippa needed. I accepted her house wasn't the tidiest I had seen but I felt she understood my needs for Pippa, and having a similar aged playmate as she grew up, she would not have the only child syndrome I had suffered.

Approaching the local secondary schools, I very soon discovered that if I could be flexible about days worked and subjects covered, I had more work than I really wanted. Later in the term I was offered a full-time post teaching English from January, initially to cover a maternity leave but with the distinct probability that it would be made permanent.

However, I did have regrets about leaving Pippa each day. She took some time to settle with Helen, and was always in tears as I left her, though Helen assured me they very soon dried up when the front door closed. I did wonder if Pippa was clever enough to try to manipulate me or perhaps, she felt she ought to show she missed me or was I just over thinking the whole situation. Paula reassured me it was quite normal with stories of Gilly screaming all the way to her child minder when Paula, whose property finding business was really taking off, had to leave her. Paula and Gilly were frequent visitors to my new house with Gilly enjoying playing being mother to Pippa. I watch and hoped Gilly and Pippa might develop the same kind of friendship I had with Paula.

Pippa and I continued to visit my mother regularly, but always on her invitation. I never pushed her, allowing Mamma to control the pace of the relationship. She seemed besotted with Pippa as a baby and enjoyed interacting with her during our visits. We talked about inconsequential things, and though I tried very hard to steer her toward the 'father' topic she had mentioned once before, but I got the distinct ' don't go there if you know what is good for you' look that I remembered so well from childhood. So, I gave up for the time being anyway. Why rock the boat when things were sailing smoothly. Mamma outwardly appeared quite well, and she never alluded to her heart condition to which Julien had alerted me, so I just had to presume the medication was doing its job.

Autumn turned to winter. The days grew shorter, and Christmas was approaching fast. Never a lover of the Christmas festivities as I had always lacked the family needed for the ubiquitous gathering, I began to dread the forthcoming holidays. Paula, of course, had invited Pippa and I to spend Christmas day at her house with her extended family. She meant well, but I tried very hard not to take part in her family events as they highlighted to me exactly what I was never going to have for Pippa, or myself. My excuse to her was that I would spend the day with my mother. My excuse to my mother was, of course that I was spending the day with Paula. I knew from previous conversations that my mother habitually spent Christmas to New Year at a small house party at Julien's country estate in Gloucestershire, and I was not going to spoil her festive season.

No, it seemed I was to spend Christmas alone with Pippa, which to be honest didn't bother me, though looking back I cannot explain my logic.

Christmas Day arrived, with the usual dismal grey weather. Pippa was content enough at first, but as the day wore on, she began to uncharacteristically grizzle and cry, not wanting to sleep or settle even when carried on my shoulder, a position she usually enjoyed. She appeared well enough, no temperature, still ready to feed, but very unsettled. I realise now she was picking up on my mood which was decidedly depressive. By 4pm dusk was falling, Pippa had not settled all afternoon, I was feeling completely exhausted and on the verge of tears. Though I had never done it before I put her to bed in her cot and left her crying, it seemed the only thing to do, though I stood at the bottom of the stairs my heart breaking at her crying until it gradually subsided, and she fell into a deep restful sleep.

I walked out into the back garden in the darkness and stood still, letting the persistent light rain fall on my head. I could see lights next door, hear their television and voices. There were people all around, yet I was alone, very much alone. The tears that had been threatening to come all day eventually broke though and I stood in the rain with tears unchecked, flowing down my cheeks. Not for the first time I wanted to scream at Philip for leaving me, leaving us.

Gradually the rain soaked my clothes and left my hair plastered to my skull, and I realised I was shivering with cold. I didn't have a blinding 'road to Damascus moment' of decision but a gradual dawning that I could just not go on like this. Things needed to change and quite honestly, I was the only one who could do this. For Pippa, rather than for me, I needed to allow, no make myself move on. Philip was the past, and of course I would never ever forget him, but he was, he had to be, the past. I had to remove him from my mind and my life as it was today. He was gone, and if Pippa was to have a future, then Philip must become a rarely visited memory. Allowing myself to wallow in my own grief must not jeopardise the future of my precious little girl, so from now on she must come first, and I must leave my memories behind.

Shivering with cold and by now with my clothing soaked through I left the garden going into the house with a resolve that I didn't know I could find some hours earlier. 1980 was just round the corner, so I needed to embrace the new decade and start a new life. Philip was not part of my new life, and though I would never forget him, I had to relegate him to my past and, albeit with difficulty, keep him out of my thoughts.

Pippa continued to sleep soundly. After a hot bath, clean dry clothes, and my hair freshly dried I gathered her up in my arms and held her tight. She was all I had, she relied entirely on me, and I must live up to her expectations. Lying on her beautiful soft, pink, wool blanket that was her present from her grandmamma, she happily rolled around the floor of the living room enchanted by the Christmas lights, as I systematically went round removing all the treasured mementos that reminded me of Philip. The photos of us together on holiday at Lake Constance, the smooth round black pebbles we had collected together, the ridiculous wooden ornament we had bought in the Black Forest. These all went into a shoe box, out of sight, to keep out of mind. My one luxury, the photo of Philip in his full-dress uniform smiling his engaging, boyish, lopsided smile, this would go in my bedside table drawer. I could look at it once a day, but that was all, and I had to do so with a happy memory, for if I could follow these self-imposed rules, I felt I could perhaps move forward. I knew I had to for Pippa.

When Paula came next to the house, she must have noticed the absence of my photos but wisely made no comment. Perhaps she could read my mind, perhaps she approved, I would never know, we just did not discuss it. This was now the way it was going to be.

Chapter 14

Stephanie. Six years later 1985 aged 40

"Mrs Legrand. Can you come to the office now to take an urgent phone call?" I looked up startled to see one of the school secretaries standing in the open doorway of the classroom with a distinctly worried look on her face. My heart immediately began to race. *What on earth had happened?* Everyone knew not to call me at school unless it was a real emergency, so it must be Pippa. She must have had an accident.

"I can stay with your class till the breaktime bell." The secretary offered insistently, "You need to take this phone call quickly." Grabbing my bag and jacket I ran, to hell with the rules, along the corridor and burst into the school office where another of the secretaries gestured at the phone lying off the hook.

"Hello, Mrs Legrand here, is it Pippa, is she ill?"

"Miss Stephanie" were the first words I heard. My mother's housekeeper was the only person who called me that.

"Mrs Bristow, whatever is the matter, I am at school at the moment. Is my mother ill?"

"I'm sorry Miss Stephanie, it's your mother. I came in the house today as usual, and I found her still in bed. I can't wake her. I'm sorry I think she may be …," She choked on the word but managed to continue, "So I have called the doctor, and he is coming. I remembered your mother telling me the name of the school where you work, so I telephoned you. I didn't know what else to do. Can you come now?" I sat down heavily in the secretaries chair as the world just stopped.

Certainly, on my last visit Mamma had looked tired, but we never discussed her health, she would not allow it. It was only because Julien had enlightened me that I knew she had a heart problem, but that was over five years ago.

"Miss Stephanie, are you still there?" I had to pull myself together.

"Yes. Sorry, it's such a shock. I will come over right away. Please don't let the doctor leave if he arrives before me." As soon as I had put down the phone a taxi was ordered, and hastily leaving the office I was reassured all would be relayed to those who needed to know in school and just to get to my mother's house as quickly as possible.

Mrs Bristow answered the door still obviously very much in shock. The doctor had arrived and was upstairs with Mamma, so I climbed the stairs and quietly let myself into the bedroom. Lying peacefully as if in a deep sleep lay my mother, my dear Mamma, with the doctor writing some kind of certificate. He glanced round at me.

"I'm Stephanie her daughter. What happened?" I asked.

"I'm afraid it seems she had of heart attack during the night. I saw her only last week and tried, yet again, to persuade her to go back to her consultant and think about surgery to try to correct the problem, but she was very reluctant to even consider the matter." I walked forward and took her hand, now very cold.

"She looks so peaceful." I could hardly believe that she would not just wake up and be annoyed with us for making a fuss.

"It would have been very quick; I have no doubt. But surely you knew she has been unwell for some time?"

"She didn't like, no wouldn't talk about it, I'm afraid. But I did know she had a heart condition." The doctor closed his consulting bag.

"She was a difficult lady at times." He said with a half-smile, "But you had to admire her for her sheer determination and independence. Most people with this condition would have retired from work years ago, but no, she wanted to continue. I think basically she thrived on work. Retirement would have meant giving up and she wasn't one to do that." A fitting epitaph I thought, as this man knew my mother all too well.

As I closed the heavy front door on the departing doctor, I suddenly felt the huge weight of the responsibility which now fell on my shoulders. What on earth did I do now? Mrs Bristow was standing by the stairs looking still very pale and shocked, which was only to be expected. "The Doctor says Mamma died of a heart attack during the night, there was nothing you, or anyone could have done, but thank you so much for all your help today. Now if you want to go home, please do. You must have had a huge shock." However, Mrs Bristow declined saying she wanted to stay and help but doing what I wasn't too sure. I eventually suggested she did her normal routine, keeping well away from my mother's bedroom and her study where I was going to be. She seemed relieved to have something to do.

First, I needed to go and say goodbye to Mamma. Entering the room all was quiet, some soft sunlight filtered through the half open curtains, so I sat on the bed and held her cold hand, kissing each cheek as was our traditional greeting. So much emotional energy, good and bad, had passed between us in the years, but I was sure of one thing, my mother very much loved me and always tried, in her mind at least, to do what was right. She was the one who had fiercely protected me and now she was gone, and I was completely alone. Tears welled up in my eyes, but I had no time to grieve, I needed to take control as she would have done and would expect of me. I kissed her on the forehead whispered goodbye and silently left the room.

Sitting in her chair behind her carved mahogany desk I felt lost. What on earth did I do next? Julien, his name suddenly launched into my head, I must tell him. He had been so close to my mother, he ought to know what had happened and perhaps he would be able to help, so I dug out his card, long ago stored in my purse. At his work number a kind and very correct lady told me he was not in his office however I ought to be able to reach him at his London home. Ringing his home number, I was surprised that Julien actually answered his own phone, somehow I had imagined a man servant at least to do the mundane tasks.

"Julien, it's Stephanie." I tried very hard to sound calm and normal.

"Stephanie! How lovely to hear from you. It's been too long, when am I going to see you and that lovely daughter of yours again?"

"Julien." I interrupted." I'm sorry but I have some really bad news." I hesitated. How did you break the kind of news I had? There is no easy way, so I just said it "I'm afraid Mamma died in her sleep last night and was found by her housekeeper this morning."

"Oh, my goodness." I heard him sit down heavily. "Cecile dead? I can't believe it. I had dinner with her two days ago. My Cecile...." The line went quiet. I could hear him breathing heavily.

"Julien, are you alright? I am so sorry to have to tell you, like this. I knew how close you were to her, but the thing is, I just don't know what to do now. Who do I tell?" Julien cleared his throat and obviously collected his thoughts.

"Stephanie, are you at her house? Stay there, I will be over to you in say, twenty minutes." The line went dead, and I breathed a sigh of relief, help was coming. Before he arrived, I realised I needed to alert Helen to be ready to keep Pippa longer after school than usual. Oh Pippa, what was I going to tell her? More panic, but a realisation that I really needn't cross that bridge right now.

"Helen." She eventually answered after the phone had rung for what seemed a long time. "It's Stephanie. Can you keep Pippa till I get back today – I don't know when that will be. It's just, well, my mother has suddenly died and there is so much to sort out. But please don't tell Pippa, just say I am held up at school or something."

"Stephanie, I'm so sorry to hear that. Are you OK? Listen for goodness' sake don't worry about Pippa she can stay as long as necessary. I'll give her some tea, and she can watch TV with mine. Its only fish fingers and chips. Will she eat that?"

"Helen, she will love that, just please don't let on about Mamma. I need to think how to do this for the best, and I can't think straight right now." I put the phone down just as I heard the front door open, interesting I thought, it seemed Julien had his own key. I met him ashen faced in the hall, and he took one look at me and held me in a tight hug. It was good to feel his strength, giving me the feeling we could get through this together.

"Mamma is in her bedroom. Do you want to see her, to say Goodbye?" Julien nodded, the news seemed to have aged him, and he went slowly upstairs. I left him to go alone, as I was not going to intrude on his parting, I knew how much my mother had meant to him, so I waited quietly in the study. Some ten minutes later he strode through the study door looking very pale and shocked.

"Whisky or Brandy Stephanie?"

"I don't drink, really".

"Whisky or Brandy? I definitely need something, and I strongly suggest you do the same." The military man taking charge of the proceedings, it had been some time since I could recall this feeling. A door tried to open in my memories, but I resisted, keeping it firmly shut, as I had to deal with the here and now. He poured a small amount of brandy into a cut-glass tumbler by the decanters and passed it to me. He took a more generous helping of whisky and sat down heavily on the sofa. He was right, of course, one sip of the strong liquor warmed me though and seemed to settle my panicking thoughts.

"What did the Doctor say?"

"He was certain it was a heart attack. He had seen her last week and tried to persuade her to see the specialist again, there was, he told me, an operation she could have had. But she refused, apparently not for the first time."

"Oh Stephanie, I should have been more forceful with her. It's my fault as I knew she was getting worse, but she just wouldn't listen. I backed off, as ever, not wanting to upset her and now she is dead. Cecile, my Cecile." He sat staring into the distance, and quite honestly, I didn't know what to say or do, so I just let the silence take its course.

"Julien." I started the conversation eventually "It's certainly not your fault, remember I didn't say anything either and she was so tired when Pippa and I came over the last time. She just couldn't cope with Pippa being a normal boisterous young child, so we left early. You and I both knew how much she hated to admit to or even talk about illness, so I took the easy way out and said nothing. To be honest that's the way she wanted it, and my goodness, she had us both trained very well." I tried to inject a lighter note into the situation and give Julien his due he smiled ruefully. Then, taking a final long swig of his whisky, he turned to me.

"Let's get going then to sort all this out. She would expect that if nothing else."

I let out a sigh of relief. Julien would know what to do. Of that, I was sure.

Chapter 15

"Julien, now we have time can you please tell me what you know about Mamma. She would never speak of the past, let alone my father. You know how she had a very good way of just closing down the conversation when she wanted." We were sitting on the sofa in Mama's study having a morning coffee some three days after the shock of her sudden death. The necessary organisation that follows a death was now well underway, so I wanted to see what information I could glean from Julien.

I had gone through her files and papers in the desk drawers. All immaculately organised and up to date. I had even searched her bedroom drawers but found nothing I didn't know already. Julien said there was a will at the solicitors, and we had an appointment next week, though I felt he knew more about Mamma's wishes but wasn't telling me.

Today, Saturday, Pippa was spending the day with Paula and Gilly. I still hadn't found the words to tell her of her grandmamma's death, and she went off thoroughly excited as Paula had promised a trip to a park with lots of ducks, geese and swans to feed. I had thought about it and decided to ambush Julien now we had the time and see what I could find out.

"Oh Stephanie, I have no idea what your mother told you, not much I understand. I never wanted to interfere, and I know she felt some things were best left in the past and, as you know, once she had made up her mind there was little anyone could do to persuade her differently." Julien sighed. It was obvious the sudden death had taken its toll on him, and being that much older than my mother, I guessed about 20 years, I expected he felt that Cecile would outlive him, but he now had to come to terms that she was gone.

"I know it's only 11 o'clock but I am going to have a whisky if you want me to talk. What about you? A small brandy again?"

I nodded if only to keep him company and he settled back on the sofa, took a swig of liquor, and began.

"Your mother, Cecile, was introduced to me in 1944, probably September. We were on the way to winning the war, but it certainly wasn't finished yet. France was being liberated and the allies needed to work with a fledging French government to ensure some kind of smooth transition once the fighting was over. I urgently required someone who had the highest security clearances, was completely discreet, and a native French speaker with a good brain in their head to work alongside me. Cecile knocked on my office door and told me she had been assigned to my department. She looked about sixteen years old, though I found out later she was over twenty. Thin and tiny, yet immaculately dressed as ever, there was a way she held her head and an intensity in her eyes which told me she could do the job. I came to realise I underestimated the maturity in her young head." He paused and took another sip.

"From the beginning she more than lived up to expectations. She could not only translate but carefully interpret the actual nuances of what was being communicated. She was very quick thinking and could read a difficult situation better than I and, being a pretty young woman, she could charm her way out of any problems. She became my invaluable personal assistant with her advice always sound and reliable, so I grew very much to depend on her. She confided in me after a couple of months that she was expecting a baby in the spring of 1945. She was so petite and dressed so well I don't think anyone had actually noticed. She never mentioned the father, so I am sorry Stephanie I can't help there, and I didn't feel it was my place to press her, as I just assumed it was a wartime romance. So many people took their opportunity of happiness as the future was so uncertain, and there were many people in her position." Julien sighed and paused again.

Was I doing the right thing stirring his memories?

"I didn't want to lose her, she was so valuable to our work, and to be completely truthful, I had also rather fallen for her." He smiled an almost embarrassed smile. "So, I helped her be as discreet as possible about the baby, arranged for the birth in a private clinic and found this house for her. I knew a little more about her background by then, with her mother coming from an aristocratic family, and her father a wealthy Jewish businessman who had made money during the first world war and specialised in innovative machinery." I could almost see the memories flash across his eyes as he recounted the story.

"Stephanie, you know I tried to get your mother to marry me, I have already told you that. In fact, I asked her before you were born, and it would have made things much easier for her if she had accepted, but she would not. She assured me I was very special to her, however she felt unable to make a marriage commitment, saying when pressed, she would never be able to fully give her heart to me and it was not fair to expect me to accept that. I would have, of course, but you know your mamma when she sets her mind against something. I thought at first, she perhaps had a fleeting hope that your father, whoever he was, wherever he was, might just come back for her at the end of the war. So, I decided to wait." Another sip of whisky and a pause, as if planning how to go on.

"Some years passed, and no one appeared, then my marriage offers almost became a private joke between us. As the years rolled on, I would propose every year on the same date, bunch of red roses in my hand and she would decline. Then we would have a lovely dinner out somewhere in London, or if the date fell at a weekend a delightful weekend away together. Yes Stephanie, I am telling you that Cecile and I had a very close relationship over many, many years. I hope that doesn't shock you too much."

As if I hadn't guessed. I almost said, but I just smiled to encourage him to continue. I was happy that Mamma had had a special friend, but sorry for Julien that she would never actually marry him.

"We were always very discreet you understand. Frankly such a liaison would have been frowned on by our superiors in the service, but being with Cecile made me happy, and I like to think I made her life more content. I realised, however; I was always at least second in line for her love, as you, Stephanie, were her reason for living, the person she held closest to her heart. I know your relationship was quite fraught at times, believe me there were times when I wanted to intervene. However, Cecile made it clear, she made the decisions regarding you, and I needed to keep out." Again, a pause, a silence to reflect before he gathered his thoughts to continue.

"I'm not really being much help to you, am I? When we met in wartime you just didn't ask questions in our line of work. You knew the person couldn't answer, truthfully anyway, so we worked on a 'need to know' basis and that very much included your personal life. I just never asked about what she had been doing or who your father was. She had come to me with the highest security clearance as I have said, so she could have been involved in almost anything. She would not, no, could not tell me, even if I had asked, but I sensed a deep emotional trauma, however that's all I know. I'm so sorry."

"Julien, please don't be sorry you have told me much more than Mamma ever did. I am so pleased she had you even if she wasn't always an easy person to live with. I remember saying a long time ago, when I was upset with her, that you were lucky she didn't marry you. But I think I was wrong to say that, please forgive me. I don't really understand why she never married you, but I do know you loved her deeply. Thank you for looking after her so well for all those years, because I realise now perhaps, I wasn't the best kind of daughter. I feel so guilty now having seen so little of her over the years." I could feel tears welling up in my eyes. "The problem is Julien I don't think I ever really told Mamma how much I loved her or showed any gratitude for her bringing me up and encouraging my education? I feel so wretched now knowing how she sacrificed things for me."

"Stephanie, please don't blame yourself. The main problem was you were too much like Cecile in so many ways, two strong women each sure they were both right. She kept you a secret when you were very young as she felt people would think badly of her, as most women with a child simply did not work all those years ago. But as you grew up, she was very proud of you, and she was always telling me about how clever you were at school, how pretty you were. You probably don't remember me, but I did see you a few times when you were very young, but after that Cecile wanted to keep you out of our relationship. I think she was worried you would say the wrong thing to someone, and our friendship would become more widely known. I know you had battles in your teenage years, she used to tell me and wonder if she was doing the right thing. You must realise she only had your best interests at heart even if you felt what she demanded of you was wrong." Julien spoke more forcefully now as if he needed me to fully understand and, of course, to reassure me. I was the one who had started this conversation and opened the 'can of worms', so I had to expect emotional consequences as Mamma's death was still so raw. A charged emotional silence hung in the room again, but this time Julien broke it.

"Why don't we go for a nice walk in the sunshine and stop off for lunch somewhere. It's been too long since I took a pretty young lady out for a meal. It will do us both good. I don't think Cecile would want us sitting round moping, do you? She was a great one for seizing the day." A grateful nodded agreement saw us strolling through the park to a favourite restaurant that he knew. He was obviously well known at the establishment and confided, with a huge smile to the owner, who had made a quiet comment to Julien about me, that I was his 'almost step daughter'. I willingly smiled back and wondered exactly how life might have been different if Julien had been around as a father figure. But I would, of course, never know.

We had a lovely lunch with Julien keeping me entertained with amusing stories about his exploits with my mother. The rather good bottle of white wine may well have helped, but I said goodbye to Julien feeling much more settled than I had been since her death and a distinct feeling that life could, perhaps, move on.

When I arrived to collect Pippa, Paula also noticed my change of mood.

"My, you look a lot better than this morning. Quite some colour in your cheeks now."

"Well, it could be the bottle of wine with the really nice lunch I have just shared with Julien. But I think I am coping better all round. But how is Pippa, I do hope she hasn't been a nuisance?"

"Pippa a nuisance! Stephanie she is so well behaved, so polite with 'please and thank you' all the time, eats whatever you put in front of her and keeps Gilly entertained. Quite honestly, she is a Godsend. I have been able to get on with my paperwork undisturbed. I don't know how you do it. I'll swap you for Gilly any day." I felt a stab of worry, was I doing to Pippa what my mother had done to me? Were my expectations of behaviour too strict? Would I drive her away as my mother had done? I just needed to be careful, being a single parent meant there was only me, no one to help with decisions, tell me what was right and if I was expecting too much of a child. I wanted to do the right thing, bring her up correctly, but I so wanted Pippa to love me as I did her. Paula saw my hesitation.

"What's wrong Stephanie? Pippa is such a lovely girl. A real credit to you. Can't you see that?"

"Paula, I just don't want to go down the same route as Mamma. Sometimes I just don't know what is for the best. Tell me the truth. Am I too strict with her? I worry that something will happen to her, and I want to protect her from any harm, but am I doing the right thing? I want her to have her own personality, feelings and desires. Sometimes I feel I stop her being herself because I try to get her to behave in the way I want her to. Can you see what I am saying? I think Mamma's death has brought all this to the fore. I don't want her to hate me like I did Mamma. Though I realise now she was doing what she thought was right for me." I could feel tears, most likely of frustration, staring to come. This was no good. Pippa must not see me upset, she still didn't know about the death of her grandmamma, and I had no real plan of how to tell her.

"Cup of tea time." Interjected Paula. "The girls are fine in the garden for a while yet. We can have a good chat, and you can get all this nonsense off your chest!" Paula was, of course right I was overthinking the whole problem, she had her feet on the ground and not for the first time was able to help me over a crisis. As she made the tea, I realised how much she had changed in the last years since I returned to England. Gone was the motherly hairstyle, and the extra pounds in weight the children had brought, as she was now successful businesswomen, with a growing Home Finder enterprise. When I saw her in her designer suits during the week, well made up with her sleek fashionable hair, I did admit to a stab of envy for her drive and purposeful thinking. She was good at her job and her success had meant that we didn't see as much of each other as we used to. But I was well respected in my profession too, I had to realise this, and I was making a good job of bringing up Pippa. I really just needed to believe in myself.

Chapter 16

I remember so little about Mamma's funeral. Perhaps it was the mind blanking out those experiences that cause too much anxiety as a defence mechanism. I always had felt a funeral was an event that brought back all the trauma that, to be quite honest, you were just getting over. Deep in my mind, and I resisted these memories as much as I could, was of course Philips's funeral that I had chosen not to attend. All those years ago my decision was taken for all the right reasons, but yet part of me felt I had not said a proper goodbye. The circumstances of his death meant that one day he was alive and with me, the next gone, just suddenly gone, without warning, and I realised I had never come to terms with that. I had coped for all these years by not allowing my mind to think of him. However, Mamma's death had brought all these feelings I could not control, rushing back to the surface.

Mamma, of course was different. I had said my goodbyes, in a kind of way, but I had to accept that many others had not and that a substantial funeral was expected. Getting it 'right' in social circumstances had always been important for Mamma, and I hoped, with Julien's help, that we would do just that, for her if no one else. Paula organised a shopping trip and a suitable elegant black dress and coat, costing far more than I would have chosen to spend, was purchased. She was right of course. I had to be correctly dressed out of respect for Mamma. I just hoped I looked the part as I did not want to let her down, because whatever our differences I loved and respected her.

I can distinctly remember Julien and I walking behind the coffin into church. I had insisted he was with me, not only for my sake, but feeling very strongly that Mamma would have wanted him close. The church seemed dark, the only light streaming through the stained-glass windows but well filled with people. The service was blur, everyone singing heartily, my choaking on held back tears, and Julien staring straight ahead controlling his emotions. As befits catholic wishes, Mamma was buried in the churchyard, the pale winter sun struggling through the bare branches of the trees and a cold stillness pervading the setting.

We then returned to her house for the dreaded 'funeral tea'. Thankfully Julien had arranged it all and known who to invite, as all the faces were strangers to me, but presumably Mamma had meant something to them. I busied myself carrying plates of sandwiches, filled savoury vol-au-vents and petite sausage rolls around the people. Some guessed who I was, or had been primed by Julien, and made comforting remarks about how much Mamma had meant to them and how she would be sorely missed at work.

Unexpectantly, I came upon a face I did recognise, older now of course, but there no mistaking Matthew. The long curly hair was tamed and no longer sat over his collar, and he had put on a bit of weight, but he looked smart, affluent and every part the civil servant.

"Stephanie." He smiled welcomingly at me. "So lovely to see you after all these years, though a very sad occasion. Please accept my condolences. Your mother will be very much missed." He touched my hand briefly.

"Matthew, my goodness" I smiled back. It was good to see a face I knew. "I am so pleased you could come. Were you still working with my mother?"

"No, not for some years now, but she always seemed interested in what I was doing and would stop to talk when we met occasionally at meetings. I realise I was so lucky to have spent time with her when I first arrived, learning so much day by day."

"And you're married?" More a statement from me than a question as I saw his wedding ring.

"Yes, yes and two children, a boy and girl, now teenagers" He laughed. "I think I am beginning to understand what my father had to put up with when my brother and I were that age. And you?"

"I have a little girl, Pippa." I wasn't prepared to elaborate. "Mamma loved her as a baby." Which of course, was the truth. However, as Pippa had grown up a little, Mamma seemed to find her more difficult, and I now wondered how much of this was

214

due to her heart condition and feeling unwell, rather than a dislike of noisy children. Matthew made his excuses and left, again repeating how much my mother would be missed by all who worked with her. Gradually, people were drifting away until a hard core of Julien with his, and presumably my mother's, close friends were drinking whisky in the drawing room.

"I ought to be going Julien, to collect Pippa." I stepped into the room. "Can I leave the caterers to clear up now? And can you lock up the house?" Julien got up and came over.

"Of course, Stephanie. Just say hello to these people. We are all going to miss your mamma terribly." He introduced me, but I simply made no attempt to remember their names, so I just smiled and wondered how much, if anything, they knew about me?

"Ah, the elusive daughter." Said one. I really didn't like his tone, but then perhaps I was being judgemental, it had been a difficult day, keeping quiet was the easy way out, so I eventually left the room, and Julien followed me to the front door.

"I'll see everything is in place before I leave." He reassured me, "and don't forget the meeting with the solicitor tomorrow at five o'clock. Why don't I collect you from school and we can drive there together? It would make more sense." I smiled and nodded a reply, it was so like Julien to think of me.

Hurrying down the street to catch the next bus to start the journey home I just felt numb, but glad the whole charade was over. I was sure Mamma would have approved, it had all gone to plan, and the mourners would surely be impressed. However, it was not, in any way a private farewell to a loved parent, and it had certainly not changed my feelings about funerals. As to the other problem I had still to face, well I put that to the back of my mind. When would I ever get round to telling Pippa that her grandmamma was dead?

Julien collected me the next day and we sped towards the solicitor's office. I was pretty sure he knew what was in the will, but declined to talk about it, rather he reminisced about my mother in his gentlemanly way. I knew nothing of my mother's financial affairs but guessed she had been well paid in her employment, and I also knew that there had been some inherited family money, Julien had said as much. Certainly, when growing up there had always been people employed in the house, and I don't think I ever saw my mother do any housework.

I had always fervently declined any monetary help, I wanted to keep my independence as I thought that would have been the way Mamma would have kept her influence over me. Yes, I accepted gifts for Pippa as I didn't wish to deny her the things Mamma's money could buy. It seemed to give pleasure to them both, but to me money was the way she could try to control me and early on in my new life I decided I wasn't having that.

In the end the Will was surprisingly simple. Some small bequests for people she had employed, and the remainder to make a Trust Fund for the sole benefit of Pippa. The trust fund would continue until Pippa was twenty-five years old, then she could do as she wished with the money. Until the age of twenty-one the income from the investments made by the Trust would come to me to use as I felt fit in the upbringing of Pippa. There were, of course, conditions, this was my mamma who had drawn up the will after all, but I felt certainly at this time, I could live with them. I could take anything I wanted from the house and then it would be sold, and the proceeds put into the Trust fund.

Julien sat quietly throughout and watched as I signed the necessary papers and arranged for monthly payments to come to my account with the main Trust Fund being held by the solicitors. On the way out he commented for the first time.

"I hope you approve of the arrangements Stephanie. They were entirely your mothers wish but I did try to guide her to allow you more say in how the income would be spent. It wasn't that she felt you shouldn't directly inherit but that she wanted her granddaughter to have the advantages you had, in education particularly. As it stands you will, more or less, have the income from the Trust to do with as you like until Pippa is twenty-one. That income is not huge but with your secure salary from teaching, it will make you comfortably well off and allow both you and Pippa to enjoy some of the nicer things in life."

"Thank you, Julien, for everything. I know I could not have done all this on my own, and I really had not thought about any inheritance. I think you know I prefer to make my own way in life, but anything that will help Pippa is good news and I am sure you know I will spend any money wisely."

Julien glanced at me.

"Oh, I am certain of that Stephanie. I see a very wise head on your shoulders. You may not resemble your mother in looks but, goodness me, you are very alike in so many ways. One thing you must promise me is to keep in touch, and not disappear from my life. You and Pippa are like my family. Why not bring your lovely young daughter down to my house in Gloucestershire for a weekend next spring? I would really enjoy that." I squeezed his arm and nodded my approval. Julien had always been special to me, and I saw no reason to end the relationship.

Part Three

Pippa

Chapter 1

Pippa, 1997 aged 18

My memories of my grandmother are all from early childhood. They are hazy recollections, like scenes viewed in a mist of jumbled remembrances. Sometimes they clear, like the lens on a camera suddenly coming into focus, and I am back in those distant days, the sounds, the smells, the intense feelings.

I realise I never really knew her, we visited my mother and I, but I can't remember how frequently. What does the passage of time mean to a five-year-old? I recall the tedious bus journey, we had to change busses in a cold damp echoing space, and the final long walk through streets with large trees alongside the pavement. Concentrate, and I can see the tall, three storey terraced house with its pastel painted facade and steps to the portico entrance.

A polite greeting, always three kisses to alternate cheeks, and a small, almost polite, hug. My grandmother was small but very correct, upright and immaculately dressed, so I often felt I shouldn't touch her in case my unwashed hands would soil her clothes. The visits followed a similar routine, after a few minutes of polite conversation I would be sent out into the garden to play, my mother stayed inside to talk, I presume.

I can clearly see the well-kept back garden with beds full of colourful flowers and a long winding lawn that led to an old potting shed that was never locked. Growing bored by the garden I used to spend time investigating the interior with old plant pots and tools stored, perhaps surprisingly, haphazardly. But, even then, I couldn't imagine my grandmother getting her hands dirty in the rich brown soil, someone else must have seen to the garden for her. I remember we never stayed for a long time, and we never had our tea there. At the time it didn't seem odd, after all I knew no different.

The camera lens in my mind comes into sharp focus. I see a rainy day when I could not go into the garden, and I was being too noisy for my grandmamma, so I was told to wait quietly and left sitting on a chair in the hall. My grandmother and mother went into one of the rooms and shut the door. Boredom overtook my ability to sit still, so I explored the delights the hallway had to offer. Highly polished wooden furniture with delicate pieces of porcelain placed carefully on top. Then I climbed the stairs letting my hand trail on the shiny, dark, intricately crafted banister, while I gazed at the pictures on the walls of proud looking people from long ago and countryside scenes from foreign places. The landing had even more great treasures in a glass fronted cabinet, I could see such beautiful figurines.

Captivated by my discoveries I failed to hear the door into the hall open, and hearing my name called sharply, I ran back down the stairs to a very stern reception. A harsh scolding from my mother, as I ought to have stayed sitting on the chair I was told, and it was clear I had disappointed her. Through my tears I could see my grandmother watching with a disapproving expression. At the time I thought it was for my behaviour, now I am not so sure, it may have been for the way my mother behaved toward me. While she collected the coats so we could go, my grandmother stepped forward and put an orange sweet in a cellophane wrapper in my hand with a conspiratorial smile, and brushed my tears away with her lavender scented, pristine white handkerchief.

That day, like all the others, my mother was strangely silent on our lengthy return journey to the little terraced house a long way south of the river Thames. I knew to mirror her silence until the immediate memories of the visit had gone, then perhaps we could resume our close and happy relationship.

It had always been just my mother and I, to me that was normal. I had my 'Aunty Helen', not my real aunt of course, but the kind lady who looked after me while my mother went to work each day. A slightly chaotic household, two children of her own and a variety of youngsters she 'minded' at different times of the day. This experience taught me tolerance of others, how to 'share' when you didn't want to, and how to stick up for yourself when really necessary. Most of the days were fun, because Aunty Helen was very tolerant, and there were very few raised voices or tears, though perhaps in hindsight these memories could be rose tinted.

I remember a totally different experience with my mother, very intense, but loving in every way. When she wasn't at work, or preparing for it, I was the centre of her attention. We played together, shared books and stories, walked out in the park, went to the shops, but mostly talked, and talked about anything and everything. Apart from the irregular visits to my grandmother we did not share our lives with anyone else, except my mother's good friend Paula who we visited from time to time, when I could play with Gilly her daughter.

I understood my mother's moods were often reflected in her facial expressions, and I soon learnt when she was tired or anxious, when to talk and when to quietly entertain myself, and when I had disappointed or displeased her. I hated her harsh, stinging, scolding words, I felt I had let her down and made a mental note not to let it happen again. So, most of the time I made sure I did the things that pleased her.

Consequently, on arrival at school aged five, I knew exactly how to cope with the sudden exposure to twenty-five other boisterous children from my time with Aunty Helen, but also could already read, maintain a sensible, almost adult, conversation, and was very aware of what others were feeling and thinking. Gregarious in nature, I soon had many friends and began to discover that there were things in my life that seemed to be missing. After school playtimes in friends' houses led me to meet not only a much different sort of grandparent but discover the role men played in my friends' lives. Why didn't I have a father who came home and played games with you in the back garden, or cooked you fish fingers and chips while your mum went out to work her shift at the local supermarket?

Carefully I choose my moment, when I best considered my mother in a good mood, and unknowingly dropped the bombshell question.

"Do I have a daddy?"

There was quite a silence, but she must have known this question would come sooner rather than later.

"Of course, you have a daddy," she simply replied. But that wasn't good enough for me, as I am now sure she would realise.

"Then where is my daddy? Why isn't he here like Gilly's dad?" Silence again, but I wasn't giving up.

"He has gone away," was her simplistic answer, the same one I was to hear occasionally in the future, learning it was a euphemism for something completely different.

"Where to, and when is he coming back?" was of course my obvious reply. My mother held me firmly by my shoulders and looked straight into my eyes.

"He has gone away, that's all you need to know." I could sense her mood changing, anger coming to the surface. "We don't need him or anyone else do we? It's just us together and that's how we like it, isn't it?" I was suddenly wrapped in her arms, a deep intense hug, and I could feel strong emotions radiating from her. I knew then that this was one subject, if I knew what was good for me, I would not be discussing with my mother again, anytime soon.

The memories become hazy again, then the lens moves into sharp focus, another deep recollection surfaces. Again, I had chosen my moment carefully for I had wondered why we had not been to see my grandmother for what seemed a long time. Our visits were irregular, but, although the passage of time is unclear to a young child, I had noticed that we hadn't made the long unexciting journey for some time. I was curious, but knew my curiosity was not always well rewarded, sometimes a sharp rebuke, but often a shared exploration of something new. My mother and I were baking in our small kitchen, and I was rolling out scones ready to cut, while she was weighing out ingredients for a sponge cake. Happy weekend afternoons were often spent like this. Dare I spoil the afternoon? However, my curiosity was too strong.

"Mum," I paused. Wondering now if it was such a good idea to bring up this subject, as I remembered how quiet and brooding, and, yes sad, my mother often was after the visits but, having caught her attention, I ploughed on.

"Why don't we go to see Grandmama anymore? It's been ages since we went there. Doesn't she want to see us?" My mother stopped beating the eggs and butter and paused as if choosing her words carefully.

"We don't need to go. Your grandmama has gone away." That phrase again, it had stuck in my mind since I had asked about my father, so now my grandmother had 'gone away' also. Of course, I wasn't letting this drop despite the warning flash of my mother eyes.

"Gone where, when is she coming back?"

"She has gone away, that's all you need to know." Again, that familiar phrase, but I hadn't the sense this time to let it go, despite the overt possibility I was about to tread into some unwelcoming territory. I clutched my rolling pin, tossed my head and felt like stamping my foot, but didn't.

"Why has she gone away? Where has she gone to? Why won't you tell me?" I was pushing the acceptable behaviour boundaries my mother had set, and I knew it. I was most likely blowing this up out of all proportion, but it felt important. Why did she have to hide things from me?

"Finish rolling out the scones please and put them on the tray over there. The oven is ready." All this said in an even voice but with an undertone of 'watch your step'. She was ignoring my questions, treating me like a baby. I should have continued to roll out the scones as asked, but of course my emotions got the better of me, and I plonked the rolling pin down noisily, stepped back from the table and probably did stamp my foot this time.

"But why has she gone away; doesn't she want us anymore?" Tears of frustration began to spill down my cheeks. I felt as if the only other person I had known as my family had disappeared and no one had bothered to explain. Of course, that was the end of the baking session, as I was sent, accompanied by stinging words, to my room, knowing I would have to apologise later and hope my mother would forgive me. But I also knew she wasn't going to tell me the real reason we had not been to visit my grandmother.

223

Chapter 2

So, I learnt at an early age that there were two taboo subjects if I didn't want to upset my mother. I had got the message, don't ask questions about ´Daddies´, or ask about Grandmamma. It didn't stop me being curious, however I knew if I dared to push my mother on either of these two topics then the consequences would be serious. I didn't really have the courage at that age to confront her, so I expect I just decided to let it go.

I suppose I was at junior school when I began to notice subtle changes in our lives. Mum bought a small second-hand car, she already had a driving licence, and we were able to spend weekend days away exploring the local countryside. We even had a holiday in a cottage on the Devon coast, two weeks of exploring, walking, paddling in the sea with cosy evenings playing scrabble while listening to the radio. I felt I had arrived in heaven, we had such fun. A new kitchen complete with built-in units arrived, along with new drop leaf table and two matching chairs. I was very impressed and was keen to show it all off to my friends. A new front door, shiny red, and double-glazed windows were installed, and after a lot of upheaval, we had central heating with cosy radiators in all the rooms. Money had always been tight, I soon learnt not to ask for frivolous things, as I just didn't get them, and although my mother had a good job, we were certainly not wealthy, so I had a distinct feeling this windfall of spending had nothing to do with her job. So uncertain of her reaction, I just didn't question any of this, deciding it was not worth the possibility, no probability, of either obtuse replies or worse still an escalation into a confrontation, which my mother always won. I would then spend some unhappy hours confined to my room until my, well-acted but increasingly insincere, apologies were accepted.

One very clear, sharp, memory is my eleventh birthday. It was a complete surprise, as my mother had made all the arrangements in secret, when we went on a day trip to France. I could barely contain my excitement as we boarded the ferry as foot passengers at Dover, watching the white cliffs drift out of view and then racing to the bow of the vessel to see France awaiting our arrival. It was just two hours on the ferry but a completely new world to me, everything was so different. My mother took me straight to a small, family run bakers shop off the main sea front and I had my first taste of buttery, flaky croissant still warm from the vast oven at the back. My eyes could not believe the array of superbly crafted delicious looking cakes on display, and I immediately extracted a promise to come back to take some home later in the day. Exploring the old town I saw sights and sounds that kept the questions coming for my mother, who equally seemed to be happier than I could recently remember.

Sunshine, smiles and laughter filled the morning all too quickly, then a real treat followed with lunch at a café on the sea front sitting out in the sun, the noisy seagulls wheeling overhead as the ferries bound for England chugged in and out. Eating out, apart from a picnic was unheard of for me, so this was a very special day. My mother expertly ordered our "Steak frites" and chatted away to the waiter, I was impressed, I had no idea she could speak a foreign language so well. Enjoying my large scoops of strawberry ice-cream while my mother sipped a very small cup of thick black coffee, I weighed up the options but felt I really had to comment about her interchange with the waiter.

"Mum, you speak French really well. Did you learn it at school?" A hesitation, a slow, perhaps wistful smile and she put the empty cup down.

"I did do French at school yes, but I mostly learnt to speak it from your grandmother. Did you not realise she was French?" Exactly how I was supposed to know that from our limited interaction, now many years ago, I didn't really know, perhaps talking about her more often would have helped. But I wasn't going to spoil the day with that kind of comment, and sensed I could learn more just letting my mother talk. So, I shook my head slowly and looked directly at her, encouraging more conversation.

225

"Your grandmother, my mother was a very busy important person, at least that was what she was always saying. But she made time each day to spend with me and we always spoke in French, it just seemed natural. I would tell her about my day, and she would tell stories about her childhood, she was a very good patient teacher, and I loved our special times together. She even said she had been a teacher in a small village school for a short while, but I really didn't believe her, as she was so full of strange, unusual stories. So, you see, even though I haven't used it for some time I can still remember how to have a conversation in French."

I really didn't know how to reply, this was all new to me, I just wanted her to carry on telling me about my grandmother and her childhood, subjects that were never openly discussed.

"So, my grandmother came from France? Please tell me more." Again, a slight hesitation, but my mother smiled and continued.

"I did come to France for a holiday when I was young, probably about your age. We stayed in Paris with some very old, vague relations I think. A big old house with lots of rooms, many of which were shut up, empty or had furniture draped in big white sheets. I remember endless museums and art galleries, but we did go up the Eifel Tower." She stopped and stared thoughtfully in the distance. "But now, come on, let's get going if we are to have our walk on the beach and get some of those cakes to take back home. The ferry goes in just two hours." The moment had passed but I tucked away the information for review later.

The day had yet still more revelations, certainly they would be life changing for me. On the deck of the ferry, homeward bound, we stared at the port of Calais retreating into the hazy mist of early evening, when my mother unexpectedly put her hand over mine holding on to the deck rail and began to explain. The next weekend we were going to an open day at a girl's secondary school in Sussex. Before I had time to react, she was enthusing about the facilities, the quality of the teaching and the opportunities it would give me. Some of the girls, like me would be weekly boarders, she hastily explained, but I could come home every weekend, and we could still have fun times together.

"Won't that be great," she stated, smiling an over broad smile, and for the second time in the day I was lost for words. I suppose my mouth opened and closed as I tried to think of something to say.

"But won't that be very expensive?" My first reaction practical as ever, because it wasn't the thought of boarding school that worried me, I think even then I quite fancied it, but how on earth it could be paid for. I wasn't naïve about money or the lack of it and knew posh schools cost money. I knew that as different options were presently being discussed among my friends at our junior school.

"Oh, your grandmother will pay for it. She wanted you to have the best education and made sure she left money and instructions just for that purpose." Past tense, so my grandmother wasn't alive anymore, which I had come to sort of realise, but never before had it directly acknowledged by my mother. I smiled weakly and turned to see France disappearing from view.

"OK, if that's what you want." Clearly the scheming of both my grandmother and mother had outwitted me at this point, and I seemed in no position to argue.

Chapter 3

In the end I enjoyed my time at the chosen girls' school. Among like-minded other pupils I had great fun and thrived in the supportive educational system that operated there. We were encouraged to follow what we enjoyed and work hard academically. There was a complete mix of girls, most from much more privileged back grounds than myself, but thrown together in this situation I made deep friendships.

I have a clear memory of my first few days away from home, feeling a little bewildered, often homesick and decidedly lonely. As weekly boarders we soon learnt to stick together, there were not that many of us, and with the help of a very caring House Mother, I managed to get though the first week. Only one other girl was completely new to being away from home, most had been to boarding Preparatory schools, and no-one seemed to have the same kind of close relationship I had with my mother. It seemed I not only lacked a 'Daddy' but a 'Nanny' in my short life. I counted the days till Friday when I skipped onto the train homeward bound, determined not to return for the next week.

Of course, my mother had other ideas, and after a Saturday of shouted arguments and many tears I was told, in no uncertain terms, that what I wanted didn't matter at all. My grandmother had decided my future many years ago, and I was ungrateful if I didn't realise what a marvellous opportunity she was giving me. I would 'do as I was told' and that unless I wanted to spend future weekends at the school, I had better 'sort myself out'. Sobbing quietly on my bed, more in anger at my seemingly hopeless attempts to get my mother to accept my wishes, than real sorrow, I knew and finally accepted, that I had hit the brick wall of parental decisions. I recognised futility when it raised its ugly head.

After that incident, for years the memories are blurred. I must have accepted the situation as, perhaps now, again through rose tinted glasses, I can only remember the good times. I was better than most of the others in class, and reasonably athletic on the sports field. Popular both with the teachers who were happy to reward talent and hard work, and with my peers, who laughed at my jokes and enjoyed my undemanding ability to grow friendships. OK, I was different, I might have encouraged mysterious theories about who I really was, but it all led to a full and happy life at school.

Weekends at home allowed special time with my mother who gave me her undivided attention. We remained very close and, even through my teenage years, rarely had substantial disagreements, for as previously I tried hard not to rock the boat. After all we had just two days together each week and I felt pressure to keep the atmosphere harmonious. Being the person she wanted me to be wasn't really so difficult, and it made life simpler for me as well, so of course, the subject of fathers or grandmothers was just not raised.

It wasn't that the subject was ignored elsewhere though. I spent various weekends and extended holidays in sumptuous surroundings with my much wealthier friends, villas in Tuscany, French country houses with huge swimming pools, and a vast country estate in Norfolk. Always the question was asked about my family, and I just learnt to suggest, somewhat mysteriously, that it was all very secretive, and that I could not possibly divulge any more information. If anything, it increased my popularity among my peers and their families, as I was rarely short of invitations.

I was however, determined to find out about my father and grandmother. I reasoned my mother just could not keep on ignoring the subject when I was no longer a child. What she was hiding became somewhat of an obsession for me as I grew older. Of course, I had furtively searched her bedroom for clues when alone in the house, not that it got me very far. I discovered her bedside table drawer was locked, so that must hold something worth hiding I decided, but had no idea where the key was. Bearing in mind I was not at home frequently never mind alone, it took too many hours of repetitive searching to locate a small key hidden in a book at the back of the drawer below.

I opened the narrow wooden top drawer with shaking hands and ears on full alert for her car returning to the house. Disappointment at first, her passport, some bank statements in a name I didn't understand or recognise, with a very substantial balance, and a bundle of old envelopes perhaps containing letters I didn't have time to read. Eventually under all this, a single photo of a young man in full dress military uniform. No date, no name, no clues. So, was this my father? I studied the photo seeking a resemblance in any way. A kind, broad, handsome face smiling out of the photo, he had short hair, was it dark or mid brown, you couldn't really tell, smiling eyes and what I could only describe as a suggestive, wide, boyish grin as I was old enough now to understand about boys. I returned to that photograph as often as I dared, I even considered taking it to a shop to have it copied but dared not remove it from the drawer. It would have been too much of a breach of trust if my mother had ever discovered what I had done.

When I was eighteen, and after my 'A' levels, we went on holiday to our favourite cottage in Devon. In the relaxed convivial atmosphere, I intended to ask some pertinent questions, and this time insist on the answers. My mother had suggested I bring one of my friends and was surprised when I declined, but I didn't want any distractions present, as I had planned the scenario for such a long time. When a suitable moment did arrive, I very nearly backed off, yet again, but I had to take this chance.

Now this memory is very clear, we are in the garden at the cottage, sitting on stripy garden chairs enjoying a long cool drink following a walk back from the beach. My mother's hair is windblown, and her cheeks flushed from the sea air.

"Mum, please, don't take this the wrong way, but I want to ask you some questions and I don't want to upset you, but I do need to know." I am not sure what I expected at this point, but she remained calm and seemed to encourage me to continue.

"Please talk to me about my father, really, I need to know, and my grandmother. Are they both connected? Is that why you never want to say anything about her? I really want to know about my family. Please, I don't want to upset you, but you must understand I want to know who I am." By now I was gabbling very fast trying to fill any chance of a silence and a point-blank refusal.

My mother raised her hand to stop me, put her glass on the wobbly wooden table beached white by the sea air, gave a resigned sort of half smile, and began to talk.

"I suppose it's time to tell you what happened many years ago."

Chapter 4

So now I knew, well most of it, and wondered why my mother just had not told me all these happenings before now. My grandmother had died when I was quite young, so why didn't she just tell me? Perhaps it actually meant more to her than she was really saying, or was it, as she suggested, one of those things that didn't get told for so long that it began to seem irrelevant. Even now I can't properly understand her logic, though she must have felt it was right at the time.

Of course, the revelations reawakened my curiosity about my father, and I had little control over that, it was surely natural that I wanted to know more about Philip and his family, my family. But Mum had made clear she hadn't wanted any contact with them, and they knew nothing about me, and she expected it to continue that way.

I did not want to lie to my mother, as it had never felt right. We always had a kind of unbreakable trust that made the truth, even when it was unpalatable, the only acceptable solution. However, as she wasn't going to accept my next move, and I knew some subtle untruths were going to be the only way to make it happen.

My birth certificate had revealed my father's name, Philip Deveraux. At last, my mother had felt now I had reached the age of 18 and was about to go to university, it was appropriate to let me see it following her long explanation of the circumstances surrounding my birth. Why on earth she had felt it necessary to keep it all a secret for so long I never would fully understand. She wanted me to be old enough to comprehend her actions I expect, and having kept so much to herself for so long that I suppose it just became the norm. Being denied any knowledge of her own father had perhaps set a presumption in her mind that it was 'for the best', but that was an entirely different circumstance.

Of course, I had secretly seen the photo she kept in her bedside drawer, though I felt sure she never knew that, but finding out his name and his background was a major revelation. The next move was to find out more, I felt it had to be possible even with limited resources, but I knew if I had voiced my desires, she would have forbidden any investigation, so keeping her in the dark was the only way forward.

Philip, of course that made sense, I was Philippa really, just Pippa had stuck from childhood. But such an unusual surname, Deveraux, French perhaps, though Mum made no mention of him being other than English born and bred. She let slip he was from a farming family in Sussex, it's all she ever knew as she had never met the family. A second son, so therefore he must have had a brother. Why did she not contact them after that tragic accident when she knew she was carrying their grandchild? I actually pressed this point with her, but she just said she didn't want them to feel any responsibility for her and the child, as it had been her decision to go ahead with what had been an accident of a pregnancy. Pride, I suspected, and a desire to show the world that she could cope perfectly well alone, especially to her mother, my rather frightening grandmother. I always felt my grandmother seemed to resent my presence in the world, at least that is what I sensed at the time, and now I know more, I realise that perhaps I just read the signals wrongly.

Anyway, the information I had was a good start. Our local library had all the telephone directories for the entire United Kingdom, something I had discovered killing time in the building some time ago, so surely it would be simple to track down any Deveraux in Sussex, with a name like that there couldn't be many. Add to that he had come from a farm, and I thought I stood a pretty good chance.

I escaped to the library as soon as I could and it seemed luck was on my side with a Deveraux listed at Longstone farm near Beckley nor far from Rye, surely this was a good omen. There were only two others, but those did not have a farm address, so I immediately made a plan that I knew Mum would not approve of, but equally was not going to know about.

This, of course, is where the lies came in and I found it was frighteningly easy to create the whole untruthful scenario.

233

"Mum, can I please borrow your car on Sunday next weekend?" I had learnt to drive at seventeen, my mother seeing it as an important skill for an independent woman. She looked up from her newspaper with a querying look.

"I don't see why not, but where are you going? Somewhere nice? Perhaps I should come too." This response was not to plan obviously, so the much-rehearsed fabrication would have to be used. I could only hope it would hold water.

"A school friend is having a special birthday lunch party at her parents' home in Sussex, and I would like to go." Being sent to boarding school had its uses, Mum didn't know all my friends. "So, I thought I could drive down as I would like to attend as we have all left to go to university now and we won't get together again. I won't drink any alcohol or do anything silly, honestly, it's just if I try to go by train I can't get there easily on a Sunday." A moment of consideration and then she thankfully nodded her head.

"That's fine, if you promise to be very careful and not drink any alcohol, or perhaps you would like me to come too and drop you at the party and come back later to pick you up?" Goodness I had to get out of that suggestion.

"No honestly Mum. That would take up so much of your day and I don't know how long it's going to go on. I think I really would be better off driving myself." My breath held at this moment as the plan could still go horribly wrong.

"That's fine then darling, I'll make sure there is plenty of petrol in the car. But you will be back before dark, won't you?" An inward sigh of relief. The first part of the plan arranged.

So here I was, parked at the lane end, the entrance to Longstone farm, on the following Sunday morning, not really knowing what I was going to do next. There was a big sign by the end of the lane, 'Longstone Farm and Cottages', perhaps they had holiday cottages, or maybe farm workers, I had absolutely no idea. I drove on up the lane which had a good surface and well-kept grass verges, someone cared about the appearance of the farm that was sure.

A large old farmhouse came into sight directly ahead, a big, impressive building, more like a manor house than a simple farmhouse. There was in addition, a track that led off to the left, signed 'Longstone Cottages', and the farmyard entrance with an array of huge modern barns to the right. There was nowhere nearby to easily turn the car without being seen from the house or I think I would have gone back home there and then.

I didn't have a real plan, just to 'play it by ear' and now I was here nerves were getting the better of me, but before I had a chance to decide what to do, striding out of the farmyard came a tall young man with dark curly hair wearing green overalls. Smiling he came towards the car, I got out hurriedly and smiled back, my hands shaking as I closed the car door.

"Hello. Can I help. Are you looking for someone?" He had huge dark eyes and a slightly lopsided mouth sporting a welcoming smile.

"Yes, well no. Um I mean I'm looking for Mr Deveraux." Well, why not, I thought, it's easier to set off with the truth anyway.

"Well now, you have a choice," he laughed. "There are three Mr Deveraux here. Which one do you want?" Now that threw me, and in my hesitation, he jumped back into the conversation. "Or maybe it's my mum you want. She's an honorary Deveraux, by marriage of course, and she looks after the holiday cottages, is that why you are here?" Saved in the nick of time I agreed readily, yes, I was here about the cottages, thankfully it was going to make a good cover story.

"Well, come on then, I'll take you up to the house and find her, she's bound to be around somewhere." He turned to go toward the big house.

"Oh, I don't want to put you out I can find my own way." I was trying to stop him, but he insisted, as he said he was going that way looking for his rather late mid-morning coffee anyway. I caught up with him and hurried to keep up with his long stride.

"So three Mr Deveraux," I tentatively began.

"Yep. Me, my dad and my grandpa and goodness knows how many before that. Been here a long time you see."

"You all work the farm?"

"Well mostly my dad now, my grandpa gives lots of advice, not that its always wanted you know, but he can't get into the tractor easily these days and me, well yes when I am at home from agricultural college." We were nearly at the house, and I was getting lots of information but not the bits I needed. Could I really come out and say, 'Did you have an Uncle Philip?' That would be rather too obvious I felt, but began to realise that just maybe, this young man might actually be my cousin.

He led the way with his loping stride to the back of the house, threw the door open and went in, so I followed. A big room with a cream Aga set into a stone fireplace, and double doors leading to a rather magnificent wooden conservatory furnished with some beautiful furniture. Set not far from the back door was large kitchen table where his mother was standing, at least I took it to be her, and an older man was sitting upright in an armchair by the window reading a newspaper.

"Mum, just found someone looking for the holiday lets." Wiping her hands on her apron she turned around.

"Where are they? I'm not expecting anyone today".

"Well, she's here", he stepped back and revealed me to the room.

"Hello, um I'm sorry I just followed this kind young man in," I said feeling rather foolish now.

" It's Johnny." He interrupted, "and this is my mum and grandpa. Mum where's my coffee I am desperate for a good caffeine hit this morning, and I need some of that cracking cake you made yesterday?"

"You are looking for the holiday cottages?" His mother said ignoring him, looking directly at me.

"Yes, I am looking for somewhere for a quiet weekend away to celebrate my mother's birthday. She loves the countryside round here, and someone in Rye recommended you so I hope you don't mind I was just passing the road end." I was quite shocked at my ability to ride out the situation with a fantasy story.

"That's no problem at all." She smiled. "I can show you round if you like after I get this starving young man his morning coffee and cake." Johnny grinned.

"Maybe you would like a coffee too, as it isn't every day we get a pretty young lady arrive on our doorstep." The elder Mr Deveraux had joined the conversation

"Now Dad you behave, or you'll drive this potential customer away," tutted Johnny's mother, but she was smiling as she pulled out a chair for me by the big wooden kitchen table. "Take a seat and have a coffee if you would like, I'm sorry I didn't catch your name." Without thinking I answered. It was just a reflex action.

"It's Pippa, well Philippa Legrand, and I'd love a coffee, thank you." The old man looked sharply up from his newspaper, then checked himself but I could see him watching my every move. Why had I used my real name? That was so stupid. However, the grandfather's reaction did tell me he had heard that name before, yet he wasn't willing to say anything. The hairs on the back of my neck stood up, and I realised I had to get the conversation round to Philip but how?

Johnny broke the silence with questions to his grandfather about the land he was cultivating, and the awkward moment passed. I tried asking vague open questions to facilitate talking about the farm and the family, but no one mentioned a Philip, but then why would they?

After coffee Johnny's mother took me out of the back door and round the side entrance to a small courtyard where there was a large converted wooden barn and two smaller single storey cottages. She was happy to chat away freely explaining the buildings and how they had recently been converted.

"So, all the family live in the big house?" I asked casually.

"Yes, it works out well. Having Adam's dad around means we can look after him and it makes him feel useful, also there's plenty of room for Johnny and his brother when they are both at home. His elder brother is in London, he's a solicitor, never been interested in the Farm very much, so it's working out well for Johnny, if he can concentrate long enough to get through agricultural college. So different the pair of them." She shook her head.

Go on take the lead here It may be your only chance.

"Yes, it must be difficult with two sons if they both wanted to farm." She nodded.

Go on stick your neck out.

"Did your husband have any brothers, or was he always the farming one?"

She looked sharply at me, and I felt a stab of intrusion. I wasn't any good at this. I just wanted to get in my car and go, to

237

stop all this subterfuge but now I had started it I had to be brave enough to continue.

"My husband's brother died quite young; it was tragic. So, of course, Adam stayed on the farm. Now, if you like I will get you a brochure and I can get back to cooking lunch, I have to have it ready for one o'clock, I can't hold up work on the farm." Muttering platitudes of how wonderful the cottages were, and how they were exactly what I was looking for, I followed her back to the kitchen where Johnny had gone back to work. Another man was standing with his back to me at the sink washing up a coffee mug. He turned and the likeness to my mother's hidden photo took me almost by surprise. Older of course, but the same broad shoulders, dark hair, square jaw, and expressive huge, dark eyes that my mother said I had inherited.

"I'll just go and get one of the new brochures from the study, if you can wait a moment. Won't keep you long." She bustled out of the room, and I stood staring at the two men, unable to think of what I could reasonably say that would not give me away. Then the grandfather spoke directly at the man I presumed to be Adam

"This young lady is Philippa Legrand, Adam, enquiring about the holiday cottages. Young Johnny found her in the lane, and I think he's taken quite a shine to her!" I just wanted the ground to swallow me up as Adam looked quizzically at me, then I saw some kind of recognition dawn on his face. Why had I told them my real name? It was so stupid. Obviously they recognised the name, and both knew something about my mother, but most probably not about me. I felt my feet rooted to the ground, but I had to bluff this out now, yet I couldn't think of anything sensible to say, so just stood there smiling, willing Johnny's mother to return as soon as possible.

Luckily the situation was saved as she appeared almost immediately with a brochure for the cottages in her hand. I took it and rapidly gave my thanks and retreated as fast as possible through the kitchen door.

Don't run, just walk normally to the car, they don't know anything. I tried to kid myself.

I was pleased Johnny was nowhere to be seen, so as confidently as I could manage, I reversed the car into the

238

farmyard and drove away down the lane, hands shaking on the wheel.

What on earth had I just done? How did you go about closing Pandora's box?

Chapter 5

'It had seemed like a good idea at the time.' How many times can you say that in your life I wonder, but this idea, quite honestly had not been a good one. What had possessed me into going on my undercover visit to Longstone Farm?

I drove away with my hands shaking as I clung desperately to the steering wheel, I just needed to get away, put miles between me and them as fast as possible. However, it quickly dawned on me I couldn't go directly home, as I had told Mum I would be out most of the day, and the last thing I wanted was to create suspicion. A road sign ahead pointed to a National Trust Property, Scotby Castle, so almost on autopilot I turned off the main highway and arrived in the car park on a busy Sunday lunchtime. Lost in the family crowds, I wandered in the garden and made my way down to the small castle in the grounds, finding a quiet bench in the sunshine. I kept going over and over in my head the encounter from just a few hours ago, yet I could not explain my stupidity of using my real name. It was just a reflex action, as I wasn't used to, or very good at lying, simple as that.

It became increasingly clear as I returned in my head to the conversations and reactions that certainly the grandfather and his son knew the 'Legrand' name. Mum had clearly stated she had never met Philip's family, as the short time she and Philip had been together was in Germany. But had Philip told his family of his new girlfriend? That much she didn't know and so neither did I. Mum had also been adamant that she did not attend the funeral as she felt she would have been unable to cope emotionally, and it would have felt like she was intruding, despite Philip meaning so much to her. Did one of his army friends mention her to the family? There were many possibilities, but I was increasingly sure Philip's family knew, at the very least, something of his relationship with my mother.

As to whether they knew about me, that was more complicated. Mum herself didn't know till about 3 months after Philip's death, so it was unlikely that any of his army friends would have known to pass the news to his family. She had left the army base in the February of the year I was born, so news via his army friends seemed a somewhat tenuous suggestion. No, I began to realise, I was as much a surprise to them, as they were to me.

I had been sitting for over half an hour mulling over the situation, knowing I couldn't change what had happened, but I needed to decide very carefully what I would do next. I knew Mum would not be happy with my news, in fact that was an understatement if I was certain about anything! But I doubted I could pretend nothing had happened and what if they, the Deverauxs used the same tactics to find me or worse still, my mother. I was going to have to face this rather unpleasant music sooner rather than later.

I realised I had eaten nothing since breakfast, so slowly walked back to the courtyard cafe for a coffee and slice of sticky cake to boost my energy levels for the drive back to London. I would have to go home sometime, but my confession might take more time to be forthcoming.

I managed to hold out for almost two days, although Mum knew almost immediately that there was something wrong. She had kept asking from the moment I had arrived back on Sunday, as I suppose I was uncommunicative and preoccupied, for which there was every reason for me to be. By Tuesday early evening I knew that the whole episode had to come into the open, while realising I had to be prepared for a distinctly uncomfortable time. I found Mum sitting reading the newspaper in the small lounge at the front of our house.

"Pippa whatever is the matter? All this quiet moping about is just not normal for you. Are you worried about your A level results? I'm sure everything will be fine. Your teachers are very happy with all your work." Gosh, my A level results; those had gone right out of my mind. But it was time to own up and clear the air.

"It's not that, but I do want to talk to you about something. Promise you will listen to my whole story before you say anything, please. I know you aren't going to be pleased so it will be easier if you can just listen, honestly."

Mum looked apprehensive and none too happy but having started I had to go through with it now. So, slowly, and as concisely as possible, I told her the whole story about what had happened on Sunday. I didn't leave out any detail, and made it clear I had planned the entire visit but had not really thought things through. When I explained my blunder of giving my real name, my mother let out a gasp, and shook her head slowly, though to be fair she did not interrupt me, just let me talk on. I tried of course to put as much 'gloss' on the affair as I could, but basically, I knew that was not going to work. I had to put up with the fact I was in some very deep water here and Mum was not going to throw any lifelines, so eventually I stopped talking.

Initially silence, I suspected Mum was trying to take in the enormity of my actions. Then she spoke in a carefully measured, but distinctly angry, tone.

"What upsets me most Pippa, is not what you have done, though God knows that is bad enough, but that you lied to me and actively deceived me. Just ask yourself, how can I ever trust you again?" She was so right, and I knew it, I had no defence for the lying and deceit. This first repost from her cut right into my heart, and I just wanted to curl up and die. I only had my mother, and I knew now I had ruined our trust. Uncontrollable tears rolled down my cheeks as I had no answer to this, yet I knew more was to come.

"I can, believe it or not, understand your desire to know more about your father. Do remember I have been in your position, but there are ways and means of going about this. What did you think you were doing just turning up on a stranger's doorstep trying to find out personal information by deception? To be quite honest I am so taken aback by your actions that I really don't know what to say to you."

"Please Mum I didn't mean any harm, I just thought I could find out something about my father. I know it was wrong, but I don't know how to put it right."

"Perhaps you should have thought about all that before setting off on this silly stupid course of action. I explained to you why I didn't want any help or recognition from Philip's family. Philip knew nothing about you, and although I wanted you desperately when I discovered I was pregnant you were, I am sorry to say, a mistake. We were two people very much in love, but we knew each other for just a few precious months, it was my decision and mine alone to keep you. Who knows what might have been if fate had not taken him away? But what happened meant those choices had gone. Philip is your biological father, but you are not, as far as I am concerned one of his family. Have I made myself clear?"

I nodded, tears still rolling down my cheeks unable to say anything, not daring to contradict my mother's wishes even though they went against everything I had been feeling since Sunday. I had a real live family out there and I desperately wanted to get to know them. Anger still flashed in her eyes, I saw there was more to come, as this matter was not closed.

"For now, please go to your room, and stay there. I will talk to you in the morning. I need time to think. But take it as read that you are in serious trouble." Leaving the room, I tried hard to walk nonchalantly as if I wasn't upset or worried, a nice try, but not actually working.

With my conscience unloaded I had a good night's sleep, however, by the look of my mother who was already seated at the kitchen table the next morning, she had not. We exchanged basic greetings, and I made myself some coffee and toast. Mum was supposedly reading the newspaper, but she hadn't turned a page since I came in.

"Pippa, I need to talk to you." Of course, I had expected this, with my mother's last repost about being in deep trouble I was as ready as you can be for another tongue lashing, for which I knew I had no defence. I sat down opposite her and noticed she looked tired and suddenly older than I remembered, and this was most probably all my fault.

243

"Pippa, I have done a lot of thinking. Yes, a very disturbed night. You need to know I am still very upset and disappointed in your deceit, because I had thought our relationship did not allow any lies. Perhaps you don't understand, but the last thing I want is the kind of mother and daughter relationship I had with my mother. I have always tried to be honest with you. So why did you lie to me?"

A huge sigh from me as I felt tears rising again, my mother's disappointment hurt more than any angry words. I felt unable to speak and keep my tears back so just shook my head, looked at the table and mumbled, "I'm really sorry."

"You see Pippa, I spent a good deal of my teenage years deceiving my mother, as she was so controlling. I think she wanted to protect me but did not realise life had moved on from her closeted upbringing before the war in Paris. I became very good at doing what I wanted without her knowing, but it put a huge strain on our relationship, and we grew apart so very quickly. She had her work; I had my life that she knew little about, so we had nothing in common. Once I had left for university, and as I have told you she didn't want me to go to York but stay in London, I spent very little time at home and even less with my mother. I just don't want that to happen to us."

I looked up from my close examination of the surface of the kitchen table, my eyes shiny with tears.

"That's not going to happen, honestly Mum." A silence, I could see she was looking to find the right words before beginning to speak.

"I have been doing a lot of thinking and accept that it is only natural that you should want to know about your father's family. I also know that I shouldn't stand in your way. I have given you my reasons for never contacting them, and they remain the same. Keeping you was my decision, Philip never knew about you so I have no idea what he would have wanted. I resolved that you were my responsibility and hated to think his family would feel obliged to help me. I didn't want or need help, as I have always made my own way in life. Your grandmother's estate was left to you in trust, as you know, for your education and any income from that trust to me to help bring you up. We've never been poor, Pippa, as I had a good job and a profession I could rely on. I just

244

wanted to you to grow up the best way possible and give you the chances you deserved, and I hope I have done that."

"Of course, you have Mum. You have always done the right things for me even if I didn't know it at the time."

"I am not so selfish as to make you take a choice, so it's not going to be me or Philip's family, as that would not be fair. I have to accept, and I have, that if you want to continue your desire to get to know them, then I should not stand in your way. But please tread carefully and respect my wishes not to be included in this matter." Emotion got the better of me at this point and I moved round the table and put my arms around my mother and helplessly sobbed into her shoulder. She stroked my hair and held me tight.

Later that afternoon, with time for reflection we sat side by side on the sofa in the living room talking, not about Philip, but life at university, my mother's reminiscences and the adventures that the opportunity would bring for me. However, that evening Mum brought me the photo that I already secretively knew she kept in her bedside drawer, and simply handed it to me.

"That's Philip," she said quietly. "That's your father."

Chapter 6

The last thing I wanted to do was upset Mum again, so I didn't mention Philip or his family after those traumatic two days. My mother gradually returned to her resilient, cheerful self, and perhaps the ghost had been exorcised, for now anyway. I did notice her photo of Philip was now clearly displayed on her bedside table, and for that I was pleased, now she could have her memories out in the open. I wondered why she could not have shown the photo to me before, but I doubted I would ever fully understand her thinking.

What she had said about my grandmamma had quite shocked me. I had only been young when she died very suddenly. It was all very disturbing at the time, and I stayed extra time with my 'Auntie Helen' for a few days, but never really realised what was going on. She had always looked after me while my mum was at work but wasn't my real Auntie. Mum sort of came and went in a frenzied manner for those days, explaining to me that she didn't know when she was going to be home, but never mentioning my grandmamma had died. I only gradually realised she was no longer with us when we stopped our ritual visits.

I had never picked up on the tension between Grandmamma and Mum, but then I was only 5 or 6 when the visits stopped. I have vague recollections of sitting on my grandmother's knee in a huge room with big windows, my mother hastily telling me to sit still and be good. Later when I was older, I spent the visits mostly in the garden, out of hearing of the conversation between them.

It seemed to me to be tragic that there was so little love between them, as I couldn't imagine not wanting to be with Mum or being unable to talk to her about anything and everything. That must have made Mum feel very lonely, and I thought back to the times I had clashed with her over small things that seemed to mean a lot to me at the time and felt ashamed I had stupidly suggested she did not love me, when she clearly was bringing me up completely on her own with no one else in her life. I resolved that, however much I wanted contact with Philip's family, I still couldn't quite say 'my father', it was not going to affect my relationship with my mother. Yet, this gave me a considerable dilemma.

So, in true Pippa fashion I did nothing about contacting the Deveraux family again. I always thought that if something was to be then it would happen, as engineering the situation generally didn't work, and anyway this way I could prevaricate for a longer time.

So, when the telephone rang one afternoon about two weeks later, I was totally unprepared for the conversation. It was a good job Mum was out.

"Hi Pippa. It's Johnny here." Johnny? Oh, my goodness that Johnny. How on earth had he got our telephone number? Come to think of it probably exactly the same way I had got his address.

"Hi Johnny, what a surprise. How are you?"

"Fine Pippa. Look I'm ringing from a phone box so can't talk for long, but how about we meet up this weekend, Saturday any good? I could meet you at Headcorn station? There are direct trains from London so that makes it easier for you. I think you and I have a lot to talk about. Please, I do want to talk to you." So, of course I agreed. I wanted very much to talk to him, though I got the distinct impression the rest of his family was most probably in the dark about the meeting.

With the meeting arranged I was back to square one with Mum, as I had promised not to deceive her again, but I was worried that informing her about the meeting with Johnny would bring back her sleepless nights and anxiety. So, this time I just went for the truth, plain and simple, and before I lost the impetus I cornered her at teatime.

"Mum please don't get upset but I have arranged to meet Johnny on Saturday." At first, she looked puzzled.

"Johnny?"

"Yes Mum, I promised not to lie to you, and I won't. Johnny Deveraux rang up yesterday, I don't know how he got the phone number, I certainly didn't give it to him, but he wants to meet to talk. So, I said yes. I don't think the rest of his family knows and I am not going to the farm. It is OK, isn't it? You said I could meet the family if I wanted. I won't talk about you if you don't want me to."

Letting out an exasperated sigh, she closed her eyes and turned her head away.

Silence. I just waited, as she had now to make a decision.

I could have made up an excuse again, deceived her, but I had promised not to, so if she really didn't want me to go, she was now going to have to tell me directly and stop pretending all this was my fault somehow.

"Oh Pippa, I just worry you are getting into a situation that is going to cause all sorts of problems."

"So, you don't want me to go?"

"I didn't say that. I, well, I……….. Oh, go if you must but don't involve me in any of the problems it is going to cause." She sounded bitter and angry.

"Mum please understand, it's not going to change us in any way if it's that what concerns you. You are my mum, no one is going to take your place. You said you wouldn't stand in my way, and I upset you by lying, so now I tell the truth you blame me again. What do you want me to do?" By now a degree of impatience and irritation had crept into my voice.

"I just don't see how you are going to keep me out of all this."

"Would it be such a bad thing for them to get to know you and me. After all I am their granddaughter and niece? I really can't follow your reasons. Yes, at the time you didn't want them to feel as if they had to help you, but you have made your own way in life now. We are 18 years further on. Don't you think Philip would want his father to know his only child?"

My mother turned to face me directly her eyes blazing in anger.

"How dare you? You have no idea what Philip wanted and neither do I, so please don't presume anything about someone you never knew. If you want to pursue this obsession then go ahead, but don't run to me when it all becomes a dreadful problem. You realise, once you start this there is no turning back."

She left the room before I had a chance to speak. It was clear she didn't want me to meet Johnny, but I was equally certain I was going to.

Chapter 7

As the train pulled into Headcorn station, I caught a glimpse of Johnny leaning his tall frame against the exit gate. He had been clad in green overalls at the farm, and those were none too well fitting, but now you could see the broad shoulders that seemed to run in the Devereux family. He looked as if he had taken some time to make himself presentable in clean jeans and a checked short-sleeve shirt. I had wavered about what to wear but eventually decided on a cotton dress with a cardigan hoping the weather kept warm.

Not many people got off the train at Headcorn, I suspected it would be busy with commuters in the week, so it didn't take long for Johnny to spot me and wave. Now as to greeting, Johnny took the lead, for which I was thankful, with his hand held out quite formally ready to grasp mine. A strong firm handshake and that ready lopsided smile was a good start I reckoned.

"Come on, I've got mum´s car so we can go to a nice pub for a drink and a chat, if that's OK." My nodded agreement, followed by a short drive which found us at a pleasant country pub with a shady garden. The conversation on the drive having been taken up by questions about my travel, we were obviously going to wait until we were established with a drink to get down to business.

"Do your family know you are here with me?" I got the question in first. I had to ask as it made a difference as to what I would reveal, and he was happy to tell the truth which was a good start.

"No. They just think I am off meeting mates for the afternoon. Why does it make a difference?"

"Well, that depends on what we talk about but having got into deep trouble with my mother over my first visit that she knew nothing about, I just wanted to know the lie of the land, so to speak." Johnny smiled, perhaps ruefully, and took a sip of beer.

"So," he cautiously began, "Why did you come to see us? It wasn't about the holiday cottages, was it? Dad and Grandpa have been talking secretively since your visit. There is something they are not telling me or sharing with Mum, and I think I have an idea but go on, answer my first question. Why did you arrive at the farm looking for a Mr Deveraux?" My turn now.

"Johnny, hold on a moment, first a question as it could change everything. Did your father have a brother called Philip who was in the army?"

"Yes, my Uncle Philip died in an accident while in the army just after I was born. Is that why Dad and Grandpa have been having quiet conversations?". Now the whispered, half heard comments Johnny had overhead in the past week or two started to make sense. "You told us your real name didn't you, I thought you must have made it up but, no when I tried it was easy to find your telephone number. Legrand is a very unusual name."

"Well, so is Deveraux."

"It's Norman, my family can be traced right back to the Norman conquest." Came the slightly arrogant reply, with a toss of his head.

"Anyway," I explained. "The problem was I just wasn't prepared or very good at lying when your mother suddenly asked my name. I realised then it was a silly thing to do, and that your grandpa recognised the name immediately."

"You are dead right he did, so did my dad apparently."

"But they didn't let on, and your mother seemed unaware of any significance, so I just lost my nerve at that moment and got away as soon as possible."

"Well," said Johnny slowly and deliberately. "How do you fit in here or am I just missing something obvious?"

In for a penny..........

"Philip Deveraux is my father according to my birth certificate." Suddenly the chatter on the nearby tables seemed loud as Johnny took all this in and remained silent. So, I continued.

"I was only given my birth certificate recently, as before then my mother would never talk about who my father was, and I had given up asking. It was the one thing that caused friction between us, it still does. She did not want me to meet you today but having discovered you all existed I needed to find out more."

"Now it really does make sense", said Johnny letting out a huge sigh. "I overheard a conversation between Dad and Grandpa in the barn. Couldn't hear properly but something about Dad knowing the name, and then something about Uncle Philip's funeral, but I was too far away to catch the full story. They went quiet as soon as they saw me."

"My mother says she and Philip were friends, well more than that obviously," I suddenly felt embarrassed, "in the summer before the accident. They spent a lot of time together and went on holiday to Lake Constance in the August. Then Philip was killed early in September, and my mother didn't even realise she was expecting me till about 3 months later. She says that Philip never knew about me, it was her decision to keep me, and she felt it was wrong to contact his family because she thought they would presume she wanted help. She was adamant it was her choice to keep me, and she wanted to bring me up without feeling obligated to anyone." Johnny took all this in and slowed the pace with a sip of beer and a thoughtful expression.

"No one speaks about my Uncle Philip anymore. I suppose at the time it would have been a shocking experience, but I was only a baby, so I never knew him. It's something now as a family that just isn't brought up in conversation." A pause here from Johnny. "So actually, you are my cousin." He laughed, again rather ruefully, "Just as a pretty girl appears in my life, I find I am related to her. That's my usual luck I'm afraid!"

I felt my cheeks burning and guessed I was blushing. I actually found Johnny's company enjoyable but wouldn't dare to admit it. Perhaps this is what a young Deveraux man was like, maybe Johnny took after his uncle, so now I could see exactly what had attracted my mother.

"Why on earth did your mother keep you secret?" He continued. "There is a readymade family here who would have no doubt welcomed her, and you, with open arms? From my grandpa's point of view, it might have helped with the loss of his son. What on earth was she thinking?"

"I understand Johnny, but you just don't know my mother. She is a very strong, independent woman, so the last thing she wanted do would be to ask for help. I think the problem is bound up in the difficult relationship she had with her mother, and the feeling she had to make her own way in the world."

"But if she loved Philip then why....."

"I don't doubt the depth of her relationship with Philip. It's only recently she has begun to talk about him but it's clear they were happy and very much in love. She just lights up when she talks to me about him. Phillip just loved life she says, he had lots of friends, was well thought of as an officer, played sports particularly rugby, and was happiest in the outdoors. In fact, mum says she kept her academic abilities hidden at first when Philip told her about his preference for sport over lessons and his mediocre school record. The army life suited him, but it seems he also had a soft gentle side when he was with Mum."

"Now I know where I get it from. My elder brother seemed to get all the brains, highflyer at school, university with a first, now forging ahead in a law practice in London, and me, well, scraped into Agri college, and always being hounded by my Mum to complete the course, even though I learn much more from Dad at home. At least it's a laugh at college with my mates if nothing else."

A relaxed silence as I think we both took in the information that had come out into the open. I caught myself watching Johnny and wondering how much he really was like Philip. I would just love to see my mother interact with him, but I guessed that was never going to happen. He had an easy confident manner, there was something engaging about him with that ever present, slightly lopsided, wide mouthed grin giving him an optimistic air which made him enjoyable company. I bet he was popular with his year group at the college but maybe not so much with the teachers.

"Your mum, she just doesn't want to know us?"

"Oh, I think that's a bit harsh. It's all about the circumstances."

" OK, but her choice of circumstances meant my grandma, who died about 5 years ago, never knew her only granddaughter." I was a bit shocked by his reply but could see his point of view, the last thing I wanted was to instigate an argument.

253

"Oh, Johnny that's not really fair. I don't want to argue but please just look at this from my mum´s perspective." He looked down into his glass and avoided eye contact for the first time. I felt had to tell him as much of our story as I could so he could see why Mum had acted that way all those years ago.

"Look Johnny, it complicated but listen, I don't know the full story myself, but it seems my grandmother was French, arriving in England just before the war, very young . My mum doesn't even know but somehow Grandmamma ended up working as a translator for the government and fell pregnant. Apparently Grandmamma would never talk to my mum about who was her father and believe me she says she tried. My grandmamma never married and brought Mum up single handed, continuing to work all the time for the government. She must have had a good job as Mum had Nannies and lived in a large house. Although she may have been small in stature, but she was very strict and controlling, though I really can't remember her much, she died when I was about 6 or 7, but she could be kind to me." The clear memory of the orange sweet wrapped in cellophane being given to me when I was crying sprang into my mind. I shook it off to concentrate, I had to make Johnny understand.

"Anyway, Mum learnt to be independent from an early age, she didn't and doesn't need anyone. At least that is what she wants the world to think. She had let her guard down to allow Philip into her life, then he was suddenly taken away. It seems her mother didn't approve of her keeping the baby, at least that's what I gather, so Mum just wanted to do things her way. She had a good profession, she's a great teacher with a good job, and felt no need for anyone's help, wanting to get on with her life and bring me up as she felt was right. She still is opposed to my seeking out Philip's family, your family, but won't stand in my way, I do hope you can try to understand." Johnny sat back in his chair and studied my face.

"Well, I'll tell you something, you Legrand women are a formidable force. I wouldn't get in the way of any of you in a hurry, that's for sure!" He let that statement hang in the air while he continued to search my face for a reaction. I just took a sip of my drink and smiled. I think he was actually beginning to understand.

"So, I said breaking the spell, "Where do we go from here? Do you think I should meet your family properly? Or what's the next step, all supposing you want there to be one?" I held my breath as I waited for a reply.

Chapter 8

Sitting on the train as I made my way back home, I thought through the day's events. Meeting Johnny had probably posed as many questions as it had answered, but I had been able to confirm that I had indeed found my father's family, though of course, the next question was, *"What now?"*

Johnny had been great company, and I really did think he felt the same. I was, I decided, going to leave it up to him to make the next step, as he knew what I really wanted, or at least thought I did, with the situation ever changing nothing was sure. I had made it clear I would like to meet the rest of the family, but only if he felt that could be done without any upset of the kind I had visited on my mother.

Our farewell had been rushed and brief, as the train was already pulling into the station at Headcorn when we got to the car park. I had grabbed my bag and was exiting the car with shouts of "thanks, hope to see you soon," when Johnny suddenly grabbed an A5 brown envelope from the door pocket and pushed it in my hand, saying "I had this copied for you." Surprise, and with no time to open it, meant I just took the envelope and ran to catch the train, with a fleeting wave to Johnny in the car.

Once on the train I opened the envelope to reveal a photo that had obviously been taken for a newspaper or magazine. It showed Johnny, his father and grandfather all standing in front of a piece of large farm machinery dressed carefully, but casually in jeans and toning, checked shirts, all smiling the ´Deveraux´ wide smile at the camera. Goodness knows what the article was about, maybe three generations of a farming family, but it was kind of Johnny to make me a copy. It was of course, thought provoking as I immediately wondered if he had really meant it to be shown to my mother, again making me wonder how much I should keep from her about the meeting. She was right of course; I had started something over which I had no control and that all this could run away with me in an instant. If I began to choose what to tell her and what to withhold then I knew I was heading for a dreadful mess, as I had already proved lying was just not my strong point. I would have to make up my mind quickly as I was nearing home and Mum would no doubt expect an update, despite claiming she wanted nothing to do with my family seeking exploits.

Opening the front door quietly, with the hope of buying myself some extra time, I found Mum in the hall with the post in her hand. No luck there then. Smiling I gave her an impulsive kiss on the cheek and a hug, just because I could, I suppose. The more I found out, the more I realised the sacrifices and sheer willpower that she had undertaken to bring me up, and the more I realised I had not always shown enough, or sometimes any, gratitude.

"Pippa," she smiled. "Had a good day?" At least she seemed in a receptive mood so now was as good as any to tell her my news.

"Come and sit down, Mum I have lots to tell you but first, would you like a cup of tea, I know I would?" We settled, eventually, either side of the kitchen table and, as I had already decided, I simply passed the photo across the table.

"This is Johnny with his dad, Adam and his grandfather. Adam is Philip's brother. Johnny confirmed he had an Uncle Philip who was killed while in the army when he was just a baby." I left the explanation at that knowing that my mother would not hear any more of what I was saying. She stared at the photo, quietly got up from her chair, and crossing to the kitchen window, held it in the sunlight, to see the detail more clearly. I could see the photo shining in the light, but my mother was sideways on to me so I could not clearly see her expression. I decided just to wait and let her have time to come to terms with the information in the photo.

The silence seemed to stretch out, then she turned, and I noticed her eyes shiny with tears. Of course, this was exactly what I didn't want, but as if she knew what I was going to say, she shook her head.

"I'm alright, honestly, it just brings back so many memories. Adam is so like Philip, or what Philip would have become, but

Johnny, oh Johnny is just a younger version of Philip when I met him. It makes it all seem like just yesterday." She looked away again and I could tell she didn't want me to see her cry. She took her handkerchief out of her pocket, blew her nose and dried her eyes before returning to the table with a fixed smile that didn't fool me at all.

I quietly went on to tell her about my day and the information I had gleaned. I told her carefully about Johnny overhearing conversations between his father and grandfather that seemed to confirm they knew about her, but seemingly not about me. He seemed to think someone at the funeral had mentioned her, but Johnny could only guess. I told her that I had given a brief history as far as I knew it about my grandmother and mother, but also that I made it clear that this was totally my initiative and mine alone.

"I didn't commit myself, and certainly not you, to anything further, please believe me and I have left it up to Johnny to get in touch again if he wants. Oh Mum, really if all this is going to upset you then maybe I should just forget it and get on with my life. Is that what you want me to do? It's just, oh I don't know, I'm not clear about anything anymore." A short silence hung in the air.

"You see, Johnny was such good company, great fun to be with, very easy going and entertaining, always smiling and so full of funny stories." I stopped talking as I realised my mother was looking directly at me. She was smiling this time.

"So was Philip. You have just described him so beautifully." Then again, she looked away lost in her vivid memories.

Chapter 9

"Are you sure you want to do this?" I asked Johnny, though really it was far too late to change our minds now, as I had already arrived.

"Well, you wanted to meet the family, so here's your chance," came the reply. It had been Johnny's idea. 'Come and watch a village cricket match,' was his suggestion, because he and his dad played, his grandpa loved to watch, and his mum would probably be involved with the teas. Perfect, a meeting on neutral territory, so it had seemed like a good idea at the time. Now where had I thought that before?

"Grandpa is really looking forward to meeting you properly. He knows you are coming but you will be a surprise to Dad and Mum if you want to see them." Johnny had it all planned, so what could go wrong?

"Grandpa is usually on my side," he explained. "Dad and I don't always see eye to eye about things, so I thought Grandpa was a great place to start. Look he is over there in the shade." Under a large oak tree at the far side of the immaculate cricket pitch sat an older man wearing a beige Panama hat. An empty folding chair was waiting beside him, so we walked slowly over.

"Here she is Grandpa. You remember Pippa?" Grandpa Deveraux insisted on getting up and taking my hand. Not a shake but a hold as he gazed into my face and smiled a huge welcoming grin. So that's where the sons got it from, I thought.

"Pippa, at last, please sit down there where I can see you." He gestured to the empty chair. "Now you can go away Johnny, I want this pretty young lady to myself." A hint of playfulness in his voice, and Johnny smiled, waving to us as he set off back to the pavilion.

"Now young lady, Johnny tells me you are Phillip's daughter and goodness me I can see you are. Where have you been for the last 18 years? But never mind you are making an old man very happy now".

"Mr Deveraux"

"Grandpa, please."

"Oh, all right, thank you, Grandpa, I don't know how much Johnny has told you, but I have only just discovered who was my father."

"Yes, yes, he has told me everything about you and your mother, mind I don't think his father knows yet, so that's a bit of a ticking time bomb there, but then that's Johnny for you. He and his dad don't always get on, so I try to make peace in the middle but sometimes I just want to bang their two heads together." He shook his head smiling. "But it's so good to meet you at last. We had no idea you even existed."

"I'm so sorry Mr Deveraux, I mean Grandpa, I hope Johnny has explained. First though, I want to apologise for just turning up on your doorstep a while back. I really hadn't thought things through, and got into such dreadful trouble with my mother, when I told her."

"She likes things done properly, does she? A woman after my own heart. But I am so glad you did, I just wish we had known all this sooner. Yes, Johnny explained, and I can see your mother didn't want us to feel obligated to help in any way, but you are my only Granddaughter." He paused and suddenly looked serious.

"You see no parent ever expects to bury their own child." He stopped and turned away. I could sense the emotion in the air, so leaning forward I grasped his gnarled, arthritic hand. After a silence as he collected himself.

"Philip lived for the moment, you see. He used to drive me mad as a youngster never settled to anything, so the army was a God send. He was happier than we could have hoped. Yes, there were girls, always one or even two on his arm, he was a handsome chap, but never anyone special he said. Then just before he died, he told Adam he had found someone, so special he was going to ask her to marry him and bring her home to the farm on his next leave. They joked about her name as Philip said she was halfway to bring an honorary Deveraux because she had a French family name, Legrand. But of course, that was never to be. At the funeral which, to be quite honest, I cannot recollect in any detail, Adam talked to one of Philip's friends who told him all about a young lady called Stephanie Legrand, and how she and Philip were about to get engaged when the accident happened. If only she had come to the funeral, we could have got to know her." He stopped, shaking his head slowly. "But she didn't, so she, and then you were lost to us." Again, a pause as he looked away gathering himself, I held onto his hand, feeling guilty for bringing this upset so close to the surface after such a long time.

"Anyway," he continued. "A few weeks after the funeral, a small box came with Philip's personal effects from the army. I didn't want to upset Elsie my wife again, so I told no one and put it at the back of the wardrobe in the spare room and quite honestly forgot about it over the years." A silence as he seemed to gather his thoughts.

"A long time later, a good 10 years on, I suppose I found it while looking for something and eventually opened it. Nothing too unusual really, his campaign medals, some books, you know the kind of thing. Well, at the bottom tucked half in a book was a photo, a holiday snap, not a formal posed photograph, and this is it." He passed me a slightly faded photograph of Philip with his arm around my mother. In the background was a large body of water and behind that some mountains. I gasped.

" It's them at Lake Constance the summer before I was born." I turned the photo over and deciphered 'August 1978.' At this point I opened my bag and pulled out a more formal photo of my mother sitting beside my grandmother with a baby on her knee.

"That's my mother, my grandmother and me in 1980." He studied it and smiled.

"Now I can see that's the same pretty young lady, for sure."

I passed Grandpa Deveraux some more photos I had brought. It had been difficult to find many, in fact any, of Mum and I together, though not surprising really, as we had no one else to take them. However there were some of me growing up and ones I had taken with my mother in. He studied each photo with great care.

"I hope I am not upsetting you, it's the last thing I want to do."

"No, love, no, not in any way, but I just can't help thinking about what might have been, if only we had known."

Our thoughts were interrupted by a muted round of applause and the two teams walked out onto the pitch. I had never watched a cricket match before and listened attentively as Grandpa gave me an introduction to the proceedings. It seemed Johnny and his dad played regularly for the village team. Today they had lost the toss and were fielding first.

"Johnny's a pretty good fast bowler, but don't you go telling him I said so! His dad is a good batsman and bowls more of slow spinner."

We watched the play and chattered away. Grandpa was easy to talk to and seemed genuinely interested in what I was telling him. He was impressed that I was off to university that autumn, especially when he found out I was to study engineering.

"I know," I said, when he expressed surprise. "Mum is pretty taken aback too. She got a degree in English and that's what she teaches, but me well, always been more scientific and practical. She says my grandmamma would have been proud, but I know so little about her and Mum doesn't like to talk about Grandmamma Cecile, so I don't really know if there is any family connection."

We both stopped chatting to watch Johnny bowl. He seemed pretty good at it to me, but then I wasn't exactly an expert, and it did occur to me that he might be trying to impress, well just a little perhaps. One particular delivery saw the ball knock the centre stump right out of the ground, and everyone clapped loudly. Adam came on to bowl next and had a completely different style but managed to get the player out with an easy catch. The teams then walked off the pitch to the pavilion.

"Off for their tea then the home side will bat. We have got a good chance of winning here if we play carefully." Johnny appeared from the pavilion, carrying a tray with a cup, a glass of lemonade and some rather good-looking homemade cake. Following behind came his father, and I suddenly felt very nervous. Johnny had warned his grandpa I was coming, but apparently, I was a surprise to his father, and I was unsure about how he would actually feel about me. I realised that the sudden arrival of Philip's daughter might, in his mind anyway, put obstacles into the succession of the farm. I didn't want anything from the family, except friendship I suppose, but legally I was Phillip's heir, and I was intelligent enough to realise that that fact could pose problems in the future.

Oh Johnny, was this such a good idea.

Johnny arrived first with the refreshments. His father close behind with an expression that was difficult to read.

"So, Miss Legrand," his father began. "You have come back to see us." Was there a hint of sarcasm? I tried not to hear it.

"Yes, hello again. Its lovely to see you all." A bit limp but I wanted to be as non-contentious as possible.

"Johnny has filled me in, eventually, as it seems you and he are well acquainted." This time I felt the barb of sarcasm. Grandpa jumped in, as I think he could sense the tension in the air.

"Pippa has brought some lovely photos to show me. She's great company and we are having a splendid afternoon."

"So long as you are happy Dad that's what's important here." He paused. No one seemed to know what to say, least of all me. Then looking straight at me he asked," Are we going to see you again?"

"Oh, I do hope so," interjected Grandpa, "and next time at the farm."

"Great," interrupted Johnny. "We will fix a date. I know, why not come for Sunday lunch. Mum does a cracking roast." Grandpa nodded in agreement and the plan seemed agreed in principle, even if a little reluctantly by Adam, before Johnny and he returned to the pavilion. I felt I had to say something to Grandpa.

"I am not sure Adam is pleased to see me, and I really don't want to make any trouble in the family. Perhaps its best I don't come to the farm."

"Don't be silly." Grandpa was firm in his voice. "He just wasn't expecting you today so it would be a bit of a shock. The trouble is Johnny doesn't always think things through, but his heart is in the right place. You are coming to Sunday lunch at the farm, whether he likes it or not! You leave Adam to me. You are my granddaughter, and I am not losing you again."

The players returned to the field and Grandpa's explanation continued. Cricket just wasn't one of my specialities, so to speak, hockey or tennis now there I was pretty good and had played for my school. Adam would be coming out to bat at number four but Johnny, who was primarily a bowler, was at number eight. We sat watching and occasionally applauding the runs with my talking most of the time. Grandpa Deveraux seemed very content to listen, and I felt very relaxed and happy in his company. Adam came out to play and was obviously a proficient batsman. He was careful and quite stylish, even I could see that, and scored a good number of boundaries pushing the home side's score along quickly.

"Adam used to play for the under 18's county side," confided Grandpa proudly. "Cricket was too slow for Philip, but he played rugby really well, always coming home covered in mud. Elsie used to make him take all his clothes off by the washing machine, even though he was supposed to have had a shower." He smiled to himself again. Not for the first time I hoped I was doing the right thing bringing all these memories to the surface.

Adam kept on scoring runs, but his main problem was keeping a batting partner at the other end of the pitch. The wickets seemed to be falling with increasing regularity to a rather clever fast bowler from the opposing side. Johnny appeared at the crease, as number eight and the home side still had sixteen runs to score to ensure victory. It was all getting quite tense, so he stopped for a quick chat to his father before taking up his position to face the fast bowler.

"No doubt Adam has just told him to play carefully and not to take any risks," confided Grandpa. "Not that Johnny will take any notice, as usual." Grandpa made me smile, he knew his family very well. He was right of course Johnny didn't have the poise and style of his father, but he followed instructions and safely batted out the last few balls of the over, so the strike went back to Adam. Between them they scored twelve runs in the next over, now just four to go, but Johnny was back facing the fast bowler. He slashed at a bouncing ball and clipped it high, but luckily no one was in catching distance. The next ball saw him push it away carefully and they got two more runs. The following delivery bounced high in front of Johnny, he stepped forward and soundly smacked it toward the boundary for a score of four. They had won. I jumped off my seat and clapped enthusiastically. It had been a lot more thrilling than I had expected.

"That was so exciting. I am so pleased I came."

"So am I my dear. So am I." Grandpa Deveraux was smiling from ear to ear.

Chapter 10

Pippa, three years later.
Summer 2000 aged 21

"Mum, Mum, I did it! I got a good 2:1! I've got my place for my post grad course next year". I knew I was shouting down the phone, but I really couldn't contain my excitement, relief, and sheer exuberance.

"Pippa darling, that's such great news. So very well done I am so pleased for you. You have worked very hard and deserve it." Mum, I knew would be as pleased as me, even more that my plans for next year were settled. "Ring me later when you have time and tell me all about it."

I had well thought out ideas for the next year, but at this precise moment everyone just wanted to celebrate and enjoy success. Three years at university seemed to have vanished so quickly, people say you don't recognise the best times in your life until they are over, and I began to understand the truth in that.

At first, I had found university life hard. Although used to being away as a weekly boarder I still had each weekend at home with Mum, but now I was hundreds of miles away and had to make a new circle of friends. With time I had come to love my academic life, so much so I was planning to stay on to get a post graduate qualification. Like minded friends became close and keeping in touch with the Deveraux family meant Johnny had enjoyed coming up to Bristol once or twice a term. Having Johnny was like having the brother I had always wanted, and I think he realised what he was missing living at home and doing his agriculture college course. We had some great adventures on those weekends, enjoyed some fantastic parties and became very close. Yes, I was going to miss all that.

After a memorable graduation, I returned home with Mum determined to do something special with my last summer of freedom. I would have liked Grandpa Deveraux and Johnny to have come to my graduation, but by now I had accepted that although I counted the Deveraux clan as family, my mother still stubbornly kept her distance and as ever I wasn't into rocking the boat. Still, I sent Grandpa a photo of the occasion, and Johnny told me how proud he was.

As we drove home after the celebration graduation lunch, Mum mentioned to me that we had an appointment with the solicitor the following day. I was surprised, though I knew about, and just about understood, the financial arrangements that my grandmother had put in place. I was very grateful for the support that had helped me though school and now university, as I didn't have to stop to think where the funding was coming from for my post graduate course. In that I knew I was very lucky, however, the solicitor's appointment was intriguing, especially so as my mother didn't really know why we were both being asked to attend. I had my 21st birthday just a few weeks ago. Did that have any significance? We would find out no doubt the next day.

The solicitor's office was all glass and shiny steel, interesting to me as I had specialised in my degree on architectural engineering, and I was somewhat distracted by the outer glass wall, which didn't appear to have a support, as he began to talk.

" Miss Legrand, err, Philippa, it's a pleasure to meet you at last. I, of course, have met your mother and your grandmother before, but never the granddaughter of Cecile Legrand."

"Actually, I have always been called Pippa but go on it really doesn't matter." Perhaps I was nervous, but I don't know why I thought that important.

"Anyway, err, Pippa, I have asked you here today with your mother to explain the workings of the trust set up for you as now you are 'of age', your grandmother was old fashioned in that respect, and stipulated 21 years and then 25 years for a dissolution of the trust."

He went on to explain what we both already knew, perhaps he needed to be sure we understood. Grandmamma's legacy had been left in a trust fund for my education. Income from this trust had paid for my schooling and university with any top up coming from the capital, any extra income from the trust had gone to my mother. The capital, and thus the income from the trust had grown substantially with careful investment in stock and shares over the years. Apparently when I reached 21 the whole of the trust income would come to me and when I was 25 the trust could be dissolved, if that was my wish, and I could take out the capital.

"But I want my mother to continue to benefit from the trust, it's not fair that I should have all the income." I interrupted his flow.

"That is, of course, entirely up to you Miss Legrand. The Will left by your grandmother is clear that all income will come to you after your 21st birthday. That is why I wanted to see you today to make things clear, and I hope, I have. What you choose to do is up to you."

My mother had sat quietly through the exchange, not offering her opinion. I imagined she was torn by wanting me to have my inheritance but aware that income from the trust set up by her mother had helped pay for lots of little extras over the years for both of us. No doubt she would try to persuade me to take the income, but I had decided very quickly that it would be shared. It felt the right thing to do.

"That only leaves one more item." The solicitor continued in a dreary voice. I was again distracted by the full height glass wall and the view over the skyline of central London.

"Your grandmother left her jewellery to you, err, Pippa, to be given after your 21st birthday. We have been keeping it safe in the bank as we have no knowledge of what the collection is worth though I imagine it may be quite valuable. However, it has been withdrawn today and it is here for you to receive." He gestured to a rather unprepossessing, medium size, brown paper parcel sitting on the desk. "If you can just sign here to say you have it in your possession now, then we are all finished for today."

Mum and I left the building each preoccupied with our own thoughts.

"There is no way Mum I am taking all the income. No, please don't even think of saying anything. She was your mother, and you have every right to all the income, never mind half. I don't understand what she was thinking when she made the will. Why did she try to bypass you? Why did she set up these conditions? I have never really understood." My mother smiled,

"Quite simply she liked to control people and their lives, no I am not trying to be hurtful, but that was Mamma. I don't think she ever quite trusted me to do, what was her eyes, 'the right thing.' The Will made sure she remained very much part of our decisions and continued her control. Well, I followed her desire for your schooling to the letter, even though it was not as I would have wished. You didn't realise at the time, but I missed you so much when you went to boarding school, even when you were coming home each weekend."

"I do remember you making me go back after the first week and being very strict with me about having a wonderful educational opportunity that you wouldn't allow me to waste. Even though I cried all weekend you never wavered."

"Well, you didn't see me cry after you left on the Monday, but I knew, Mamma's wishes or not, it was for the best and you see it was. Look where you are now!" We walked on with the unremarkable brown paper parcel under my arm.

"Grandmamma's jewellery. What do you know about that?"

"No more than you Pippa. At the time of her death everything was so strange and quite frankly distressing, the last thing I thought about was the jewellery. I do remember Mamma wearing some pieces, but I really can't tell you more. We will just have to have a good look at them at home and decide what it is best to do. If there are valuable pieces, then we need to think about insurance if you want to keep them."

Ever practical Mum I thought, feet well and truly on the ground. I was very intrigued by the idea of the unknown jewellery in the box we had been given, and as soon as we reached home, I was at the kitchen table undoing the brown paper parcel, while Mum put the kettle on.

The package revealed a beautiful inlaid wooden box. Highly lacquered, it shone in the afternoon sun that poured through the window, with tiny pieces of different coloured wood surrounded by gold and silver laid in patterns. It was actually an heirloom in itself.

"Have you seen this before?" I asked Mum. She nodded.

"It stood on Mamma's dressing table in her bedroom. I think I once asked about it and she said something about it coming from the Middle East, maybe Iran, a gift to her mother, my grandmother, I don't really remember but I always thought it very special."

I opened the metal clasp to reveal several small black velvet pouches and leather covered boxes, it was like discovering a treasure trove. I picked up the top black pouch and tipped the contents onto the table, and out fell a string of tiny pearls set as a delicate necklace with a shiny diamond clasp.

My mother took a sharp intake of breath.

"Those are Mamma's special pearls. She wore them a lot." Mum picked them carefully up and fingered the tiny smooth beads. You could see the memories arriving in her mind.

"When I was very young, I remember sitting on her knee and touching them on her neck and being told to be careful as they were very precious."

"Then you must have them and wear them Mum, please I would really like that." Mum smiled and fingered the pearls again very gently.

"Thank you, Pippa, I would love to have these. They do so remind me of Mamma."

I picked up the velvet pouch to pass to her and felt there was something still inside. Tipping it out again revealed a small piece of folded paper. When opened, in faded writing we managed to decipher 'fur Meine Liebling, O.' I looked at Mum. This certainly wasn't French, even my poor grasp of languages told me it was German, and that it was a message of love.

"Goodness, I wonder what this means about the necklace?"

My mother smiled, "I have absolutely no idea. Mamma used to whisper secret words to me in German, I didn't know what they meant but they seemed to express love. Mamma always had secrets you see, but maybe that note is why she wore them so often. Perhaps they held a special memory of someone?"

She tucked the note securely back into the velvet pouch with the pearls.

We continued to open the boxes and pouches marvelling at the contents. So many sparkling jewels set in different items. Some, if not most, were obviously old and Mum suggested they were perhaps her mothers who had died when Cecile was young. We knew that Grandmamma had come from aristocratic parentage so that did make sense, and quite honestly if the jewels in the settings were real, then this collection was very valuable.

Some of the pieces Mum recognised as Grandmamma had worn jewellery every day as part of her normal routine. Certainly, the box of earrings contained some magnificent pieces, as apparently, Cecile didn't feel dressed without earrings and always wore a pair.

Eventually we took out the last leather covered box. It contained another spectacular ring, set with an emerald centre piece surrounded by white diamonds. This was part of a set we had already found with matching necklace, earrings, bracelet and broach. All emeralds were set with diamonds in gold, it must be very valuable we decided.

"My word, I do think these need to go back to the bank as soon as possible don't you Pippa? Insurance for these will be very costly."

But I was distracted and didn't reply, as at the bottom of the padded wooden box was a brown dog-eared envelope. Carefully I took it out and found a small, obviously old photograph of a young man looking intently at the camera. It had been taken some time ago, and the man was just about smiling. What was most noticeable were his slightly hooded dark eyes and a distinctive set of these eyes in his face. A mop of curly dark hair topped the portrait, and he was wearing a rough looking open necked shirt. I turned the photo over, now oblivious to my mother's chatter, and read the name in florid old-fashioned French script, 'Etienne'.

"Mum, look at this. Just look at the eyes and the hair. What do you see?" My mother, Stephanie, stared at the photo with the same dawning recognition I had.

"Those are your eyes and the way they are set in your face Mum, and the hair. Look at the curls. Can't you see that?" She just kept staring at the photo and turned it over as I had done.

271

"Mum. Who is Etienne? Do you know anything about this photo?"

Chapter 11

"I really don't know who Etienne is, Pippa. I never even heard Mamma say the name." We were now both sitting down at the kitchen table. Mum had her favourite mug in her hand, entwined pink roses, now worn with constant washing, the word MUM in large letters drawn on it. A birthday present some time ago from me if I remember, she has kept that a long time, I thought. The small photo sat on the Formica surface between us.

"But you look so much like him, surely you agree? This must be your father." I wanted Mum to see what I was seeing.

"Pippa, I don't know what to think. I used to fantasize about finding out about my father when I was your age and younger. But then, after Mamma died, I knew I would never find out anymore, so I stopped thinking of it, as even her friend Julien couldn't give me any clues."

I decided to stop pressurising my mum. I knew she could see the striking resemblance but just did not want to admit it. Mum, I realised very early in life, liked stability. She hated change and making difficult decisions, that was maybe because she was always having to make them by herself, or perhaps that was just her character, I couldn't tell. Experience had taught me that pushing her in these situations only led to more reluctance and indecision on her part.

"Shall we clear this lot away and I'll make some tea?" We had stared at the photo for long enough, so it was a sensible suggestion from Mum, and her way of dodging the question. I picked up the photo ready to put it back in the envelope only to discover inside another item, that in my astonishment at finding the photo, I had not noticed. I carefully took out a folded piece of light brown card with type written words on it and a tiny photo in the dog-eared corner. It was all in French and the photo, although small, was surely my Grandmamma Cecile looking very young.

"What on earth……..?" Mum turned back from the sink where she had been washing up the mugs.

"Now what, Pippa?"

"Look Mum, its Grandmamma. But it's all in French. Come on you can translate. What is it about?" Mum dried her hands on her apron and took the document. She put her reading glasses on and took it to the kitchen window to get more light. Looking puzzled she turned it over and re-read both sides.

"I don't understand. It's some kind of identity card for a 'Cecile Andre' dated March 1944, issued somewhere called Apt in department 84. That's before the end of the war. It certainly looks like Mamma, but it can't be. What would she be doing there in wartime? I know for certain she came to London with her mother before the war broke out." Cooking tea forgotten, she sat down at the table again.

"I thought she was Cecile Legrand." I remarked.

"Yes, well, Cecile Antoinette Isabella Andre Legrand was her full name, it's quite a mouthful and apparently Andre was after her father. So it all could add up I suppose. She would have been about 22 in 1944, I think. But where is Apt? Can we find out?" My trusty school atlas was retrieved from my bedroom, and we poured over the page about France getting nowhere.

"I don't think the French departments have change much since the war. Can we find where 84 is?" I suggested. Some scurrying around the European section of the atlas brought up a departmental map of France, and we found department 84 down in the south-eastern corner, one departmental region north from the Mediterranean. With a better chance of spotting the town, we searched the previous map and found Apt set in a river valley east of Avignon, where the Calavon river curved up toward the start of the Alps and Sisteron. We then both sat back and looked at each other. It made no sense to either of us, then the same thought struck us both. The photo and the identity card must be linked, so had Etienne lived in Apt?

I looked at my watch, it was now almost 7pm. We had been occupied with the jewellery box contents all afternoon.

"Mum why don't we go down to the pub by the park and have a meal and a good think about this. Save you cooking." I saw my mother open her mouth to protest, she never willingly went out for a meal. Habit, I expect, I knew money was tight when I was younger, and old habits die hard. However, ten minutes later we were sat in the pub garden at the back, sipping a drink with a meal ordered. Try as we might we could not come up with a logical reason for Cecile to be in occupied France in 1944.

"Unless," my mother suddenly suggested, "I remember Julien saying when he first met her that she came with 'the highest security clearance', that phrase stuck in my mind. I do wish he was still alive to help us. But what if, and I just don't have any idea if this is even possible, what if she was in France for a reason, maybe to gather information. I never really knew what Mamma did for a job during or after the war, always 'a secret' I was told. Am I just being too fanciful?" I couldn't comment but I was absolutely sure I was going to try to find out.

So, I started my research the next day. Luckily mum had, for no particular reason, kept Grandmamma's address book, so via a number in that I reached her old office and was passed to someone who remembered her, called Matthew. When finishing the conversation, he asked to be remembered to Stephanie, so my mother did have a secret past I thought, and I was sure I detected a blush when I passed on the message later that day. Anyway, he put me onto a department at the war office and I arranged to go up to see them the following day.

By the time I returned the next day it all began to add up. The identity card was recognised and a very old file on my Grandmother Cecile retrieved. Just like the espionage films it still had 'Top Secret' stamped in the top corner, so it was not passed to me to read, however the facts soon became apparent. Cecile had been recruited to the Special Operations Executive in 1943. As a native French speaker, and a young pretty girl she was ideal, as apparently the Germans didn't suspect pretty young women so easily of being the enemy. The S.O.E. operatives had the job of helping the local resistance disrupt the enemy, hoping to occupy as many soldiers as possible, keeping them away from the front line that would eventually be trying to repel the Allied invasion.

It seemed my grandmamma demonstrated a natural ability at inventing small explosive devices and was therefore ideal for the job. She was certainly in France in March 1944, returning in late July the same year, and it appears she was either very lucky, or very clever, as few S.O.E operatives made it back to the UK safely. The file confirmed she had been in the department of Vaucluse 84, and in the region near Apt, staying at a village called St Saturnin les Apt just a few kilometres to the north. However, they could not tell me anything about a man called Etienne.

I recounted all this to Stephanie, my mum, when I got home. She was completing the last week of school before the summer holidays but had been thinking about me all day.

"Mum, your birthday is in April isn't it? Well that is just about nine months after Cecile came home." She knew what I was saying, and it all pointed to Etienne being her father in my opinion, but Mum was more cautious.

On the way back on the train I had made a plan. I had been hoping to take Mum on a holiday this summer, just the two of us before I started my post graduate studies. It now seemed a great idea to go to France, to St Saturnin les Apt and see what we could find out, maybe nothing, but we could have a holiday as well.

Resistance at first from Mum, but as I said I would organise and pay for it, well my grandmamma's trust income would, all she had to do was to come with me, so in the end she agreed. By the end of the next day, we were booked on the TGV via Paris to Avignon with a week at a B&B run by an English couple set in the countryside just outside St Saturnin. A hire car from the TGV station would give us the chance to explore.

Our departure was in just one weeks' time.

Part Four

Stephanie and Pippa

Chapter 1

Stephanie and Pippa in Provence, July 2000.
Pippa

We arrived at the new TGV station outside Avignon in the middle of the afternoon. The station was newly built, and not quite finished, but it was a fantastic structure of glass and steel. The trains arrived in a glass curved bubble set above the modern station concourse, with subterranean tunnels joining the two railway lines going north and south. I was transfixed by the structure, as this was exactly the kind of project I hoped to be involved in when I had completed my post graduate training. It may not have appeared beautiful to everyone, but the symmetry and simple structure of the glass allowed the building to nestle unobtrusively in the landscape. Mum, on the other hand, didn't seem to notice anything and was determinedly wheeling her suitcase to the exit doors, so I had to run to catch her up.

The slightly offset automatic doors launched us into the bright light and intense heat of a July Provencal afternoon. Work on the exterior landscaping had still to be completed but I saw a long rectangular pool with walkways either side and a planting scheme of olive trees and lavender. Someone had really thought about this, and the effect would be, in years to come, a stunning arrival point for Avignon, gateway to Provence. However, at present we had to struggle across an unmade car park to collect the hire car, a small, ubiquitous white Renault. We were both glad it had air conditioning at the very least, and I elected to drive, Mum to navigate. Soon we were passing the walls of the ancient city and concentrating hard to cope with the wide road, speeding traffic and multiple roundabouts following the signs for Cavaillon and Apt.

Once clear of the built-up area and on the correct road we relaxed a little and began to enjoy the scenery. Driving along a flat fertile plain we were surrounded by fruit trees that had the autumn crop of apples already set. The road was straight, and to the south we saw the hills of the Luberon begin to appear running west to east forming the horizon. The route continued straight across the plain, following the line of the ancient roman road the Via Domita, and later a river valley eastward towards Apt. The landscape changed to silver green olive trees, rows of deep purple lavender and clear views of small villages scattered like stones, on the hillside. Turning north and climbing gradually we caught sight of the white stone mountain top of Mount Ventoux in the far distance, dominating the landscape as we had entered the foothills of the Ventoux range.

Our B&B hosts had sent a clear sketch map of their location, and we turned west just short of St Saturnin les Apt which was starkly visible, its large church with octagonal bell tower at the heart and the old castle and chapel climbing up the hillside to the rear. The azure, blue sky highlighted the landscape perfectly, and the air was so clear, this was most certainly the place to be if you were an artist.

'Mas des Olives' was set in its own olive field and clearly of some age. The outer walls coated in a gentle ochre colour and a large faded blue set of doors opened to the courtyard. Greeted by our hosts, they explained they had spent three years renovating the place, a lot of it themselves. Marianne had been an interior designer and that showed in the simple cool stone interior of our room. Outside they had created small gardens with simple seating and a magnificent walled swimming pool with plenty of shade. Once settled in our room I couldn't wait to try out the pool while Mum had a snooze. This was just perfect.

After a delicious dinner eaten out in the courtyard our hosts came to chat with us. Over coffee and a small brandy nightcap for Mum, we told them exactly why we were here in Provence, and they seemed genuinely interested in our quest for information.

"We know the local Resistance was very active here during the war. There are numerous plaques on buildings and out in the countryside commemorating various actions taken by the local 'Maquis' as they were known." Marianne seemed to have a good understanding of local history. With her long, now slightly greying, blonde hair tied up loosely in a bun, she managed to look elegant even though she had just cooked dinner for ten hungry guests.

"There's an old boy in the bar I sometimes frequent." Began David her husband.

"Sometimes." Interrupted Marianne her eyes sparkling with humour. "You are in there a lot, at least every time you are sent on an errand into the village." Her husband smiled. She knew him too well.

"Well, you need to be seen supporting local businesses, and don't forget Pierre sends clients our way when they are looking for accommodation. The least I can do is have a drink when in the village." David had a rather more bohemian appearance. His full head of steel grey hair was unfashionably long onto his collar and in contrast to his wife he preferred a more relaxed dress code. His faded cotton shorts and once black tee shirt had seen much wear but were obviously comfortable. His laid-back manner probably revealed who really did most of the work at the B&B. However, David was obviously good with the guests, and when motivated an excellent handyman which was exactly what they needed in their situation. In fact, it seemed they were a perfectly matched pair. They had apparently been married for over 40 years so they must have learnt to live with their differences.

"Anyway," David returned to his story. "Pierre told me this old guy was in the local Maquis. Quite a hero apparently, but you can't get him to talk about those times. 'Best forgotten' is his stock reply if you can get him talking at all. Goodness knows what he feels about the numerous German visitors we have arriving during the summer."

"He will be pragmatic like the rest." Marianne continued. "People make their living round here from the tourists, wherever they come from, so it pays to welcome everyone the same. However, it is good to have English guests to have a chat to, I hope you don't mind us joining you this evening." We all smiled and took a sip of our drinks, I was finishing a rather nice, very pale, local rose wine we had had with dinner, and I began to feel ready for an early night.

"Marianne, where would you start our search for information?" Mum was more awake than me. Marianne paused, playing with a loose strand of hair.

"Quite honestly there is nowhere better than the Town Hall, the 'Mairie' in the village. Someone there will point you in the right direction. If you park down by the new school and swimming pool you can walk up through the old streets and find the Mairie easily. It's just by the church. That's exactly where I would start."

Chapter 2

Stephanie

I lay in bed hearing the early morning silence relishing the ability to enjoy a relaxed start to the day. School had been its usual hectic self by the end of term and having all this luxury arranged by Pippa was the perfect antidote. I smiled inwardly as I thought about Pippa. Such a grown-up young lady now, having inherited her father's height and her grandmother's physique she was tall with an enviable figure. Pippa was one of those people who enjoyed their food and yet never put on an ounce of weight. She used to be self-conscious of her height when younger, but now I was proud to see a confident young woman ready and able to enjoy the world. I don't think she realized how attractive she actually was, I had watched yesterday how heads had turned to admire her as we travelled across France. I allowed myself a small bit of self-congratulation at having achieved the seemingly impossible task twenty-one years ago of raising a daughter alone, actually not just raising a daughter, but one I could justifiably be proud of.

So now we were here in Provence, close to St Saturnin where perhaps Mamma had been. I had said nothing to Pippa, she would no doubt have thought me mad, but since arrival I had this distinct feeling of belonging, coming home. Which of course was ridiculous as I had never been here before, most probably my overactive imagination was playing tricks on my psyche. However, I did feel a great sense of peace.

Today was going to be busy and a good chance to get my rusty French up to speed. I had been helping for a number of years at the after school French club after I admitted to a fellow teacher that I had spoken French at home with my mother. Certainly, that had kept my skills up to date. I even took one of the younger year groups for basic French, and I had enjoyed a number of day trips and exchange visits to France. All this had allowed me to keep my knowledge of spoken French alive. Pippa had just not inherited the language gene, so the talking was going to fall to me.

Cecile, my mamma, always gave unusual presents to Pippa when she was young. Never the run of the mill dolls or 'toy of the moment'. A chemistry set when she far too young in my mind, lots of construction sets, and adult books on historic buildings. Pippa enjoyed all these things, and this may have set her on her course to the architecture in which she was now so engrossed. Perhaps Mamma knew her potential better than I, or she was hoping to direct her learning, but like so many things about Cecile we would never know.

Pippa stirred. The sun was now peeping through the lavender-coloured shutters. I quietly crept to the bathroom leaving her to wake up gently.

Fortified by a leisurely and substantial breakfast of croissants with thick lavender honey, coffee and slices of local juicy cantaloupe melon served on the shaded terrace, we set off in the car to the village. The sun was already climbing high in the brilliant blue cloudless sky. It was quiet, and we found the car park Marianne had described and set off uphill, across the road and into the narrow winding streets of the old village. The rows of tall, three storey houses on both sides of the street cast some welcome shade. Most had closed shuttered windows against the heat, and solid wooden, sometimes ornate, front doors. Ahead the magnificent octagonal bell tower of the large stone church came into view. Then the street widened to a small square, the church directly ahead, a large plane tree, casting a pool of shade in the centre and the tricolour flag, hanging limply above the entrance to the Mairie off to the right. To the left was a rising stone footpath signed to the chapel, which no doubt Pippa would want to explore as soon as possible.

On entering the Mairie, it was like stepping back in time. Overcrowded notice boards full of sheets of typewritten paper were behind the desk, French bureaucracy was infamous, and the local town Mairie was the heart of the local complex administrative procedures. However, the young lady behind the mahogany counter smiled a warm welcome so I thought we might be in with a chance. I found my French returned quite quickly, and the young lady listened, replied and then disappeared into a room behind.

"Where's she going?" asked a frustrated Pippa, waiting for me to translate.

"Apparently there is an older lady who may be able to help in some way. She has gone to find her." Just then a round, cheerful looking lady with immaculate coiffured grey hair appeared, bringing with her a cloud of expensive perfume. With concentration I could understand what she was saying, she didn't help with the speed of the delivery, and she handed me a piece of paper containing a name and address. I profusely thanked her for her time and even Pippa managed "Merci" as we left the building.

"So?"

"Apparently there is a man in the village who has started an archive of local history. She suggests we go to see him. He lives in a street behind the church, and I have got his name and address, look Gerrard Dupont, 11 Rue Castel. So, let's go now and see if he is in."

Following round the back of the large church the nameplate 'Rue Castel' told us we were going in the right direction. Looking for number eleven wasn't easy as small side alleys dived down to lower levels with well-worn steps, and the street, like the others seemed deserted. Having found the right house, the closed shutters and solid front door of number eleven didn't appear to hold out much hope. However, after ringing the doorbell, and wondering if it was in fact working, the front door opened wide to reveal an older man with grey hair, a well-trimmed moustache, tortoiseshell framed glasses and a pleasant smile. It seemed the lady from the Mairie had phoned ahead and we were expected. He led us through a dark hallway to the rear rooms that were flooded in light looking onto a large south facing terrace with an ancient creeping vine covering the trellis. I notice piles of paper and boxes stacked against the walls in the room.

After formal introductions, Gerrard suggested that we spoke in English as he was a recently retired teacher from the College in Apt and loved to practice his language skills. This was a relief. At least this way I wasn't constantly translating for Pippa and having to concentrate on getting my French correct. He insisted on getting us coffee before we started talking and disappeared to the kitchen.

"Goodness look at all those boxes and papers," exclaimed Pippa. I frowned at her, I didn't want him to overhear, as his English was obviously excellent. So, I made some pleasant observation of the view over the rooftops toward the Luberon, just as Gerrard returned with the coffee.

"I am sorry about the untidiness," he began. "It's easier to keep the material to hand that I am working on at the moment. There are many more boxes untouched in a room upstairs." He smiled and his face lit up. "You see once people know of my hobby or as we would say 'passion', they keep turning up at my door with boxes of old photos and documents, quite often after an aged parent dies and they need to clear out the house. Not everything is of use but it's easier to take the boxes in and sort them just in case." He took a sip of coffee, we both followed suit. It was very black and very strong.

"Since my wife died some three years ago this project has kept me busy. Now I am retired I can really get going with it, as there is so much to document. I hope to produce a working historical archive for the village with regular exhibitions in the summer for the visitors." When Gerrard talked about his work his face lit up and he was obviously immersed in the whole enterprise. His enthusiasm was infectious.

"But now, Mrs Legrand......"

"Oh, Stephanie please and Pippa"

"Well then its Gerrard for you as well." He chuckled and his smile grew broader. "What can I help you with. Anne-Marie at the Mairie was pretty vague, but I will do my best." I went on to explain as concisely as possible the whole story, beginning with Cecile, our recent discovery of her wartime record with the S.O.E. in St Saturnin, and finishing by showing him the photo and the identity card. Pippa had the photo enlarged and although it was now slightly blurred it gave a better overall image of Etienne. Gerrard rummaged for a magnifying glass in an untidy box of pens, pencils, rulers, elastic bands and other assorted debris he kept on the end of the table. He looked carefully at the identity card first.

"I have seen a some of these before. They were issued in the Nazi occupied territories. It does certainly seems to suggest the lady in the picture was here in St Saturnin in March 1944. It's a bit damaged but look here in this bottom corner it says she was working as a teacher." Neither of us had seen that and Gerrard carefully pointed to the relevant part of the card where it was very creased and smudged. He then looked at the photo.

"Yes, again very much of that era, and a handsome young man if I may say so. However, simply a first name Etienne tells us very little. Has he got a connection to the lady on the identity card?" Of course, that was the question we all wanted answered.

"Gerrard, we simply don't know. But my mamma Cecile had kept the two items together and we can only suppose so. You see, I understand that I was born just nine months after Cecile returned from France. I could never get her to talk to me about my father, and I did try, so I can't be much help, but we do suspect now it may have been this man Etienne. Where do we go from here? What can we do next to find out any information?" Gerrard sat back in his chair, drained his now cold coffee, and pulled as slightly quizzical face.

"Well, if you are ready to help, we could go through some of the old photos I have of wartime in the village and see if we can spot him. It's about all I can think of right now, but I think it's worth a try." I looked at Pippa who nodded enthusiastically.

"Unfortunately, I have got to go to Avignon this afternoon to the Prefecture, some administrative problem with my pension." He rolled his eyes expressively. "But if you can come back tomorrow morning, I will have the right boxes out for us to search, but it might take some time. Also, I will have a think about where else I can glean any information. Does that help?"

"Gerrard that is wonderful, but we mustn't take up all your time."

"Quite simply it will be a pleasure." He smiled and he seemed genuinely enthusiastic. We left, by that time exchanging the Provencal three kisses to alternate cheeks, leaving Gerard waving on the doorstep.

"Well," exclaimed Pippa. "What a great start. Mind that house could do with a bit of a clean. Did you see the layers of dust on the mantelpiece?"

"Pippa that's a bit mean. He obviously had a wife who use to look after him and, like most men of that age, hasn't a clue how to do housework. He's actually a very pleasant, articulate person and I am glad we have met him." Pippa replied to that comment with a knowing perhaps, suggestive glance. I chose to ignore her.

Chapter 3

Pippa

I realised it was early as the sun had yet to peep through the shutters, but I felt awake, and after another huge, delicious dinner provided by our excellent hostess, I thought a bit of exercise would be a good idea. Slipping out of bed I grabbed some shorts and a tee shirt, dressed in the bathroom, and exited the bedroom hoping not to wake Mum. There were some quiet sounds from the kitchen as I passed, probably Marianne was already preparing breakfast. Certainly, running a B&B was not to be undertaken lightly. During their summer season they would have to exist on very little sleep, seemingly content to socialise with guests into the small hours and still have breakfast on the table for the early risers. Of course, they got to live in this wonderful part of France all year round, but I had to admire their stamina.

I walked briskly to the front gates and along the track. This time I turned right, away from the village and set off, half jogging, on the country road. On each side were rows of vines now covered in dense, mid green foliage and small dark bunches of grapes just beginning to swell. A small, thin, noisy tractor was weaving its way along the rows in the distance, with this the only sound breaking the silence of the early morning. The air was deliciously cool, belying the heat that would gather later during the day. By the time I had reached the top of a small hill my jogging legs had given up and I sat on a rock by the roadside. The sun was just now over the top of the mountains to the east casting rosy shadows on the stone buildings of the village. Yesterday had certainly been exciting, and we seemed to have made great progress in our quest, finding Gerrard was key to that, and I was pleased he was as enthusiastic as we were. On reflection he was a very charming gentleman, and it was clear my mum thought

288

that too. We had arranged to meet again today at 10am at his house. Yesterday afternoon had been taken up by sunbathing, swimming and rather a lot of sleep. All that relaxation had felt very good for us as we guessed today was going to need a good deal of concentration.

By now the sun was fully over the horizon and the idea of breakfast changed my mind from going any further. Walking briskly back I wondered if Mum was still asleep, perhaps I ought to have left a note to say where I had gone, as the last thing I wanted to do was to worry her. However, as I quietly let myself into the room she was just waking, so I dived into the bathroom first.

Breakfast again was superb, and we set off for the village in plenty of time. Mum suggested we call at the Boulangerie and collect something to share with Gerrard over coffee, so I chose some small lavender flavoured biscuits which were freshly baked and smelt very appetising. Gerrard answered the door with his usual expected smile, and as we exchanged kissed greetings. I noticed a clean and well pressed shirt this time, with the back room just a little tidier.

"Entre, Entre, ladies." He showed us through to the big outside table in the dappled shade on the terrace, where three boxes of papers and photos were ready for us.

"But before we start, I have our coffee almost ready and some news to relate. Just wait while I get it and put these delicious biscuits on a plate." He disappeared into the next room.

"Gosh, there is plenty to sort through here." I was having a quick look into one of the boxes, where there was a complete mix of papers and photos of different sizes.

"Can't wait to get going?" Gerrard caught me having a look as he returned. "But just wait a little as I have some more information." He went on to explain that on his way back from Avignon he had called to see one of his few remaining contacts who had been active in the local Resistance during the war. Most were long gone and those few who remained often lacked the will or desire to recount what had happened all those years ago. The majority felt it was best forgotten and were unwilling to engage in talking about those times, however as he explained, Raymond on a good day, enjoyed a good glass of red wine, and a chat about old times.

"Thankfully, it was a good day, and worth the deviation on the way home." Gerrard explained that Raymond had spent most of 1944 in the hills above St Saturnin with other young men avoiding the Nazis and carrying out small but significant attacks on the occupying forces. They could not return to their homes, or they would have been taken as forced labour to the munitions factories in Germany as had many of their contemporaries.

"Anyway, when I asked, he remembered talk of a young woman, I am trying to remember your English saying. Ah yes 'a young slip of a girl' am I right? Anyway, he remembered the girl had produced small transportable explosive devices to help their attacks. She had also apparently invented a simple explosive trap that could be laid near their various hideouts in the hills that not only alerted them to the arrival of the enemy but caused significant injuries to those arriving. Unfortunately, he personally never met her but thought he remembered her being around in the late spring and early summer of 1944." He sat back while we digested the information.

"So, you think that was Cecile, my mother?"

"Yes, I do Stephanie, it's all beginning to add up. The various stories seem consistent with her being here in 1944. But, yes, it's still guesswork at the moment." He paused, sipped more of the rather strong black coffee, and helped himself to another lavender biscuit.

"Now let's get going with the boxes. I suggest one box each. Look at the photos first and just see if you can see anyone who resembles Etienne."

I must admit to finding the next hour fascinating, though I had never much enjoyed history at school it had seemed useless to have to learn about people long ago, this was extremely interesting. Real people in photographs who had lived not that long ago in St Saturnin, and I soon became distracted from the main task by the unfolding social history in front of me. We had been scanning photos for Etienne for about an hour when my Mum let out a gasp.

"I think I have found him. Look, at the end on the left at the front." She pointed to a young man staring intently at the camera among a group taken outside the church in the centre of St Saturnin. He had those slightly hooded eyes, set recognisably in his face with dark curly hair. Gerrard and I crowded round, both agreeing that he looked very like the Etienne in our photograph.

Gerrard turned the photograph over and found some faded writing, as luckily someone had written not only the date, 1943 but the names of the men outside the church, though as it was written so long ago the writing was almost illegible.

With a patience that Mum and I did not feel, Gerrard found his magnifying glass, moved out of the shaded light on the terrace and examined the back of the photo. We held our breath, as this was the best lead we had, but we needed more than a first name.

"Well, I can see his name Etienne, that is easy as I have an idea what it should say, however the second name, well its more difficult but I think its Fournier. Now that's not a common name round here and it sticks in my mind I taught at least one Fournier at the College in Apt, so there still may be a local family connection in the area. I'll ring my friend at the Mairie, she will know if there is a Fournier family in the commune." He disappeared into the hall to use the telephone, while Mum and I poured over the photo.

The men were all similarly dressed in what looked like working clothes, certainly open necked shirts, long dark trousers with boots on their feet. No one was smiling, but then maybe you didn't smile at the camera in those days. Amazingly the front of the church and the area around with the plane tree looked almost exactly the same as it did today, with the tree a little smaller of course.

But our eyes kept returning to Etienne, was it our Etienne? Who was he and how did he know Cecile? The more we found out, the more questions rose in our minds. Gerrard returned smiling, but then he always had a smile on his face, he was that kind of optimistic man.

"How is it you say, 'Got it'." We smiled at his attempts to use idiomatic English phrases.

"There is a family Fournier living in the commune just outside St Saturnin at a small farm, not far from Les Andeols. Ann-Marie at the Mairie is sure they have been at the farm for generations.

She even found their telephone number for me." He flourished a piece of paper, and he seemed almost as excited as we were.

"I will phone right away and see if we can visit, as all this is best explained in person I think." He disappeared to the phone again, with Mum and I exchanging glances, as this was all moving very fast now. Gerrard returned quite quickly.

"Well, that was interesting. I caught Jean Fournier who is the proprietor of the farm now. He is happy to see us all later this afternoon. Yes, he had an Uncle Etienne, his father's brother, but he was, I am afraid to say, sadly killed toward the end of the war."

Silence. I think we all knew that finding Etienne himself was most unlikely, but to hear so certainly of his death was a damper on our spirits. Silence continued in the room as we all held our own thoughts. My mother spoke first.

"Julien, my mamma's close friend, once said he felt Cecile was waiting for someone to come to her after the war. This is so sad. I wonder if she ever really knew what had happened to Etienne." My mother's voice betrayed her nearness to tears, so I took her hand and then felt tears well up in my eyes. Gerrard looked a little embarrassed at first but sat down beside us.

"I'm afraid this is the nature of war." He eventually said. "The consequences flow out over many generations. I am so sorry Stephanie, as it would have been so wonderful to have actually found Etienne, but I am afraid I always thought it improbable. Many needless young lives were lost in those years, but perhaps we will be able to find out more from his nephew or would you like me to go alone this afternoon?"

"Oh Gerrard, that is so kind but most certainly not, we must follow this through. I know it was a silly idea that perhaps we could find Etienne himself, but somehow, I just held a little bit of hope, but no, I'm fine and so is Pippa, and we can't thank you enough for your help so far.   In fact, why don't we take you out to lunch in the village then we can all go on to the farm later?"

"What a great idea Mum." I leapt in before Gerrard could reply. "There looks to be a nice little café bar by the Boulangerie. Do they do lunch Gerrard? Shall I pop down and book a table?"

In the end we all walked down together as it was by now almost midday and gradually the mood of the group lightened. We ate a splendid lunch, shared a bottle of local wine, and silently toasted Cecile and her Etienne.

Chapter 4

Stephanie

Gerrard led the way in his small, rather battered white Citroen, while I let Pippa drive again, she had much more confidence than me at being on the ´wrong´ side of the road. We soon left the main road toward Apt and travelling west, we moved along a small country road with vines either side. The tiny hamlet of Les Andeols was, as seems usual in the French countryside, deserted. Just past the last house, Gerrard turned down a gravel track toward a group of farm buildings, which had an air of neglect from outside, but we had learnt that often the interior of such houses would belie this. There was wall around the main part, mostly ochre rendered, with a huge arched doorway leading to an inner courtyard. Gerrard turned in beside an old tractor and parked, with Pippa following his lead.

Before we had got out of the car a tall, slim, older man with greying close-cropped hair strode out of the courtyard. He must have been in his 60's but still appeared fit and active. A handshake with Gerrard and an exchange in French but with a heavy regional accent, which was going to prove a challenge for me. I had already briefed Pippa that she couldn't expect instant translations and that I would keep her up with the conversation as much as possible. However, it now looked like Gerrard was going to have do a translation for me.

Introductions and handshakes followed, as this was indeed Jean, who was Etienne's nephew. I noticed the same slightly hooded brown eyes that Etienne had in the photo. He led us into the courtyard which was dominated by a huge plane tree giving shade to almost the entire outside space, and there under the plane tree was a large iron table and chairs with gaily coloured fabric cushions. It was a relief to be in the shade of the courtyard and

Jean gestured for us to sit as he disappeared into the house, also ochre rendered with faded lavender shutters closed against the heat. Returning with his wife carrying a tray with a large jug of iced water and glasses, Jean introduced us to Helene. Gerrard had a quick conversation regarding their two sons, each of whom he had taught at the College in Apt, which was a good idea I thought, as it broke the ice somewhat. He then went on to a general explanation of who we were and why we were looking for an Etienne Fournier.

Jean and his wife listened intently, then they both looked at the enlarged photo we had brought. Jean replied in a fast guttural dialect to Gerrard, and I was by now struggling to comprehend, so Gerrard quickly translated.

"Jean says he cannot be sure. He has only seen a few photos of his uncle, but he seems to look a lot like his father Pierre when he was young. There is definitely a family resemblance." Jean left the table and went into the house.

"He is going to see if his mother is awake, as she is now rather old and infirm, she can't see too well and has difficulty hearing, but her mind is all there. He is hoping she will come out to join us, as she will know much more." We all took a long sip of water, and I think Pippa could sense my anxiety, we were so close but so far from certainty.

Eventually Jean came back with his mother. She was determinedly walking with a stick, waving away his proffered arm, obviously having taken time to brush her hair and put on some perfume. She may have been elderly, but she still took care of her appearance. We all were introduced, and her handshake was frail but firm. Jean explained slowly and clearly what we had told him, then showed her our photo of Etienne. She held it close to her eyes and then looked at Jean with a nod we all could see.

"C'est Etienne." She clearly said. "Le frere de mon mari, Pierre." I glanced at Pippa, she had got the meaning, it was her brother-in-law. I looked at Gerrard and passed a photo of Mamma taken just after the war, holding me as a very young baby. Gerrard asked the old lady carefully and clearly if she recognised the young woman in the photo, explaining it was my mother. Again, she held it up close to her eyes, taking her plain rimmed, quite thick glasses off for a closer look. She looked carefully then announced, "C'est Cecile, une de ses copines." Pippa looked at me puzzled.

"She says 'its Cecile one of his girlfriends'". I gave an involuntary shudder, as it was the almost careless way she had said it 'one of his girlfriend's'. How many did he have? What was she trying to tell us? Gerard spoke again asking if she could remember when Cecile was here. Jean's mother thought for a while, then replied quite firmly,

"Peu de temps avant de se faire tuer." It was said in an almost callous way. Pippa looked worried as she could tell the tone was odd but didn't understand the meaning. She glanced at me.

"She says 'just before he got himself killed'." Gerrard had also picked up on the tone of the remarks and looked a little hesitant. However, before he could say anything Jean interrupted, looking embarrassed himself and suggested his mother go back inside as it was much too hot for her in the courtyard. Helene, his wife, helped her this time and they slowly made their way indoors.

Jean gestured to see the photo of Cecile, and all the time looking at me, went in a flood of French to Gerrard, where I got lost very quickly. Gerrard got him to pause while he explained that Jean thought he recognised Cecile as she had been his teacher at the village school for a short while. I began to realise now how talented Mamma had been, being able to simultaneously translate while you were listening, she must have been so quick thinking with her brain able to work in different languages at the same time. Jean continued to talk quickly while Gerrard nodded his encouragement, but none of it made any sense to me.

Before Gerrard had a chance to translate the rest of the conversation for us, Helene appeared and with a nod to Jean suggested perhaps we all might like to come back tomorrow for lunch. Jean would look out some old photos of his father and uncle for us to see. She explained it would just be a simple lunch, but we would be most welcome.

Luckily, Helene spoke without too much of an accent and more slowly, so I had a fighting chance of understanding. We gratefully accepted and then felt it was time to leave, so with warm handshakes all round and promises to return at noon the next day we made our way to the parked cars.

"What was all that about?" asked a totally bewildered Pippa. "I really think I should have taken more notice in my French lessons at school."

"Don't worry Pippa, I understood only a small part of it. What did Jean say, Gerrard?" I was eager to know but dreading a little the knowledge it might bring, as the attitude of the old lady had shaken me.

"We need to talk, but not here." replied Gerrard firmly, so we hastily arranged to go back to the B&B and have the chance to quietly discuss what had gone on.

Some fifteen minutes later we were sat in one of the shady walled gardens with a jug of iced water to share.

"What was that all about Gerrard? I just could not follow the long conversation you had with Jean, after his mother had gone indoors. She clearly recognised Mamma, but why did she have that attitude toward Etienne?" I had become increasingly concerned on the drive back with questions circulating in my head. Had Jean put the facts we had presented together and realised that Etienne could be my father? I had seen him watching me closely, though we had never specifically mentioned the possibility. I had hoped if Cecile had been recognised, we could have then broached the subject, but a turn of events we just hadn't predicted took over and there was no opportunity. Gerrard held his glass of water and began.

"A lot of those who lived through the war just do not wish to discuss it, I have found this many times before. It was a terrible time in so many ways for them and they would rather forget, and sometimes if you dredge up a memory the hurt returns to the surface. Jean was embarrassed by his mother, but he candidly told me why she behaved like she did."

Gerrard went on to explain that Jean's father, the elderly lady's husband, was taken from the farm as forced labour to the munition's factories in Germany in 1943. Etienne, his younger brother, returned to the farm from his mechanics training in Cavaillon and, so the mother said, promised to keep the family and the farm safe till his brother could return. However, Etienne soon began to work for the Maquis in the area.

"To be fair," explained Gerrard, "it would be expected of any able-bodied men remaining to 'do their bit', but Jean's mother thought he should put his family first, and not get involved. When he was killed taking part in an attack, she lived in fear that their farm would be taken from them in retribution. She also had to take over, do all the physical work, and look after her son and an elderly parent. According to Jean, she never forgave Etienne for risking his life when he had family responsibilities. Pierre, the brother, did come back at the end of the war to eventually take over the running of the farm, but his wife still blames Etienne for putting the whole family in danger."

We sat mulling over the information. The old lady's point of view was very valid, we had not even considered that way of thinking. We all thought we were looking at a resistance hero, not a man who abandoned his family responsibilities, it was really all a question of perception.

"Goodness," sighed Pippa. "We have opened a Pandoras box here, haven't we?"

"I agree Pippa, it's so difficult. We don't want to further upset that family. You could see Jean was so embarrassed, so perhaps we should make an excuse and not go to lunch tomorrow. What do you think Gerrard?"

"I firmly believe we should go, Stephanie. Jean would feel he had upset you both if we don't turn up. I got the impression his mother can be a bit 'difficult' at times, but he is hoping to get her to join us for lunch and perhaps tell us a bit more about what she knows. He is also going to find some photos. I very much think we should go and see what happens."

Chapter 5

Pippa

Waking early again with daylight just beginning to creep through the shutters, I lay thinking. Last night, Mum was very quiet, and I sensed, upset after our meeting with Jean and his family. Though I tried to get her to talk, she kept saying she was alright just a bit tired, but I knew from experience that when she was worried, she just wanted space to think and that talking just annoyed her. So, I had encouraged her to go to bed early, leaving me with our hosts who, by now, had got used to a good chat at the end of dinner. They wanted an update on our quest.

"Well," I started, when all the debris of dinner was gone, and we had a glass of something to lubricate the proceedings. "Lots happened today, some very positive, but some knowledge that has rather upset Mum, so I have encouraged her to have an early night." I went on to explain our finding of Etienne in a village photo, our discovery of his family name and visit to the farm to meet his nephew.

"Sadly, we found out that Etienne was himself killed not long after my grandmother left, fighting with the Maquis. To be fair we really didn't expect to find him still alive, but it was sad for Mum to finally know this." I stopped. Perhaps the emotion of the day was getting to me, but I felt tears well up.

"Anyway, we met Etienne's sister-in-law who is still alive and living at the farm. She is old and rather infirm, but still very much 'all there'. She recognised Cecile from a photo as a girlfriend of Etienne. So, now we definitely know Cecile was here and knew Etienne." I paused and Marianne and David looked eager to find out what happened next.

"The thing is that the old lady, Etienne's sister-in-law seemed quite well, offhand about him. It seems she felt let down as she thought he was supposed to look after the family when her husband was taken away, not get killed fighting with the Resistance. Well, that what she said anyway. Actually, it was all became a little embarrassing." David looked at Marianne and took a sip of his ruby red wine.

"I did warn you that you may find it difficult to get people to talk about wartime around here, and I would say that's not an uncommon reaction. I don't think any of us can even try to understand what people went through. Perhaps personal survival and that of your immediate family was more important for some people, and it's not for us to judge." We all nodded. He was so right; we had never been in that situation.

"So, what now?" asked Marianne.

"Well, we are invited to lunch tomorrow. Jean says he will look out some photos of his father and Etienne and try to get his mother to tell us more, but Mum feels she doesn't want to go as she is upsetting the family, which I can understand. However, Gerrard says we must go as Jean has invited us and wants to make up for his mother's rather callous remarks." I shrugged my shoulders. "So, I hope Mum has a good night's sleep and we can face the lunch together with Gerrard. She has agreed to go, so let's just see."

Anyway, this morning Mum seemed to be sleeping peacefully enough, and as there was now some daylight, I quietly got dressed and went out for a walk, not wanting to wake her. The trouble with Mum was she was very good at hiding her feelings and putting on a brave face. I suppose she had to when I was little, and she had no one else. You just get on with life whatever it throws at you she once told me, and so we did. Was I beginning to regret having started all this? I was having my doubts now as I wasn't sure anymore where this would lead, coming back of course, to the old adage 'it seemed like a good idea at the time'. I just hoped that today would not bring any more difficult revelations.

Walking in the relative cool of the early morning and seeing the magnificent countryside all around made me realise that I wanted to see more of the world and despite what was happening with the search at the moment, I was right to bring Mum away on holiday to at least experience new horizons.

She appeared well rested when I returned, and we had a convivial breakfast on the terrace with the sun shining in the blue sky all around us. Gerrard had suggested we tried to visit Roussillon before lunch and that we should set off as soon as possible after breakfast as the village was small and got very crowded in the summer. I thought it was a great idea and would take Mum's mind off the forthcoming visit.

We parked at the top of the tiny village by the cemetery, having carefully negotiated the narrow streets. The view over to the village, all differing shades of yellow, red and orange, was spectacular, however as advised by Gerrard, we ventured first onto the Ochre Trail. Quite honestly it was so unexpected, neither of us had ever seen anything like it before. The old ochre mine workings had been transformed into a walking trail where, from the first viewpoint and flight of wooden steps down into a sandy bowl, we were surrounded by weird rock formations of brilliantly coloured stone. From dazzling orange through yellow, deep red, purple and even white, the dusty rock contrasted vividly with the bright azure sky. As we walked new vistas opened with pine trees impossibly clinging from cliffs of the coloured ochre stone. My camera worked overtime, but it could never do justice to what we were seeing. After that we explored the village, with the buildings reflecting the shades of ochre we had seen on the trail. Gerrard was right, as the morning wore on the visitors continued to arrive until the narrow streets were thronged with people. We had enjoyed our visit but needed to get back to the car or we would be late for lunch.

Following a quick stop at the B&B we did arrive nearly 10 minutes late, to find Gerrard's car already parked. Hurrying into the courtyard we found him sitting with the Jean's mother in cane chairs set well into the shade.

"So sorry Gerrard," started Mum. "We were so enthralled with Roussillon we didn't leave ourselves enough time. We've got some flowers for Helene and a bottle of wine for Jean."

"Don't worry at all. The Provencal idea of time keeping is generally very lax, so you really don't need to apologise, anyway Jean is still out working in the fields. Helene is preparing lunch in the kitchen, and we are just having a quiet conversation. Put the flowers and wine on the table and come and join us, there are some interesting photos here."

Mum took the chair next to the old lady and I stood behind to get a good view. An old photo album had been found and as the pages turned, we saw Etienne and his brother growing up on the farm. There was lots of conversation, in French, of course, though I could sort of get the meaning, with Gerrard translating anything Mum didn't seem to understand. I did find it rather frustrating and not for the first time decided I should have tried harder with French at school.

Helene came out to start to lay the table and thanked us profusely for the gifts, so I decided to help her, leaving a deep conversation, of which I had no idea of the content, going on between Jean's mother, Gerrard and Mum. Helene seemed happy for me to help and with gestures and smiles we got on with sorting out the table and putting together dishes of salads, charcuterie, and cheese ready to bring outside. Their kitchen had an old-fashioned rustic feel, with a large stone fireplace on one wall with a strategically placed upright chair to the side. For Jean's mother I suspected, and suddenly I had a flashback image of Grandpa Deveraux, the first time I had seen him at the family farm, sitting by the window that Sunday morning. Finding my father's family had meant so much to me that I really did understand Mum's anxiety and desire to actually know about her father. The whole experience of finding the Deveraux family had not always gone smoothly, but I was so pleased I had undertaken the quest.

Jean appeared in the doorway and was chased amicably by his wife to get changed while we took the food out to the big iron table now transformed with a pristine while cloth and place settings. This wasn't, whatever they had said a casual lunch, and I felt that perhaps Helene felt she had a point to prove.

Mum looked up and called me over. I sensed there had been some further revelations, not perhaps so directly spoken as yesterday, as Mum looked sombre but somehow more relaxed.

"Look Pippa at this photo. It was taken when Jean was at the school and around seven years old. Look who is sitting on the front row." I took the slightly faded photo and saw a standard school scene, two rows of pupils with an older man in a grey suit in the middle of the front row and a petite young woman sat by his side. That woman was clearly Cecile, my grandmamma, and the photo was dated June 1944 on the reverse. So Jean had been right when he said he recognised Cecile.

"Goodness, so it is all true. Exactly as you said Gerrard, she was working as a schoolteacher at the village school. That's incredible. Do we know any more?" Mum nodded. Did I read too much into her face? I began to wonder what had really been discussed by the three of them while I helped out in the kitchen.

"Lots to tell Pippa, but it will have to wait, sorry, till we can have a good chat later." At that point Jean appeared in a clean shirt and began to help his mother to the table. We all sat down ready to partake of the lunch set out before us. Bottles of their own red wine appeared and soon the conversation was flowing freely. I, of course, lost the thread very quickly but was happy to eat the delicious food and watch the proceedings.

I had taken, in my first year at university, a subsidiary course in Psychology, as it seemed to me if I was going to design buildings for people it was a good idea to understand the way they thought. So 'people watching' had become hobby. You could actually learn so much just observing, and so long as I smiled and nodded occasionally, the rest of the lunch party were happy to ignore me. Mum was in deep conversation with Gerrard and to a lesser extent Jean, who was also talking to Helene. Helene was much involved with ensuring Jean's mother had everything she needed, as the old lady had given up on communication, but was clearly enjoying her lunch.

I watched Mum and Gerrard, observing that they were obviously relaxed in each other's company, with a lot of direct eye contact when speaking. I remembered being told that was important for effective communication. Their arms brushed together often, and I witnessed Gerrard gently touch her hand, perhaps to reassure her with Mum seemingly happy and at ease in his company. He had clearly become a special friend in the past few days.

On reflection I realised Mum had dedicated her life to looking after me, and there had not been any men in her life, that I knew about anyway, since my father. I understood she had been deeply in love with him, so perhaps no other men ever lived up to his standard, or she never really looked, as I was always there taking up her time and energy. It was good to see Mum interact with Gerrard who could only be described as the epitome of a perfect gentleman.

Once we had demolished the wonderful array of meats, cheeses and salads, Helene brought out trays of ripe cantaloupe melon. She explained slowly that these came from their neighbour who grew them in his fields. They had been harvested just that morning and that the ones that were the ripest had been selected for us at lunch. They were the best melons I had ever tasted with so much ripe juice flowing from the slices we all needed the napkins provided. Strong black coffee followed, and then Jean helped his mother indoors for her afternoon nap. Mum caught my eye, and I got her meaning, it was time to go, and for me I hoped, to find out what the deep conversations with Jean's mother had revealed.

We left soon after with Gerrard, following many Provencal farewells and a promise to come and see the family Fournier if we were ever in the region again. It appeared the lunch, though previously dreaded by Mum, had gone well, and I was now eager to find out what new information had been gathered.

Chapter 6

Stephanie

I could tell Pippa was eager to know what had been discussed as I did understand how difficult it was for her with her lack of French, but decided it was impossible to continuously translate. It was much simpler and easier to talk to her later after I had had time to mull over the information we had gathered. Gerrard had been right of course, we needed to attend the lunch, and it had certainly cleared the air. I now understood a lot more about Etienne and his relationship with Cecile and had sympathy for Jean's mother who had been left in a dreadful predicament.

"So?" Pippa had hardly got into the car following lunch.

"Just hold on, darling, please. Let's get back to the B&B. I have arranged for Gerrard to come as well just in case I have misunderstood anything. Gerrard understands the situation clearly and has his point of view. So, just wait a few more minutes please?" Pippa let out a long, exasperated sigh, but she knew I was right, not that this happened very often I would be the first to admit. Pippa had her own opinions and was perfectly happy to express them. Now I wonder where she got that from?

Gerrard followed and soon we were out of the oppressive afternoon heat on our favourite chairs in the shady part of the walled garden. A large jug of iced water stood on the table, and as Pippa poured us each a tall glass, she looked impatiently at me.

"So, we know Cecile was teaching at the school and she knew Etienne. But what else, please tell me all, as you were having a very long deep conversation with Jean's mother while I helped Helene." I looked at Gerrard, he nodded slightly as if to suggest I did the talking. I just hoped he would correct any misunderstanding and steadily began to tell Pippa what we had gleaned.

305

Jean's mother had been more forthcoming this time. She still harboured a sense of grievance against Etienne for not putting his family first, but had talked openly about him, his role in the Maquis and his relationship with Cecile. A handsome young man, never short of a pretty girl on his arm, he had strong opinions and was determined that what he was doing was right. He was clever, brave and quick thinking, soon having an important role in the local Resistance. Jean's mother really didn't approve and didn't want to know, as she felt that she could not be held responsible for the things of which she just did not have any knowledge. But she was aware Etienne disappeared often at night and could sometimes be gone for days at a time. Cecile visited the house on a few occasions, and of course she was known as the village schoolteacher, with Jean being in her class. Then I hesitated.

"She went on to say that apparently there was talk in the village at the time, that Cecile was being courted by a Nazi officer. She had been observed in his car and out walking in the countryside with him." I said this now in a matter-of-fact way, but I had been very shocked when this had been revealed.

"What? But surely that's not true!" exclaimed Pippa.

"She may well have had little choice," interrupted Gerrard. "If the officer concerned decided he wanted her company, then Cecile would realise she would draw unwanted attention from the occupying forces if she resisted. Perhaps she thought if she played him along it might keep her safe. We just don't know."

We all sat in silence trying to comprehend what it must have been like for my Mamma. How could she make the choice? She would realise the community would turn against her if she was seen as a collaborator but, rejecting the officer's advances brought dangers of a different kind.

"Gosh, she was brave." Pippa remarked. "I don't think I could have done this. She was leading not a double but a triple life, with one mistake and she would be in grave danger. I always thought Grandmamma was a strong determined character, but this is really something else."

"Yes." Agreed Gerrard. "Jean's mother remembered Cecile as being petite but very determined. She once overheard Etienne and Cecile arguing about another man but can't remember the detail. You have to remember that Jean's mother tried very hard not to get involved in any way. She had her young son Jean and her elderly mother to care for, and those were her priorities." Gerrard wanted to keep the record straight, then he continued with concern in his voice. "All this must be very difficult for you Stephanie. I really don't want you to be upset."

"Gerrard that's so kind." I smiled as best I could. "But we started this, so none of this is your fault in any way. Yes, its unsettling, but at least now I know a lot more about Mamma and most probably my father. Jean had apparently suggested to his mother that I may well be Etienne's daughter, as he had told her I had the 'Fournier eyes and curly hair'. It seems the old lady thought so too, so it all appears to fit into place." A silence again and I think we all needed time to take in the information revealed so far.

"So?" Pippa brought us back to reality. "Anything else?"

"Well, yes, with a bit of prompting she was able to tell us that she thought Etienne took Cecile on his motorbike to get her safely away, coming back with a superficial bullet wound to his shoulder having met a roadblock. We can only imagine Cecile did in fact make the rendezvous with a light aircraft and was taken back to England, as that's the way agents were repatriated if they survived." Gerrard informed us.

"And Etienne. Do we know what happened to him?" Pippa wanted to know it all, but who could blame her, as this was beginning to sound like something out of a wartime novel.

"Yes." I continued. "A few weeks later, around the end of July 1944, she thinks, Etienne simply went out one evening and never came back. Word was got to her he had been killed in an ambush in the hills above St Saturnin, with his body being buried in an unmarked grave. She had to pretend he had gone to help a relative on a farm near Marseilles if anyone asked, and she lived in desperate fear, for many weeks, that the farm would be taken from them in retribution if the occupying army found out the truth. Of course she also had all the farm work to manage, so you can understand her anger at Etienne, even if you feel he was doing the right thing for his country. It is all so very sad."

We sat thinking, the silence continued, and I could feel the tears that I had managed to control all day arriving and, not wanting to embarrass Gerrard or Pippa, I made a quick excuse and left to go to our room, where I stood by the window, allowing at last, the tears to flow.

Tears for Mamma, for the man she loved, my father, who I never knew, and for the whole damn war that meant Mamma had lost the man she wanted to spend her life with. I understood that feeling only too well and could feel a desperate sadness for Mamma. Why, oh why, had she not told me all this herself?

Pippa appeared in our room about ten minutes later, and I tried to hide my tears as I didn't want to upset her. However, she wasn't fooled, coming over and putting her arms around me.

"Mum, Mum please don't cry. I know you are upset, and now I feel awful for bringing you here."

I controlled my emotions sufficiently to reassure her that she had most certainly done the right thing, for I knew now what I should have been told many years ago. I was sad for what had happened to Mamma and how she had lived her life most likely not knowing what had happened and waiting for Etienne. I felt so tired and emotionally drained, but pleased it was now all out in the open. However, I certainly didn't feel I could face going to dinner that evening yet didn't want to let Pippa down.

In the end she was happy to go to dinner herself and to let me have an early night. She had also promised to telephone Gerrard to reassure him that I was alright as he had gone away most concerned about me. That was very nice of him, Gerrard was such a kind, thoughtful man.

Chapter 7

Pippa

I was glad to see Mum looking rested the next morning. I had reassured Gerrard yesterday evening that she was more settled after the somewhat fraught, emotional day. He readily suggested we had a day off from our quest giving me an idea that he thought would be fun for us both. So over breakfast I suggested we headed for the little town of Isle sur la Sorgue for some exploration. Mum agreed, especially as Marianne, clearing a breakfast table nearby, endorsed the idea commenting that the town was so pretty and so different from the others around. I surreptitiously put a small bag on the back seat as we were leaving.

"What's in that?" Mum enquired.

"Oh, nothing much, some things we might need later." Thankfully, it was left at that.

A straightforward drive along the flat plain with fruit trees growing on each side saw us arrive at Isle sur la Sorgue. Known as the 'Venice of Provence' it had the crystal-clear waters of the Sorgue river flowing through its heart with many small side streams crossed by metal pedestrian bridges linking the narrow streets. Having successfully parked the car, we walked along one of the main streets with the clear water of the river flowing gently at one side. The colourful buildings were reflected in the river, and as ever, the sun shone in a clear, azure blue, sky. Turning into one of the many side streets we found shade and an eclectic mix of shops, from the ever-present Boulangerie through chic ladies' clothes to dusty antiques laid out for people to rummage and find a bargain. Gerrard had told me how to find the small, but iconic Central Park with the huge moss-covered water wheel, the river sliding over a small wear, and stone benches placed in the shade.

I spied the narrow metal bridge that led over the wider river and guided Mum to the park. Standing at one end was the magnificent ornate Italianate, ochre-yellow building that had once been the major bank in the town. Grateful for the shade we sat on a cool stone bench and allowed the tranquillity of the setting to wash over us.

"This is just wonderful!" exclaimed Mum. "Mind everywhere is wonderful here. I could fall in love with all these places and live here happily." I nodded and smiled my agreement, pleased to see Mum so rested. I knew she worked very hard at school and had become integral to the running of the very successful English department. I was, of course, very proud of her to have achieved that but began to wish now that she would perhaps take things easier and maybe even think of early retirement. As I was more or less 'off her hands' and with Grandmamma's legacy available, I really wanted her to have time for herself. The sudden death of Cecile, her mother, was always in the back of my mind, and I was sure Mum thought about it too. Apparently, Cecile had a chronic heart condition and eventually I had persuaded Mum, when I found out the details, to visit a good heart specialist to make sure she had not inherited the same problem. Luckily, she had a fit and healthy heart, so both of us could stop worrying, well in theory at least.

I glanced at my watch, we needed to be moving toward lunch if the day was to go as planned.

"Come on Mum, Gerrard has not only recommended a great place for lunch but has booked us a table, so we had best get going." We retraced our steps to the riverside street and a simple restaurant with red gingham covered tables set at the water's edge. Our table had been reserved in a shady corner and we sank into the chairs with some relief. Our choice for lunch was easy, as we had both taken an instant delight to the hot goat's cheese salad served as a local delicacy. Circles of mild creamy goat's cheese toasted on baguette drizzled with local honey with a freshly tossed green salad had become a firm favourite. I had to have an ice-cream to finish, but Mum preferred the rich thick black coffee. Again, a glance at my watch.

"Are we in some kind of hurry?" asked Mum raising her eyebrows.

"Well, we do have somewhere to go this afternoon, and I think we ought to get going. If that's OK?" Mum looked expectantly as if I was going to elaborate, but I just kept quiet, as I thought that if she knew of the plan for this afternoon, she may well resist. So much better to present her with a 'fait a complis'.

We drove out of the town along the valley toward Fountain de Vaucluse, itself a tourist hotspot, with the famous 'fountain' bubbling out of rocks high up in the valley, though Gerrard had explained that actually during the summer it was only a dribble, if you were lucky, and not at all worth the clamber up the rocks to see. Just before the village we passed under a huge Roman viaduct and turned right down a track toward the river Sorgue. Pulling up in the carpark Mum spotted the brightly coloured canoes on the riverbank and looked directly at me.

"Please tell me you are not expecting me to get into a canoe. You have to be joking."

"Well, actually yes, I am. Just listen, Gerrard told me all about this and he has booked it for us. It's not difficult or at all dangerous but great fun. He came with his tutor group from the college as an end of term outing a few years ago and they had great fun. Come on Mum, I'll look after you. Promise."

Shaking her head but complying with my request, I grabbed the bag from the back of the car, checked in with the reception, thank goodness they spoke good English, and hurried Mum to the changing rooms. Emerging dressed in swimsuits with shorts and tee shirt on plus old trainer type shoes kindly lent by Marianne, we stood on the riverbank and donned a life jacket each. Two families, Mums and Dads plus two children each were also on our departure.

"I can't believe I am doing this." Whispered Mum. "If you had told me….."

"That's exactly why I didn't, now listen I think we are going to get some instructions. I hope they are in English as well." Luckily, they were, but very brief, apparently the French are not well known for health and safety regulations being followed. However, we managed to clamber into the yellow plastic canoe without capsizing with Mum at the front and myself at the rear. We had each been given a double ended paddle with strict instructions not to lose it. The two families, now in four separate

311

canoes had a little more difficulty with some of them ending up standing in the shallow water trying to get into their canoes. I heard Mum giggle and wondered if we had been clever or just lucky.

Once the convoy of canoes were ready the leader, in his single kayak, proficiently pushed off from the shore and set off downstream. We followed, catching the gentle current, starting to float back toward Isle sur la Sorgue. However, keeping straight wasn't quite so simple, though we did at least manage to stay pretty much on course, which is more than could be said for our fellow adventurers. We rounded the first bend and saw a concrete weir right across the river and were astounded to watch our kayaking leader step out of his kayak, the water was only knee deep and lift his vessel over the weir. He then gestured that we should all do the same.

Steadying the canoe with one hand I got out first into the deliciously cool water, my feet slipping on the smooth stones on the bottom. I helped Mum out and somehow, without mishap, we lifted the canoe over the concrete, stepped carefully over ourselves and got back in, paddling away to join the leader who was waiting in the lee of the weir. Needless to say, the two families had greater problems not helped by constant hilarious laughing when the majority of them slipped on the stones and ended up sitting in the river. We couldn't help but join in and laughed out loud too. I leant forward to Mum and whispered,

"The Mums are not really the right shape to fit into a canoe, are they?" Mum giggled.

"That's a bit mean, but actually true. Mind 'pride comes before a fall' so watch out for the next obstacle." She did at least seem to be enjoying herself, for by then with the sun on our backs, the clear water running by, and the tranquillity of the landscape, it would have been difficult not to.

With everyone back in their canoes we set off again gently moving down the Sorgue. Mum and I decided the safest place was directly behind the leader. Some of the other canoes managed to get off course and got tangled in the overhanging trees by the banks, even going round in circles as the two voyagers paddled in opposite directions. At one point one of the canoes drifted toward a fisherman standing thigh deep at the side of the river happily minding his own business, his rod having cast his line out into the flow of the river. Moving sideways towards him, its occupants shouting a warning and, with the rest of us trying not to collapse with laughter, the collision was just avoided. A shake of his head and the fisherman peacefully resumed his afternoon's activity.

Ahead we could see an island in the middle of the river. The flow of the water seemed to be speeding up and with a wave of his hand to indicate 'follow me' the leader expertly guided his kayak round the right-hand end of the island, picked up the faster current and disappeared from sight.

"Goodness me!" exclaimed Mum. "Do we have to do that?"

"No choice, and let's get going before one of the others messes it up and gets in the way. Take your paddle out of the water and let me guide us round." Using my double ended paddle, digging one end deep into the water and pushing off toward the faster flowing current, I kept the paddle on the left side of the canoe and guided us round the corner into the swift flow. We bounced along, then popped out into the calm waters beyond the island. I steadied the pace with my paddle as our leader waved us over with a thumbs up sign.

"OK Mum, you can breathe again now."

"How did you do that Pippa? That was exciting if not a bit frightening."

"Actually, I joined the Canoe Club at university for a trial afternoon in freshers' week, but I hated the wet and cold. However I did learn how to steer, but I never thought I would use the skill." Screams of laughter could be heard as the first of the following canoes came round the island, actually all in one piece even if the last one managed to come through backwards.

After that it was very calm and easy, as we more or less floated with little need to steer just enjoying the tranquillity, scenery and bird life. After one last turn at Partager Les Eaux, the parting of the waters, we expertly beached the canoe, disembarking with just our feet rather wet, dragged our yellow vessel up the sand and hanging onto our paddles. The two families eventually arrived smiling broadly and we all stood holding our paddles for the official photo. I don't think I have ever seen a group smiling so much. Clambering onto an old, but serviceable, coach to return

313

upstream still holding our double ended paddles proved the last obstacle, certainly not helped by more hysterical laughter as the paddles proved difficult to get in through the coach door.

However, as I sat down beside Mum for the short return journey to the start, she turned to me and gave a broad smile.

"I don't think I have had as much fun for years, and I certainly haven't laughed like that for ages. We must thank Gerrard for his idea, but no more surprises please!"

Chapter 8

Stephanie

I woke refreshed after our canoeing adventure. Certainly, it had been a very different day yesterday, it had been just what we needed, and I felt much better physically and emotionally. Lying in bed savouring the opportunity to think, I tried to put the events of the week in perspective. Pippa's bed was empty, and I presumed she was out on her now regular morning walk, knowing she wouldn't come back till the sun was well up over the horizon and spilling through the shutters.

So much about the past had come to light, though I still felt Mamma should have told me all this herself, but no doubt she had her reasons. I well-remembered not talking about Philip to Pippa when she was young. I don't really know why but I think I may have done it as a self defence mechanism, as putting all memories of Philip to one side, I felt I could get on with my life. I had told Pippa everything when she was older, and that of course led to her quest of 'Deveraux Finding' which at the time caused me great upset and worry. I understood her feelings of needing to know much better now, as I had been going through the same gnawing anxiety all week. It had just come much later in my life.

So, I think we were all pretty certain now that Etienne was my father. Of course, we could have done medical blood tests, but that intrusion on the lives of family Fournier was, in my mind, unacceptable. They seemed content with my sudden appearance and the evidence we found made our supposition all the stronger. However, niggling in the back of my mind was the knowledge of the 'German Officer'. We had no conclusive evidence that he even existed, but old Madame Fournier was pretty emphatic that Cecile was known in the village to have a German officer as a companion. I had a sudden thought last night of Mamma's pearl necklace that she wore so frequently. Who was the 'O' in the loving message that accompanied them and why was it in German? Was it indeed a gift from her German Officer friend? It had obviously meant something special to her or why keep the dedication? I had the distinct feeling that Mamma's time in Provence would go on keeping us guessing and certain happenings may well remain a mystery.

I had spoken with Gerrard yesterday evening to thank him for organising our day, and he seemed delighted we had enjoyed ourselves and was his usual jovial self. He had become a good friend over the past few days, and he mentioned he had yet more information for us, so we arranged a rendezvous for the following day later in the afternoon. In the meantime, his suggestion for today being Friday, was a visit to the renowned street market in Lourmarin.

With Pippa confidently driving, we made the journey over the Luberon massif via the winding narrow road through the Combe de Lourmarin to the small town with its Chateau to the south. The market was a popular attraction, and we were directed to park in the big field below the Chateau, the streets of the town being thronged with market stalls and people. As I stepped out of the car looking at the splendid Chateau walls, an overwhelmingly strange feeling almost took my breath away, and I needed to put my hand on the car to steady myself.

"Mum, are you alright?" Pippa was startled by my actions.

"Yes, yes, it's nothing, just I felt very strongly, so strongly in fact my breath was taken away, that I have actually stood here before. But that's silly I can't have done."

"No." Pippa agreed. "But who knows if Grandmamma did. Maybe something important happened here?"

"But I'm not Cecile, so it doesn't follow that this could happen."

"There are more things in heaven and on earth Horatio." quoted Pippa.

"So, you have remembered your Hamlet I see. Well, maybe. It's OK, I feel better now, let's just put it down to experience and go and enjoy the market."

We plunged into the streets with market stalls at each side under the welcome shade of the huge plane trees. From brightly painted pottery, to carved wooden utensils via mountains of fresh vegetables the market just kept on surprising us. Fresh meat and fish jostled for a place alongside clothes and spices with rotisseries of cooking chickens enticing the thronging customers. As we turned a corner more stalls led out along the next street. We paused at a particular stall with hundreds of pashminas of so many different colours hanging on display.

"I do so want to take Paula a present." I said fingering the soft material. "Do you think she would like one of these?"

"Who wouldn't?" was Pippa's reply. So, we eventually came away with three such garments, one each and one as a present.

"I also want to get something as a 'Thank You' for Gerrard. Pippa what do you think he might like?" She came back in a flash with a suggestion which was a brilliant idea, so we retraced our steps to a large stall with pretty, colourful plants. We could both visualise something bright with flowers living on his terrace, being a lasting gift and reminder of us both. We choose a large climbing plant with bright pink, trumpet shaped flowers and bought a ceramic pot to complete the present.

By now we had quite a lot to carry, but also managed pate, cheese, tomatoes and some bread for a picnic lunch on the way back. How we actually got it all to the car I am not sure and fitting the rather large plant in was also interesting, but with a bit of ingenuity we eventually had everything successfully stowed inside. By now the sun was at midday heat and retracing our steps, we drove up to the Luberon ridge and found a stone picnic table in the shade, where tomatoes, cheese and pate had never tasted so good.

Later that afternoon as the heat of the day was receding, we set off to meet Gerrard. He had suggested we rendezvous by the old windmill just on the edge of the village of St Saturnin. Standing on its vantage point, the sails no longer turned in the breeze, but it was a landmark for the village and must have been there when Cecile had lived here. We both assumed it was to grind corn for bread, but it had actually ground the olives produced locally for oil until quite recent times. Gerrard was waiting in his little white car and jumped out to greet us with his usual enthusiasm. He then suggested we went with him in his car so he could explain en route.

We set off uphill, out of the village along a narrow road with open views to the plain, with the Luberon mountains to the south and the scrub land to the north. Boulder strewn and covered in stunted local oak trees with prickly undergrowth, there were paths and tracks leading away into the rising ground. It was obvious why this was the stronghold of the Resistance during the occupation, with great cover, miles of rocky ground and paths known only to the local inhabitants. The local fighters could reach their targets with little chance of being seen. Gerrard explained he had spent some time in the previous day's doing research into the actions of the local Maquis in July 1944. He had been able to speak to another of the few remaining men who had actually taken part in that fighting.

"He has 'good days and bad days' I think you say? He cannot really remember what happened last week, but his memories of wartime are often so sharp and clear." He went on to explain his friend had remembered Etienne Fournier as an important Resistance member taking part in many missions. July 1944 was one of their most crucial times as they plotted and executed actions almost daily to keep the German troops occupied and unable to move north to help to stop the allied invasion. Gerrard continued.

"One such mission was particularly difficult, he remembered, and they lost a number of men at an ambush on the road to Sault. My friend says he cannot be sure but feels that this may well have been where Etienne was fatally wounded."

We were both quietly taking in all the information, when the car turned sharply north into a gorge where the land fell away steeply to the left and high stone walls hemmed in the road to the right. It looked like perfect territory for an ambush, then about halfway along there was a small layby where Gerrard stopped the car. Just beyond was a stone plaque on the wall, and I suddenly felt my legs tremble as we walked across to read it.

The message it gave was stark and clear. *30th July 1944 an ambush on a convoy to Sault, five resistance fighters killed. 12 soldiers of the occupying forces dead.* At the top of the plaque was the double cross of Lorraine, the emblem of the Resistance.

"We can't be sure Stephanie, but it seems this may well be where Etienne was killed." Gerrard's voice was quiet and matter of fact, but I could sense emotion behind the words. Pippa grasped my hand, and I felt tears rise again, as I looked around a barren, bare, almost soulless place, but I felt that sudden connection again. We stood looking at the plaque and saying nothing, as high above two buzzards circled in the clear sky with their eerie cries. Eventually I broke the silence.

"Gerrard, thank you for all your work. It is sad, but you have helped us find out so much. If this is where he was killed, then he must be laid to rest somewhere in these hills, so I can at least feel close to him up here." We all stood in silence, caught up in our own thoughts. Pippa and I had entered this search with an open mind as to what we might find. Sometimes the facts discovered were not always easy to accept but, certainly some ghosts were at last laid to rest. Then Gerrard spoke quietly.

"Stephanie, I do have some more and perhaps better news. My friend had heard about Cecile but as with our other old resistance man he never met her. However, he suggested a name of one of the young resistance helpers who he feels may know more. Young teenage boys they really were, helping out in many ways, taking messages, carrying small items to deliver, even just confusing the soldiers by their sheer petty vandalism." Pippa looked directly at Gerrard.

"Do you think this boy may have actually known Grandmamma?"

"My contact seemed to think so and I managed, with the help of Ann-Marie at the Mairie, to track him down. Still living near St Saturnin, he was only about fifteen in 1944, and he wants to meet you and, if that's alright with you, I have arranged to meet in the café at St Saturnin tomorrow morning. I feel it will be interesting to hear what he can tell us."

I managed a smile, this quest seemed never ending.

"That's great Gerrard. If we bring the photos, he can tell us what he remembers. Thank you so much yet again."

It was rather a sombre ride back down to collect our car, as no one spoke much, we all had too much to think about and Gerrard seemed very perceptive to my moods. However, we all cheered up a little when we reached the windmill, and Pippa brought the large pink plant out of the car and presented it to Gerrard who appeared a bit overwhelmed. We had decided carrying up to his house was going to be difficult, so a car-to-car swap seemed the solution.

"This is so kind and not at all necessary." He protested. "But I will stand it on my terrace, and it will always remind me of my special English friends." We exchanged kisses and hugs and arranged to meet the next morning.

Chapter 9

Pippa

Perching on my now familiar rock, I watched the sunlight stream over the Luberon and cast early morning shadows on the village. We were due to return to England tomorrow, back to our normal lives, though whether they could ever be quite normal again might be a different matter. We had arrived with a photo, lots of questions and hope of finding some answers, but we could never have imagined how much we were to discover. We both freely admitted that without Gerrard it would have been impossible. Gerrard, such a delightful gentleman, I hoped very much that he could remain in our lives and felt Mum wished the same.

A rollercoaster of a week, but despite the emotional toll, I knew Mum would not have changed anything. She still felt that her mother Cecile should have told her many years ago what was known about her father, but the tears and anxiety that had arrived in the past few days were, however, an acceptable route to the knowledge that she had been eager to know for so many years. I had always been very close to Mum, being able to read her moods and joining in her sorrows from an early age. I hated to see her upset and as a young child tried very hard to behave well and do what she wanted. I had felt tears rising this week as the story unfolded, but like Mum was glad that at least some ghosts could be laid to rest at last.

Remembering anything about my grandmamma was quite difficult for me. She died apparently when I was seven, but for reasons best known to herself, my Mum just didn't tell me until much later. I can picture her as a small, slim, very elegant lady in a cloud of perfume. She was kind to me, but the atmosphere was very strained whenever we visited, and I sensed I needed to be on my best behaviour. Mum always seemed ill at ease at Grandmamma's house and then moodily quiet as we travelled home after our visits. I soon learnt to keep my thoughts to myself and not to ask questions. The Cecile we had now discovered was amazing to me, such a brave young woman when she was only my age. I tried to imagine what she must have felt and how she summoned up the courage to undertake those tasks, I was only too well aware I would not have been able to manage any of it.

Etienne, of course, was an entity we just really didn't know or understand, but both of us felt how unfair it was that Cecile had lost the man she had loved. This meant so much to Mum having lost my father Philip so suddenly. Yesterday, Mum had mentioned to me her thoughts concerning the pearl necklace, as it seemed Cecile certainly had a connection to a German officer. That much old Madame Fournier had made clear however, we felt perhaps it was too insensitive to pursue this angle of investigation. The declaration of love so carefully kept with the pearls clearly meant something to Grandmamma, or why else keep it? Agreeing that this aspect was most likely to be one step too far and that Cecile perhaps needed her secrets, we stopped digging, for now anyway.

Yet there was still more to come. Our meeting set for today was with someone who claimed to actually know Cecile from all those years ago. That he could possibly tell us more was intriguing, and I knew Mum was looking forward to meeting him.

Gerrard was already sitting at a shady table at the corner café in the village when we arrived. A meaningful hug and kiss for Mum and three Provencal kisses to each cheek for me. Already having ordered our coffees, Gerrard began his explanation.

"Rene is meeting us here soon and he has a story to tell. He was just 15 in 1945 but like so many of his age was active for the Maquis. My friend yesterday suggested he may have some information, and it seems Rene is very willing to come and talk."

At this point a slim, tall, athletic looking man walked over the road toward the café. We had realised he must be around 70 years of age, but he looked well for his years and carried a broad smile on his suntanned face. Gerrard beckoned him over, and with handshakes, introductions and more coffee ordered, Rene spoke in rapid French to Gerrard. I knew was not going to understand anything but also saw my mother straining to keep up with the conversation. Gerrard seemed to sense this immediately and explained to Rene he would translate as we went along, at which point Rene smiled and nodded with a comment to Gerrard that he was sorry that his English was very poor. Taking a sip of his black coffee Rene spoke quickly and confidently to Gerrard. His story was not unusual in the dark days of war, his father was taken from his home early one morning, put against a wall and shot in full view of his family for supposedly being active with the Resistance. Rather than subdue the population these actions fuelled further dissent causing Rene and many of his friends to work for the Resistance from an early age. They acted as messengers, lookouts, and caused petty nuisance distractions that helped to disrupt life for the occupying forces in the village. Rene went to the village school and remembered well the arrival of Mademoiselle Andre to teach the younger children in Spring 1944. At this point Mum passed the photo of Cecile taken soon after the war. Rene looked at it and smiled.

"C'est Mademoiselle Andre." He confirmed. He remembered her well and commented how all the boys thought she was very pretty. He continued saying that she had been very kind to all of them and that the younger children loved coming to school as she made her classroom an interesting and safe place during that awful time. Rene then looked very earnestly at Gerrard and seemed to be making a very important point. Gerard translated.

"He wants to say, 'Thank you' directly to you, Mademoiselle Andre's daughter, Stephanie, as he says she saved his life." Mum smiled at Rene, encouraging him to go on, as all this was getting very interesting if not a bit emotional.

Gerrard continued to translate, as Rene spoke clearly about his first real Maquis mission with two other young boys helping to make a diversion to draw the German patrols away from other important Resistance activity. Although in dark men's clothing with a cap pulled down over her face, Rene recognised Mademoiselle Andre as she led the three young teenagers to lay explosive devices near the barracks at Apt. Rene was injured as he returned to a device that had not exploded on time, falling and breaking a bone in his leg making it very difficult, and painful for him to walk. Mademoiselle Andre had waited for him and helped him get away, half carrying him a long distance to the disused mine workings near Roussillon where she hid him in a cave.

"I was so frightened." Gerrard translated for him. "I could not walk, and it hurt a lot. Mademoiselle Andre was so kind and promised that someone would come to help me, but I had to stay in the cold, dark, cave alone. I remember, even now holding her hand and begging her not to leave me."

Mum and I shivered despite the warm summer's day, for Rene was telling the story as if it was just yesterday, not over 50 years ago. Eventually Mademoiselle Andre had managed to leave him, again promising someone would come, or she herself would return. It was many hours later, but a man did come and got him to a doctor who put his leg in plaster and then took him home. By the time he was ready to return to school Mademoiselle Andre had gone, and he was never able to say thank you or tell her how grateful he was.

This time Rene looked directly at Mum.

"I say 'Thank you.'" He managed in obviously carefully rehearsed English, and Mum leaned forward and grasped his hand, smiling through the tears in her eyes, and we were all silent for a while. It seemed my grandmother had made a real difference to this village in so many ways during her short time here. Then Rene then made his excuses and left with generous handshakes all round and copious grateful goodbyes.

"I don't know what to say," began Mum. "An amazing story and so much more information about Cecile's time here, she obviously made a great impression on Rene, and how brave to put her life in danger getting him away. I am beginning to think I didn't know my Mamma very well at all." Gerrard put his hand on my mothers and quietly said,

"I don't think we can ever know all the secrets in another person's life, but I think you should be very proud of Cecile." As Mum and I walked back to our car we each reflected in silence on the story we had heard. It seemed the more we knew, the more we wanted to know.

Following a restful few hours in the gardens and around the pool at the B&B we welcomed Gerrard for a final dinner with us before our return to England the next day. I noticed Mum made an extra special effort with her appearance that evening, and Gerrard arrived suitably well dressed for the occasion. I knew I was not the only one who felt a growing emotional connection between them, but both appeared too reticent to mention their feelings. We had a great dinner reminiscing about exploits of the week with David and Marianne joining us for drinks after dinner. I tried as hard as I could to engineer some time alone together for Mum and Gerrard, however David and Marianne kept the talking going as was their usual habit with the wine freely flowing. We didn't exactly have an early start in the morning but had to be away in good time to catch our TGV train at Avignon at 11am.

Eventually I suggested I might go to get some sleep and that broke the party up. Marianne exclaimed at the late hour and rapidly disappeared, knowing it was her job to get the breakfasts ready the following morning. I tried to slip away and let Mum go with Gerrard back to his car, as I was sure more than ever before that their fledgling relationship should be allowed to develop, but someone had to make the first move. Mum, however had other ideas and called me over to 'say a proper goodbye' to Gerrard and so we all walked to his car. Hugs and kisses, huge thanks with promises to keep in touch, then the car departed up the track. We walked back in silence, each with their own thoughts.

The next morning, I was packing our suitcases into the car with Mum saying goodbye to Marianne in the courtyard when an engine noise and a cloud of dust alerted me to a car coming down the unmade track rather fast. It was clearly Gerrard's small, battered white Citroen, and almost skidding to a halt, he jumped out, looking around for Mum.

"Stephanie?" He simply enquired.

"She's in the courtyard, Gerrard, talking to Marianne." He walked determinedly through the gates, and I watched as he approached Mum, touched her in the shoulder and led her back out of the courtyard towards the track. I watched as I really did not want to interfere, but neither did I want us to miss our train.

"I won't be long Pippa." Mum called over her shoulder. "Gerrard wants a word." Checking our room was empty of our belongings I returned to the courtyard to say my goodbyes to Marianne and David.

"What was that about with Gerrard?" asked Marianne. I just smiled.

"Well, put it like this I would not be at all surprised to see Mum back here as your guest very soon." Outside standing at our hire car I could see Mum and Gerrard walking back down the track, now holding hands. At his car, a few words were exchanged, a hug and a brief kiss then Gerrard got into his car, waving as he drove away.

"Come on Mum." I shouted. "We really don't want to miss the train. I've got all our things, and we need to get going." Carefully negotiating the narrow roads that led from the B&B I waited until we reached the main road before questioning Mum.

"Well?"

"Well, what?" was her reply.

"You know only too well what I mean." I pressed my case. "What happened with Gerrard? Why did he come to see you this morning? What did he want?"

Mum smiled.

"Oh, nothing, just to say 'Goodbye' really".

"Really?"

Mum continued to smile.

"What do you think?" She added.

She could be so infuriating at times, but I think I understood the meaning of their conversation. I had a very strong feeling Gerrard would continue to figure in my mother's life in the future. Perhaps our search for knowledge of the past had opened an unexpected door for the future. I very much hoped so.

Chapter 10

Rothenberg ab der Tauber, Bavaria, Germany. July 2000

There was camaraderie in the crowds of people he had decided. Certainly, he could feel lonely in a throng of strangers but the mere fact of seeing so many, quite ordinary souls, helped him to feel the world was, at the very least still functioning and therefore, so perhaps should he.

Rothenberg ab der Tauber was just twenty or so minutes' drive from his now resoundingly empty house. He had begun to counteract his loneliness by just walking around its exceptionally pretty painted buildings, the cobbled streets with quaint shops and the fortified walls giving impressive views out over the Bavarian landscape. Whatever season of the year there were visitors of many nationalities, always other people to notice, enabling him to feel as if he were, at the very least, sharing this moment in time.

The main town square with the highly decorated 'Rathaus' town hall also had numerous pavement cafes, and he had taken to one in particular, located on the sunny side where he could sit and enjoy a tall glass of beer. Discovering their 'Taggesmenu' of daily specialities at a very reasonable price encouraged him to eat there on most of his visits and he became well known at this particular establishment. His favourite corner table located against the white rendered wall, usually reserved especially for him.

Today, it was late July, and the sun was hot as he sat in the shade of the parasol sipping his beer and watching the crowds. His mind slipped, as it frequently did, to the past, for at over four score years there was plenty of past to reflect upon.

Still a striking, handsome, tall man with now thinning white curly hair, that had once been blonde, he kept in good shape and enjoyed good health. He knew he had been luckier than many, probably most of his generation. Now, as the world began the new millennium, he realised so many of his contemporaries were not here to experience it. The war, so bitterly fought, had taken many and broken the lives of thousands of others. He had been able to survive the fraught last hectic months and return to his home in the Rhinelands, though his father never came back.

Germany was then in ruins and needed rebuilding, so with his artistic flare, good education and business sense, he set about designing and building homes for the people of the now defunct fatherland. Never had the need been greater and his company flourished, expanded and merged over the years to become a nationwide force in construction. He needed a wife and married Helga, pretty, blonde, and sensible, who he grew to love. She gave him two fine sons, stability in his life and looked after the house he designed and built overlooking the rolling Bavarian countryside with huge glass walls set in strong oak beams, all very radical and avant garde at the time. Johann followed him into the business having inherited his artistic flare and commercial acumen, expanding the firm to include large projects with inspirational designs. Luca his son, conceived with Johann's turbulent Italian wife, was now following in their footsteps, with international innovative architectural projects ensuring the future of the firm. He still enjoyed a seat on the board monitoring all aspects, rarely intervening these days.

Helga, the thought of her brought his sadness back, even though it was now over three years since illness had taken her. He missed her presence greatly, the house seemed empty, but he also knew, hoping she never realised that though he dearly loved her, she had never been able to capture the piece of his heart given to his first love, all those years ago.

He rarely thought about his war service, it wasn't something he enjoyed reflecting upon. He had served his country out of necessity rather than desire with the influence of his father, who had followed a very successful military career, ensuring he was stationed as safely as was possible, away from direct action.

Something recently had stirred these memories, opened a door that had been firmly closed over fifty years ago. What had caused this he didn't understand. What was that theory about a butterfly flapping its wings in South America causing an earthquake in Asia? Someone, somewhere was digging into the past and disturbing the equilibrium.

For he had now seen her twice, each time visible across the square, just recognisable. Obvious to him in her outdated clothes, but seemingly invisible to those around her.

It was Cecile, his Cecile, he was certain. She had stood looking directly at him, just as he remembered her from many years ago, their eyes meeting with an instant mutual recognition. The first time he moved to go to her, but immediately she was gone. The second time he kept the eye contact as long as he could, but when he blinked she had disappeared.

He had loved her so deeply, an aching first love of infatuation from the moment of setting eyes on her. She had returned his feelings, at least so he had blindly thought, and yet still held out hope that she had in fact given him her heart in a bond of true love. Three months of soaring emotions and unrivalled happiness had come crashing down to leave him destitute at her betrayal. Even then he couldn't quite bring himself to hate her, ensuring as best he could, her escape by directing those searching for her in the wrong direction. He never knew what became of her but hoped that indeed her repatriation and safety had been achieved.

In those early post war years, he even countenanced the idea of going to England to look for her, however the obstacles were too great and the realisation of the enormity of the task had eventually persuaded him to close that chapter of his life, to be pragmatic and look ahead. Yet, in his soul he could never quite forget his Cecile and a piece of his heart would always remain hers.

Almost completely lost in his thoughts he was brought back to reality by the arrival of his lunch, a brimming plate of sauerkraut and large round, spicy, sausages.

He smiled up at the waiter, realising it was in fact the owner of the restaurant taking time to engage with a valued client and thanked him for his excellent service.

"No problem, Herr Kaufman," was his reply.

"Oh, please call me Otto."

Epilogue

Pippa, 4 years later, June 2004

Transatlantic flights are pretty mind numbing I decided. Going over to the US had been exciting with so much anticipation of the forthcoming events, but this return flight seemed endless, and any form of sleep was completely evading me.

My first real overseas project had been so fulfilling, even if I really was only there for experience. I had, at least, some input in the presentation and the working up of the computer models of the possible finished scheme. If all went to plan, I would be doing this round trip for a few years to come so I had better get used to it. Working in an international firm of architects had been my dream and being lucky enough to land a job straight after my post graduate course, a complete bonus. Hard work and long hours were expected but the job satisfaction was immense. So now my life seemed well mapped out for a good number of years.

I began to plan my two weeks off work on my return, at least that might pass the time. Gilly knew I was due back around now, with our flat share working well, for as old friends we knew and trusted each other. Gilly, quite a highflyer in her way, followed her parents into accountancy after getting a first-class degree, and was now working hard with a top London firm. The flat her mother had so conveniently found for her, had a spare bedroom exactly when I needed somewhere in London to live. However, I didn't plan to stay long this time though. I had people to see and places to visit.

I needed to go down to see Grandpa Deveraux. Johnny's last email said his arthritis was playing up and he wasn't too well, being pretty fed up with not being able even to get into the Land

Rover and drive it easily, having given up trying to climb into the tractors some years ago. Grandpa had always been special. His remaining son Adam, my father's brother, may not have been too welcoming at first, but had eventually accepted me as part of the family, especially when he saw how happy it made his father. He took some time to understand I was looking for a family, not a family inheritance, though you cannot really blame him for wanting to protect the farm for his son.

I tried to go down regularly to help cheer Grandpa up. Johnny, by now having finally completed agricultural college, was doing what he loved, working full time on the farm and seemed blissfully happy. Recently moved into one of the holiday cottages with his long-standing girlfriend Lizzy he appeared completely settled. The fact that there was an embryonic new Deveraux on the way made Grandpa all the more pleased, though like his son, I think he would have preferred a ring on the finger of Lizzy before his first great-grandchild actually made an appearance. Grandpa was old fashioned in that way, making me smile, as finding my father's family had been very important to me.

Then, I must sort out some travel to see Mum, as that was equally high on my list of priorities. A rush of happy feelings made me feel better about the long flight and the lack of sleep. I was so pleased to see Mum settled and happy now. To think that a chance encounter could change the whole direction of your life was still quite amazing to me. If I hadn't found that photo at the bottom of the jewellery box none of this would have happened.

Mum had indeed kept in close touch with Gerrard following our holiday, returning to David and Marianne's B&B the following Easter, spending the week with Gerrard enjoying each other's company. By the summer she spent a month in St Saturnin staying with Gerrard. On her return to England, she negotiated early retirement from her teaching post, sold the house she had bought all those years ago before I was born, and by the New Year of 2002 had begun living contentedly with Gerrard in St Saturnin. I, of course, had been out to stay and was so happy that at last Mum had found a soulmate. Gerrard seemed totally devoted and Mum continually had a smile on her face.

They worked together on the archive of local wartime history, and just last summer had their first exhibition in the 'Salles des Fetes' in St Saturnin. It was so well attended that the Mairie had asked for a repeat this year, as it had been such an attraction for the tourists. Mum and Gerrard were also working on a small book to sell alongside the photos and wartime memorabilia they so carefully displayed on the walls of the village hall.

But, like Grandpa Deveraux they wanted things to be right, so a small wedding took place the first summer after Mum had arrived, in September 2002. I smiled and remembered the occasion with such happy feelings. It had been a glorious late summers day, with the ceremony in the big stone church in the centre of the village, following the visit to the Mairie to complete the civil proceedings. Mum looking so elegant in a knee length cream satin, fitted dress, with three quarter length sleeves and a square neckline. This was all set off by a wide brimmed cream hat with vibrant red poppies in the red band. Gerrard in a dark suit with bright white shirt and a startling red bow tie complimented her perfectly. I was touched that Jean had offered to accompany Mum down the aisle at church, it seemed so fitting. Mum and Gerrard were often visitors at the farm at Les Andeols, being counted now as part of the family it appeared.

Then we all went back to the B&B with David and Marianne for a leisurely celebration meal set out so colourfully in the courtyard. I was pleased to see Paula and Ronnie had been able to come, I knew Paula was delighted to see her best friend happy and settled even if it did mean losing the close contact they had for so many years. I recognised Rene, who had become a good friend and walking companion for their winter forays into the hills of the Luberon and was introduced to some of Gerard's friends from the village. It was a wonderful meal and a convivial atmosphere.

As the evening light began to fade Marianne lit a host of small candles in glass jars around the courtyard, the effect was calm and yet spectacular. With the meal over, people began to mingle and I left the main table to take some photos before the light had completely disappeared. Standing with my back to the outside wall deciding which were the best angles I became aware, out of the corner of my eye of two people by the main arched entrance, watching the proceedings.

A young man with dark curly hair, dressed in brown working clothes and heavy boots, the sleeves on his shirt rolled up to expose suntanned arms. A pretty young girl at his side, small by comparison, with brown hair pinned and rolled in an old-fashioned style, wearing a simple cream blouse and calf length dark skirt. He had his arm protectively around her shoulders, as they were looking intently at the celebrations. I knew, almost as soon as I did, that if I looked directly at them, they would be gone, and of course I was right. There was no one there, but I knew who it had been. Cecile and Etienne had come to watch and, I like to think, give their blessing to Stephanie and Gerrard. I told no one else of the 'visitors' but I was sure about what I saw.

"This is your captain speaking. We are about to begin our descent into London Heathrow. Please return to your seats and fasten your seatbelts." The announcement woke me, so I must have had some sleep after all.

As we descended through the grey clouds to a cold and wet London, I thought about my life to come. Hopefully, I would make my mark in my chosen profession and eventually be lucky in love. Whatever life threw at me I knew I had to make the best out of any situation, as I was following in the footsteps of two indomitable women, not only my grandmamma Cecile but my mother Stephanie. Nothing was ever going to be easy.